PAUL S. FRITZ is a member of the Department of History at McMaster University, Hamilton.

Since the rise of the modern nation state in Europe, political leaders have had to cope with the problems of conspiracy and internal securtiy. *The English Ministers and Jacobitism between the Rebellions of 1715 and 1745* is a study of the response made to these twin problems by the British central government, under Stanhope, Sunderland, and Walpole. Faced with the prospect of assassination, internal rebellion, and conspiracy, the ministers naturally took all necessary measures to protect the security of the state. Nor did their worries end with the successful defeat of the Jacobite Rebellion of 1715; an examination of the anti-Jacobite campaign after this date clearly demonstrates a continuing dread of Jacobitism. At the same time, their action in the years 1715-45 against Jacobite plots for a restoration betrays an acute awareness on their part of the political advantages to be reaped through careful exploitation of those fears.

Professor Fritz's study is a valuable addition to the existing literature on Jacobitism. It uncovers new documents revealing the workings of the conspirators, and it illuminates how the threat of conspiracy was used successfully by imaginative politicians to retain power.

Robert Walpole

PAUL S. FRITZ

The English Ministers
and Jacobitism
between the Rebellions
of 1715 and 1745

UNIVERSITY OF TORONTO PRESS
TORONTO AND BUFFALO

© University of Toronto Press 1975
Toronto and Buffalo
Printed in Canada

Library of Congress Cataloging in Publication Data

Fritz, Paul Samuel, 1938-
  The English ministers and Jacobitism between the
  rebellions of 1715 and 1745.

  Bibliography: p.
  Includes index.
  1. Jacobites.   2. Great Britain – Politics and
  government – 1714-1760.   I. Title.
  DA813. F7   320.9'41'071   75-33706
  ISBN 0-8020-5308-4

To the memory of my Mother

Preface

The subject of Jacobitism has received wide treatment by professional historians. Their general attitude, however, has been to view the Jacobite threat as one not to be taken seriously. Since Jacobite endeavours were unsuccessful, most historians, in the true Whig tradition of historical writing, have treated these efforts with the contempt they feel should be showered on any lost cause. Certain recent studies have begun to alter this view, however. The late Archibald S. Foord, in *His Majesty's Opposition, 1714-1830* (Oxford 1964), showed very conclusively the real importance of parliamentary Jacobitism in the years immediately after the rebellion of 1715. So, too, in the late Romney Sedgwick's introductory survey to his *The House of Commons 1715-1754* (London 1970, vol. I), the Jacobite factor is presented as a genuine threat to the British government. And most recently John Brooke in his *George III* (London 1972, p. 5) has stated: 'Looking back from the distance of two hundred and fifty years it seems that King George I and his ministers exaggerated the danger of Jacobitism. But at the time no one could be sure. The long vista of history is deceptive. Nor are timely precautions to be despised because the danger they guard against never materialises. In the event there was no Jacobite restoration. But two armed rebellions were to take place before the Hanoverian monarchs felt secure upon the throne.'

It is hoped that this study of Jacobite activity in the years following the rebellion of 1715 and the concomitant response of the English ministers will further substantiate this viewpoint. In addition, this enquiry shows that, although the Whig ministers genuinely feared Jacobitism, they were able to use the threat of conspiracy with great effectiveness to maintain their political power.

In the preparation of this book I have incurred a great many debts of gratitude and I welcome this opportunity to acknowledge them formally.

I am most deeply indebted to Professor J.H. Plumb of Cambridge University who directed an earlier version of this study as my doctoral dissertation. He has remained throughout my most constant critic and guide. I should also like to express my debt of gratitude to three other historians. The late Professor D.B. Horn of the University of Edinburgh read an earlier version of the manuscript and the copious notes he passed on to me have saved me from a number of errors. I also benefited enormously from advice given me by the late Professor A.S. Foord of Yale University and Professor R.M. Hatton of London University. Needless to say, the remaining errors and shortcomings of this study are my own.

To the owners of private manuscript collections I must also record my gratitude: Her Majesty the Queen for graciously allowing me to make use of the Stuart papers, the marquess of Cholmondeley for permission to use and quote from the private archive of Sir Robert Walpole, the earl of Stair for the use of the papers of the 1st earl, the Earl and Countess Waldegrave for placing at my disposal the papers of James, 1st Earl Waldegrave, and Lieutenant Colonel J.H. Busby for the manuscript journals of Mrs Charles Caesar.

The staffs of a number of archival centres and libraries have helped me enormously. In particular, I wish to express my appreciation to those of the Public Record Office, the Scottish Record Office, the Manuscript Room of the British Museum, the Anderson Room of the Cambridge University Library, the Royal Archives at Windsor Castle, and the House of Lords Record Office. I am also indebted to those persons who aided me in any way during the course of my research at the Archives du Ministère des Affaires Etrangères, the Haus-, Hof- und Staatsarchiv, and the Archivio Segreto Vaticano.

I wish to thank the Imperial Oil Company and the Canada Council for providing me with financial assistance to undertake the research for this study. The publication of this work was made possible, in part, through a grant from the Humanities Research Council, using funds provided by the Canada Council, and a grant from the Andrew W. Mellon Foundation to the University of Toronto Press.
PSF
January 1975

Abbreviations

Add. MSS Additional Manuscripts
Arch.Aff.Etr.Corr.Pol.Angl. Archives du Ministère des Affaires Etrangères,
   Correspondance Politique d'Angleterre (Quai d'Orsay)

BM British Museum
Caesar Journals The Manuscript Journals of Lady Caesar, 1714-1740
HLRO House of Lords Record Office
HMC Historical Manuscripts Commission
PRO Public Record Office
RA Royal Archives, Windsor Castle
SRO Scottish Record Office, Edinburgh
SP State Papers
Stuart Stuart Manuscripts, Windsor Castle
Waldegrave MSS (Chewton House) The papers of James, 1st Earl
   Waldegrave, at Chewton House, Chewton Mendip,
   Somersetshire.

NOTE ON DATES
All dates, both in the text and in any commentary in the footnotes, are Old
Style, except that 1 January, not 25 March, is taken as the beginning of the
new year.

Contents

Illustrations

THE ENGLISH MINISTERS AND JACOBITISM
BETWEEN THE REBELLIONS OF 1715 AND 1745

Prologue

Since the rise of the modern nation state in Europe, political leaders have had to cope with the dual problems of conspiracy and internal security. For Britain, the Catholic problem following the Protestant Reformation, the Spanish threat culminating with the defeat of the Armada in 1588, and the Jacobite menace created by the Revolution of 1688 brought not only the horrible prospect of assassination, internal rebellion, and conspiracy but also produced a natural and instinctive response from the government to take all necessary measures to protect the security of the state. This study is concerned with the last of these problems – Jacobitism.

The birth of Jacobitism dates from the Revolution of 1688. With the flight of James II to France and the transfer of the crown to William and Mary, the English government faced a disputed succession that was to plague successive ministries until the middle years of the eighteenth century. Open rebellion, Jacobite plots, assassination attempts, projected invasions from the continent, endless Jacobite intrigue at foreign courts, the listing of military support for the Pretender, the interminable comings and goings of Jacobite agents to and from the continent, a growing proliferation of Jacobite pamphlets and broadsheets, numerous declarations of intent from the Pretender himself, growing obstructionist tactics from Jacobite supporters in parliament – these were the marked characteristics of Jacobite activity over the next several decades. As a result, fear of Jacobitism became a central element in the shaping of English domestic and foreign policy.

Above all else, the ministers feared the possibility that the Jacobites might achieve the restoration of their candidate by obtaining the support of a foreign power. And their fears were well justified. In the decade following the revolution – the 1690s – not only did the ministers have to contend with a spate of Jacobite intrigue but also faced the spectre of a foreign power supporting the rebels. During the summer of 1690 and the winter of 1691 two widespread Jacobite plots were uncovered by the government and, during the course of the investigations that followed, a number of prominent members of the English and Scottish nobility were implicated, among them Clarendon, Ormonde, Arran, Dartmouth, Devonshire, Macclesfield, Dorset, and Tarbat. An even more dangerous plot was revealed in 1696 when a scheme was drawn up by Sir George Barclay and several others to murder the king. A week after the plan was to have been carried out more than three hundred persons were lodged in London prisons alone, charged with complicity in the plot.[1] In the course of the ministers' vigorous and wide-ranging enquiry Sir John Fenwick implicated, by his testimony, Shrewsbury, Russell, Godolphin, and Marlborough.

Moreover, Louis XIV, until his death in 1715, at various stages supported the Jacobites. In 1689 and again in 1692 and 1696 he made public his attachment to the Stuart cause and, in each of these years, entered actively into plans for an invasion attempt. Indeed, in the latter year plans were so well advanced from the French side that the duke of Berwick, James II's illegitimate son and an officer in the French army, was dispatched to England to direct the rebellion that was to precede the invasion from France.[2] William III and his ministers lived out the decade of the 1690s, particularly after the death of Mary in 1694, in a state of increasing uncertainty that was relieved but little by the Peace of Ryswick of 1697. Although by that peace Louis XIV had recognized William III as king of England and thereby accepted, by implication, the revolution settlement, he absolutely refused to agree to the expulsion of James II or his supporters from France. The acknowledgment proved to be of a temporary nature dictated by political expediency, for upon the death of James II in 1701 Louis immediately recognized his successor, James III, as king of England.

French recognition of the Stuart claim, together with the outbreak of the War of the Spanish Succession, once again ushered in a new period of hope and a new wave of activity on the part of the Jacobites within England and on the continent. For the English ministers, however, it meant increased unease and fear for the Protestant succession. Jacobite goals in this first decade of the eighteenth century culminated in the invasion attempt of 1708 in which Louis XIV supported them with money and the promise of 6000 troops

1 G.H. Jones, *The Main Stream of Jacobitism* (Cambridge, Mass. 1954), 47-8
2 Ibid., 47

and arms and ammunition for several thousand recruits.[3] In addition to this open activity, the closing years of Anne's reign were taken up with secretive negotiations by certain members of the Tory party, particularly Viscount Bolingbroke, to bring back the Stuarts after her death.[4]

The death of Queen Anne meant a change of dynasty. George Lewis, elector of Brunswick-Lüneburg and arch-treasurer of the empire, succeeded, by Act of Parliament, to the throne of Britain and Ireland. Seven weeks elapsed before he finally set foot on English soil on 8 September 1714 and, in the interval, a mood of uncertainty permeated every aspect of official life; a rival claimant, with a better blood-right to the succession, existed. That rival claimant was James Stuart, known as James III to his followers and as the Old Pretender to the formulators of the Act of Settlement of 1701. John Byrom, a fellow of Trinity College, Cambridge, expressed that mood well when he wrote: 'God bless the King, – I mean the Faith's Defender; God bless – no Harm in blessing! – the Pretender; Who that Pretender is, and who that King, God bless us all! is quite another Thing.'[5] There was, however, but one interrogative on the lips of the Hanoverian Tories and Whigs – what would the Jacobites do to further the cause of their candidate, James III? They waited expectantly for some attempt in favour of the Pretender during that crucial interval between Queen Anne's death and George I's arrival. The Jacobites did nothing. Their only attempt at concerted effort amounted to little more than the wrangling indecision that was to be a marked feature of Jacobite activity over the next thirty years. At this critical point the strength of Jacobitism was not openly expressed and hence the element in England, Wales, Ireland, and Scotland that favoured a Stuart restoration remained unknown. But not for long. Within a year of George I's accession, the British government was faced with an open Jacobite rebellion.[6] On 6 September 1715 John, earl of Mar, raised the Pretender's standard at Perth. Through this and the next year the British government was fully occupied in putting down a major domestic insurrection. In a dispatch from the earl of Stair, ambassador in Paris, on 20 July

---

3 Ibid., 78
4 J.H. Shennan and Margaret Shennan, 'The Protestant Succession in English Politics, April 1713-September 1715,' in *William III and Louis XIV: Essays 1680-1720 by and for Mark A. Thomson*, eds. R. Hatton and J.S. Bromley (Toronto 1968)
5 John Byrom, 'An Admonition Against Swearing. Addressed to an Officer in the Army,' *Chetham Society Publications*, New Series, XXX, 1894, 572
6 For the Jacobite rebellion of 1715 see Jones, *The Main Stream of Jacobitism*, 108 ff; Sir Charles Petrie, *The Jacobite Movement* (London 1959), 208-84; Basil Williams, *Stanhope* (Oxford 1932), Chapter VII.

1715 to James Stanhope, one of the secretaries of state, the government was aware of plans for this rising. Immediately a spate of emergency measures followed: the recruitment of twenty-one regiments and the addition of a half-battalion of Guards were approved by parliament, the Habeas Corpus Act was suspended for six months, Admiral Byng was ordered to head up a squadron in the Channel, customs officers at all major centres were ordered to examine all persons entering England, troops were dispatched to the West Country, garrisons hastened to Bristol, Plymouth, and Southampton to guard against any attempt for an invasion via those ports, and the Guards encamped in Hyde Park.

The successful handling of this rebellion must be attributed to three ministers in particular – the two secretaries of state, Charles Townshend and James Stanhope; and the first lord of the treasury and chancellor of the exchequer, Robert Walpole. These three strove ceaselessly and diligently to allow not the slightest degree of success to crown Jacobite endeavours. Each hint or whisper of Jacobite activity in the counties was immediately followed up by letters hurriedly dispatched to the justices of the peace or the lord lieutenants. So, too, all reports from British ambassadors abroad were acted upon with speed. Each of the campaigns was closely watched and, during that at Preston in November 1715 Stanhope sent almost daily instructions to General Carpenter. Earlier in September, acting on information communicated to them by Stair about the projected rising in the West Country, the ministers issued warrants for the arrest of a number of the English Jacobites. Within a short space of time Lord Lansdowne, Sir William Wyndham, and several others were committed to the Tower charged with treason. By April 1716 the rising had been suppressed in England and Scotland. The punishment of the rebels followed. Twenty-six of the captured officers received the death penalty; about 700 of the rank and file were transported; and, of the seven English and Scottish lords captured, tried by their peers, and sentenced to death, all but three – Lords Derwentwater, Kenmure, and Nithsdale – were imprisoned.

Although the British government was successful in defeating Jacobite designs at this stage, the ministers knew that the defeat of a Jacobite uprising was not to be equated with the defeat of Jacobitism. Continued support for the Pretender did not terminate in April 1716. 'The rage and spirit of the party is still far from being subdued,' declared Townshend a year later. It was to be feared, he said, 'that the fire of the whole rebellion is rather smothered for a time than totally extinguished and that it is ready to catch hold of the first convenient matter that shall be offered it, and may break forth with fresh fury.'[7] That a fresh rebellion did not 'break forth' was due, in large part, to the vigilance, penetration, and meticulous care that the English ministers took in the years after 1715 to preclude such a possibility. Future Jacobite attempts were to rely heavily for their success on the element of surprise but never were the ministers to be taken unexpectedly. To be off their guard for a moment, where Jacobitism was concerned, was but an invitation to invasion by the Pretender aided by a foreign power. The reaction of the English ministers to Jacobite projects in these years demonstrates clearly their dread of Jacobitism, and the harsh retaliatory measures they took appear as but external expressions of their genuine fear of a Stuart restoration. In addition, their action betrays a keen awareness of the political advantages to be reaped through a careful exploitation of those fears, for in engaging to do battle with the forces of Jacobitism the ministers were not only protecting the Hanoverian succession but themselves as well. The nature of the Jacobite challenge in the years immediately after the 1715 Rebellion and the response of the English ministers form the subject matter of the ensuing chapters.

7 William Coxe, *Memoirs of the Life and Administration of Sir Robert Walpole, Earl of Orford* (London 1798), II, 52

1

The Swedish-Jacobite conspiracy of 1717

The chief aim of the Jacobites was to restore their candidate, James III, to the throne of Great Britain and to overturn the Hanoverians. To accomplish this objective certain requirements had to be fulfilled. The formula for doing so was clearly set forth by the earl of Mar as early as 1715. He wrote:

. . . there is no hope of succeeding in it [a restoration] without the assistance of a regular force, or without a general raising of the people in all parts of England, immediately upon the King's landing, and that the latter depends very much upon the former. For though the generality of the people are extremely averse from the Court and Ministry (whom they hate and despise) and well inclined to a restoration; yet it is not to be expected that they should declare themselves all at once, unless they see the King attended with such a force as will give some reputation to his undertaking, and encourage the country to come in to him.[1]

At least two conditions were vital for a restoration attempt to have any prospect of success – a general uprising within England and foreign support. It is significant that Mar places the emphasis for his former prerequisite not on Scotland or Ireland but on England. Even Bolingbroke saw this as essential, for he was convinced that if Scotland and Ireland to a man were prepared to flock to the Stuart banner, the throne could never be disposed of by these two alone.[2] In addition, the failure of the Jacobite Rebellion of 1715 should

---

1 HMC, *Stuart MSS* I, 520
2 H.N. Fieldhouse, 'Bolingbroke's Share in the Jacobite Intrigue of 1710-1714,' *English Historical Review*, LII, 1937, 453, 455

have taught the Jacobites, among other things, that, regardless of the disposition of their supporters within Great Britain, foreign support must be a *sine qua non* for the success of any further venture. Throughout the next several decades they were to exhaust much time and energy in attempting to enlist arms and men from abroad.

Of this one reality the Pretender himself was fully conscious. 'I find myself unable to flatter myself with the hopes of any foreign assistance,' he lamented in a letter to the duke of Lorraine in July of 1716.[3] Six months later, however, his mood of despondency changed to one of buoyancy and great urgency because he was convinced that Sweden was about to become the instrument for his restoration to the throne of Great Britain. In a letter to Baron George Görtz von Schlitz, the king of Sweden's chief minister, he urged: 'Take your measures, choose your canals, rely on my secrecy, but lose not a moment.'[4] By early January 1717 Sweden, acting through three of her ministers – Baron Sparre in Paris, Baron Görtz at The Hague, Count Gyllenborg in London – had undertaken serious discussions with the Jacobites. As a result a plan was concerted and agreement reached for an invasion of England on behalf of the Pretender.

Between 1706 and 1716 the Jacobites, with little success, had worked with great earnestness to win the support of Charles XII, king of Sweden. In the former year negotiations of some sort had been initiated at Paris with one Count Bielke, a Swedish major-general, and the following year Ker of Kersland, a Scottish Jacobite, endeavoured to further these discussions but seems to have made little or no headway.[5] The next serious effort came in 1715 when Baron Sparre actively engaged in talks for a Stuart restoration. In July of that year he met at Marly with the duke of Berwick and Torcy, the French secretary, and early in the course of their discussions Berwick urged Sparre to write to Charles XII. For his part Sparre assured them his master would look with great favour on such a project and would give tangible proof by placing his fleet and troops at their disposal, providing an appropriate sum of money was advanced from the Jacobite side. Matters would be greatly facilitated, he felt, if the Pretender wrote personally to Charles XII and offered him 50,000 crowns. Accordingly the offer was forwarded in late June via Torcy to his brother, the comte de Croissy, the French ambas-

---

3 *Stuart MSS*, II, 255

4 Ibid., III, 441

5 N. Hooke, *Correspondence of Colonel Nathaniel Hooke, Agent from the Court of France to the Scottish Jacobites, in the years 1703-1707*, ed. W.D. Macray (London 1871), II, 39, 446, 449; HMC, *Portland MSS*, IV, 307

sador extraordinary to the court of Sweden, who was to use his offices to enlist the support of Sweden for the venture.[6] The money was duly advanced via Torcy's agent and Jacobite hopes mounted, for in return they anticipated the use of the twelve battalions in the region of Gottenburg under the command of Major-General Hugo John Hamilton, one of the many Scots in the king of Sweden's service.[7] Their expectations for an invasion via Newcastle were destined to be short-lived, however, because the efforts of Croissy to convince Charles XII to champion the Stuart cause, on the grounds that he was now an enemy of George I, fell on deaf ears. As Britain had not yet declared war on him he was not prepared, he stated, to provoke her into such action. Henrik Müllern, his chancellor, claimed also that his master already had enough enemies and was unwilling to add George I to his list; furthermore, were they to embrace the Pretender's cause at this juncture it would only serve to excite great mistrust among the other Protestant powers.[8]

Although troops had been refused and the money returned, the Jacobites did not waver in their anticipation of support from Sweden. In late December 1715, after the Pretender disembarked at Peterhead, he wrote (but did not send) a desperate appeal to Charles XII for immediate aid.[9]

Following his return to France after the failure of the 1715 Rebellion, James III could look only to Sweden as his potential deliverer. The regent of France, the duc d'Orléans, had now turned his back on the Jacobite cause, and it became obvious that the Pretender would no longer be allowed to remain at Bar-Le-Duc in French territory. Ormonde and the earl of Mar, the Pretender's secretary of state, held meetings with Sparre in late February 1716 to sound him out on the possibility of James taking up residence in Charles XII's territory of Zweibrücken. With no power to treat on this subject, the most Sparre could do was to promise to write to his master, but before a reply was received the Pretender moved his residence to papal territory at Avignon.

As nothing had been heard by mid-July, it was decided to send a special envoy to the court of Charles XII and to this Sparre agreed, providing it was a person of 'consequence and character.' Although Ormonde was proposed, the task finally fell to John Erskine of Alva, cousin to the earl of Mar. With

---

6 *Mémoires du Maréchal de Berwick* (Switzerland 1778), 146; J.F. Chance, *George I and the Northern War* (London 1909), 77-9; *Stuart MSS*, I, 372-4

7 *Stuart MSS*, I, 413

8 Chance, *George I and the Northern War*, 78

9 For Charles XII's bitter dislike of George I see 21 and 29 below.

him he took a memorial in which the Pretender requested immediate aid from Charles XII in order to check the ambitions of their common enemy, George I. Once arrived in Hamburg, Erskine was to establish contact with Major-General Hamilton to have his opinion on the disposition of the Swedish court and, if the situation was judged to be favourable, he was to go forth and use his utmost powers to bring Charles XII 'into such measures as may conduce to our service.' In addition, he was to seek refuge there for the Pretender and his court; to secure his assistance with troops, arms, and ammunition sufficient to ensure a restoration; and to promise Charles the return of all his dominions taken from him by George I. The venture itself was a bold and imaginative one but it never materialized and by mid-September Erskine received orders to terminate his mission.[10]

The Jacobites were aware of one stark reality in their endeavours to win support from Charles XII – he had to be in need of money and they had to be in a position to supply it. In 1716 Charles desperately needed liquid capital, a need which set in motion a chain of events which could have proved very serious for the British government. Concurrently with Erskine's mission, another emanated from the court of Sweden – Baron Görtz arrived at Amsterdam on 2 July 1716 in search of capital.[11] Failing to secure the moneys there, he proceeded to The Hague in the hope of persuading the United Provinces to make a loan on the security of the Swedish iron and copper mines, but for both political and economic reasons he met with no success. The United Provinces were experiencing their own financial strains following the War of the Spanish Succession, and, even had they been in a position to do so, it is most unlikely that the United Provinces would have jeopardized their good relations with Britain by such an action. The Treaty of Westminster had been concluded on 25 May 1716 between Britain and Austria, and, in addition to guaranteeing the Dutch Barrier Treaty, provision had also been made for the transport of 8000 men from Denmark and 10,000 from Prussia to be used either in Britain or Holland as the case might require it. Görtz's efforts to raise capital met a similar fate in France, where finances were as precarious as in the United Provinces. On his arrival in Paris in late August he met first with Sparre and explained to him the urgency with which capital was needed. Unless it were forthcoming by Octo-

10 *Stuart MSS*, II, 155, 213, 283-4, 288, 359, 402, 500-2. In the margin of the papers sent by the Pretender to Erskine empowering him to negotiate such a treaty is the notation that he got only as far as Lübeck.

11 For further details of these transactions see R.M. Hatton, *Charles XII of Sweden* (London 1968), 436ff; J.J. Murray, *George I, the Baltic and the Whig Split of 1717* (London 1969), 285-317.

ber, he claimed, Charles XII would be left in a critical situation with no money to pay his troops.[12] Görtz then had an audience with the regent but was able to elicit only vague promises for the payment of subsidies due to Sweden by conditions of the treaty of April 1715. Unable to secure funds from either France or the United Provinces, Görtz was left with one other source – the Jacobites.

Up to this point he had demonstrated an extreme reluctance to engage in any transactions with them. Quite unlike Görtz, however, Baron Sparre and Count Gyllenborg had given them all possible encouragement. Sparre had always shown a warm sympathy for the Pretender and his adherents, one of whom, General Dillon, had been a close friend for over twenty years. Count Gyllenborg, who had been Swedish ambassador in London since 1703, had demonstrated a like enthusiasm. Married to Sarah Wright, a distant relative of the English Jacobite, Charles Caesar, he had been a party to most of their plans and secrets.[13] The Jacobites were certain of the support of these two men, but did not feel fully confident of Görtz's whole-hearted support until early January 1717. Görtz's failure to secure liquid capital elsewhere was to unite him with Sparre and Gyllenborg and together they agreed – as a last resort – to a plan for a Stuart restoration. The triangular web of a Swedish-Jacobite conspiracy between London, Paris, and The Hague was initiated in a two-hour meeting between Sparre and Dillon in Paris on 29 August 1716.[14] At this session Sparre, acting with the authorization of Görtz, announced to Dillon that the king of Sweden was now 'most inclined to enter into amity and union' with them. He requested him to make all haste to prepare a memorial to Charles XII in which he should mention 'the succours of all kinds that Arthur [the Pretender] expects and hopes from his friends in Bernard [England], as also the advantage and benefit this union may prove to Humphry [Charles XII].'[15] Once it was prepared, Baron Görtz would take it back to The Hague and communicate it to the king of Sweden. As soon as the king had considered it, Sparre assured Dillon, he had no doubt whatsoever that his master would then dispatch to him full power to make a treaty for their mutual interest. Once these credentials were received, the necessary troops and supplies to undertake the venture would be forthcoming by the end of November or early December 1716.

12 C.J. Nordmann, *La Crise du nord au début du XVIIIe siècle* (Paris 1962), 68
13 Caesar Journals, Book I. Mrs Caesar records that there had been a long and intimate friendship between her husband and Count Gyllenborg. After Gyllenborg's release he gave Caesar his picture and upon his return to Sweden sent him one of Charles XII.
14 *Stuart MSS*, II, 427-8
15 Ibid., II, 428

No doubt ebullient at the progress they had made, Dillon hurried off that same afternoon to inform the queen mother of the outcome. That evening, at her command, he discussed their good fortune with Charles Middleton and Father Lewis Innes, the queen mother's confessor, at Avignon. Accordingly Father Innes penned the memorial which was duly presented to Sparre. In it the Pretender declared that he had 'positive and repeated assurances from the heads of the English Church and the heads of the Tories . . . that they will unanimously join him [the Pretender]; on the following conditions: – (1) That 6,000 regular troops be sent, which will be sufficient to occupy a suitable position, and thereby give the well disposed time and opportunity to resort thither; (2) that means of arming 30,000 men be sent at the same time with the requisite munitions.'[16] In return for military aid the Pretender pledged himself 'to put his ally and benefactor once more in possession of all his just rights.'[17] However, before any agreement was reached, even in the most general terms, divisions of opinion arose among the Jacobites themselves over the number of troops necessary for a successful operation. Although Mar agreed in general with the scheme, he was insistent on one thing: the number of troops should be raised to eight or ten thousand since such a force would enable them to land troops in both England and Scotland.

Before leaving for The Hague, Görtz and Sparre agreed on Sweden's terms and at a second meeting on 15 September Dillon was presented with their conditions. They demanded to know what amount of money could be offered immediately to assist any endeavour and, in the event of its success, insisted on the restoration to Sweden of Bremen and Verden, a treaty of union and commerce, and such other treaties 'as it shall please the King to dictate.'[18] It was obvious that a substantial supply of money was their first and foremost need. 'The King of Sweden is in absolute need of money to pay his troops in the exigency in which he finds himself,' wrote Dillon to the Pretender. 'If Your Majesty, by means of your friends in England, would satisfy him on that point, it is the essential stroke, and one that will engage that prince to make the utmost efforts to restore you to the throne of your ancestors.'[19]

In reply to the Swedish proposals the Pretender restated his demands: 8000 foot and 2000 horse and dragoons, 30,000 firelocks of an equal calibre, 30,000 bayonets, 6000 swords, 500 cwt of powder for muskets, twenty field

16 Ibid., II, 430
17 Ibid., 430
18 Ibid., IV, 76
19 Ibid., II, 477

pieces, ten four-pounders, and ten eight-pounders. With respect to money, all he could claim was that he had written on it.[20]

Indeed, the machinery for collecting the money had been established by mid-July. As a supply from France was now out of the question, it had to be gained from Jacobite supporters in England, among whom were listed Francis Atterbury, bishop of Rochester, and Robert Harley, earl of Oxford. The middleman acting between them and the court at Avignon was John Menzies,[21] the Pretender's chief agent in London, while Captain John Ogilvie, the earl of Oxford's messenger, carried the majority of communications to and from the continent. At an early stage not only Atterbury and Oxford but also the earl of Arran, the duke of Shrewsbury, and Sir William Wyndham were informed of the good disposition of Charles XII towards their cause. The earl of Arran, brother to the earl of Mar and soon to be elected to the chancellorship of Oxford University, was constituted commander-in-chief of all the forces in England and Scotland.[22] The management of the collection of money – variously referred to in their correspondence as 'the factory trade,' 'the muslin manufacture,' 'the woolen trade,' 'the staple trade' – was entrusted to Francis Atterbury. On 10 September he was created official resident in England 'to and by whom he [the Pretender] will from time to time transmit his pleasure, commands, and directions to all his subjects of that kingdom.'[23] Previously a full and separate power had been sent to him making him responsible for the collection of all money. It had been delivered to him by John Menzies with whom he worked very closely.

Francis Atterbury was to remain at the very heart of Jacobite activity within England until his banishment in 1723. Educated at Westminster and Christ Church, Oxford, in 1713 he had been made dean of Christ Church and the very next year was named by Queen Anne to the bishopric of Rochester and the deanery of Westminster. On the day of Anne's death Atterbury had met with several of the leading Tories, among them Ormonde, Bathurst, Bolingbroke, and Wyndham, and insisted that they take immediate action by seeking aid from Louis XIV and proclaiming James III king of Great Britain. At this meeting he declared: 'he would at the Royal Ex-

20 Ibid., III, 544-5
21 John Menzies, alias Bradbury, Abraham, Monsieur de Magny, was a native of Aberdeenshire and one of the impoverished rebels of the 1715 rebellion. Between 1716 and 1718 he was a pensioner of Mary of Modena and in the former year came to England to act as agent there. One of his sidelines, apparently a fairly lucrative one, was selling chocolate to the French nobility.
22 *Stuart MSS*, II, 305; W.R. Ward, *Georgian Oxford* (Oxford 1958), 57-8
23 *Stuart MSS*, II, 466-7

change read, in his lawn sleeves, the Proclamation. Upon this Lord Bolingbroke said that all our throats would be cut. To which the Bishop reply'd
that if a speedy resolution be not taken, by God all will be lost. Lord Bolingbroke harangued upon this subject, and the Bishop fell into a great passion
and said that this pusillanimous fellow will ruin our country; so he quitted
them.'[24] From the outset, however, Atterbury was reluctant to enter fully
into his new duties and not until mid-1717 did he finally commit himself to
the Pretender's cause.[25] In this procrastination lies the explanation for much
of the haphazard Jacobite activity during these months, for he gave no firm
direction. He himself wished that full power had not been sent to him, and
many others shared this view. In addition, from the beginning Atterbury
and Oxford seemed unable 'to submerge old quarrels' and to unite in the
common endeavour before them.[26] The earl of Mar pleaded with Menzies,
on more than one occasion, to use his persuasion to gain 'a mutual trust and
confidence between them' and to ease Oxford's bitterness over full power being granted to Atterbury. Mar even wrote personally to Oxford, begging his
advice and direction, and stating that he had always looked on him as a 'father and director in those matters.'[27]

With reports flowing in from Menzies of the slowness with which money
was being collected, the court at Avignon decided to send an emissary to
England to hasten proceedings. Accordingly, one Downes arrived in late
October and went first to the earl of Arran and then to Atterbury requesting that £50,000 be dispatched immediately.[28] Considering this amount to be
exorbitant, Atterbury pledged himself to raise £20,000; by 19 November he
had secured some £5,000 but did not turn it over immediately as he awaited
further instructions from General Dillon at Paris. Once these were received
he would then give it to the earl of Arran to be delivered to Count Gyllenborg in London.[29] Since Atterbury was reluctant to give signed receipts for

---

24 Add. MSS, 35,837, f 509. Quoted in Basil Williams, *The Whig Supremacy 1714-1760* (Oxford 1962),
150
25 According to J.H. Glover, Atterbury did not send his first letter to the Pretender until
August 1717. See *Letters of Francis Atterbury, Bishop of Rochester to the Chevalier St. George and
Some Adherents of the House of Stuart*, ed. J.H. Glover (London 1847), I, 1-2.
26 The animosity between Atterbury and Oxford stemmed largely from the division of
opinion as to what action the English Jacobites should take at the time of Queen Anne's
death. Atterbury had headed a group demanding immediate action and Oxford had opposed him.
27 *Stuart MSS*, II, 459, 465
28 Ibid., III, 243; V, 527-8
29 Ibid., V, 528

the money, he allowed the power sent to him to be used not only by Menzies but also by Jerningham, a banker in Fleet Street.

Although the earl of Portmore and the duke of Shrewsbury were sympathetic to the project and great hopes were entertained of gaining substantial sums from them, there is no evidence that they ever contributed. Menzies worked ceaselessly to secure their services but even by late January they had not committed themselves. Unless, they argued, some guarantee were provided from the emperor, Charles VI, that he would draw his troops out of the Austrian Netherlands, in order 'to puzzle' Holland and curb her from sending immediate aid to the Hanoverians, the entire project was doomed to failure.[30] Charles Caesar, however, engaged actively in the collection of money and guaranteed £5,000 from among his friends. Oxford and his colleagues formed a separate group with respect to 'the muslin trade.' In addition to acting as Atterbury's right-hand man, Menzies also collected from the Catholic interest, but with this latter group the principal director was Thomas Southcott, a Roman Catholic priest. By the end of the year Southcott remitted some £8,000 to Avignon.[31]

In Scotland the collection of money was entrusted to Captain H. Straton, the Pretender's agent in Edinburgh, who was also expected to furnish him with details regarding the number of troops available and advice for an invasion attempt.[32] Straton duly forwarded lists of the army and appointed Alexander Macleod, a Presbyterian, to communicate the general plan to the Highland clans. There was, however, little prospect of gaining money from this source as many of those who might have contributed were now in exile or had forfeited their estates. Moreover, the heavy burden and losses they had sustained as a result of the 1715 Rebellion had left many of them penniless and unable to aid even their distressed friends at home and abroad.

The main direction of the affair was from England through the English Jacobites and their negotiations with Count Gyllenborg. Although Atterbury engineered the plot, there is no evidence that he ever directly negotiated with Count Gyllenborg. It would seem that the earl of Arran acted as his go-between. Gyllenborg informed Görtz on 29 September that he had held several meetings with the Jacobites, but that without an express order from Charles XII he could proceed no further.[33] He had received assurances

30 Ibid., III, 494

31 Ibid., III, 338, 401. The £3000 mentioned by Mar in his letter is probably the same amount as referred to by Southcott in his to Mar.

32 George Lockhart, *The Lockhart Papers: Containing Memoirs and Commentaries upon the Affairs of Scotland from 1702 to 1715*, ed. A. Aufrere (London 1817), II, 7-8

33 The main source of this aspect of the conspiracy are the intercepted letters of Görtz, Gyllenborg, and Sparre. Copies of these are to be found in PRO, SP 107/1A and 1B. Another set

that money would be forthcoming if, in return, they could be guaranteed the services of Sweden to the extent of 10,000 men. Writing from The Hague, however, Görtz cautioned him not 'to make any mention in your letters to the King, or to your correspondents in Sweden, of what has been secretly proposed to you about the Pretender.' But he did authorize him to find out particulars. On 16 October 'two of the principals' made the rather high estimate of £60,000 as their contribution for Sweden's services. At this stage Görtz was still firmly against any sealed bargain. There must, he told Sparre, be no 'formal treaty,' for when the money was collected would be time enough. He was most definitely opposed to any suggestion that the Pretender should retire to Stockholm, since it would be like 'blazing abroad our intelligence by sound of trumpet.' In no uncertain terms he stated his position: 'Your friends must place so much confidence in us, as to furnish us with what we want, to put ourselves in a condition of becoming useful to them; the sum required is not exorbitant, three hundred thousand crowns may satisfie us at present, for we want nothing but to augment our naval force at Gottenburg.' Similar instructions were sent to Gyllenborg, but Görtz did tell him that if a plan were prepared he would forward it to his master.

The English Jacobites were not, however, to be taken in so easily. Upon receipt of these orders Gyllenborg went almost at once to the home of one of the leading English Jacobites, probably the earl of Arran, and told him Görtz's position. Gyllenborg was told explicitly that a loan with no prospect of aid was out of the question. 'Why,' asked this Jacobite, 'should we run the risk of making a loan to the king of Sweden when we can invest our money here in England at seven or eight percent?' 'Let us be assured,' he said, 'that by our money we shall merit his help and actually have it.' This attitude on the part of the English Jacobites hastened Görtz, it would seem, to reverse his position. This, and, at least, two other factors. He had just received word that Sweden was in the midst of a harvest failure and, as the situation had become serious, money was needed even more desperately. Appeals had already been made to have as much oats, rye, and barley as possible sent from England and aid had been sought from the court at Avignon. Mar had requested Captain Straton 'to have 5,000 or 6,000 bolls of meal' sent to Sweden, but fear of arousing the suspicions of the British government had hampered efforts in both areas.[34] At the same time Görtz had received a much broader

is located in the HLRO, Records 1716/1717, item 249. The originals of these, which are to be found in the Upsala State Archives, have been printed in full in *Handlingar rörande Skandinaviens Historia* (Stockholm 1822), X. For this section I have used those in the HLRO.

34 *Lockhart Papers*, II, 7

treaty power from Charles XII. On 25 October he had informed the king he had been offered the sum of 300,000 thalers; accordingly Charles sent him the power 'to treat and conclude in our Name, with all singular persons of what condition soever, and all matters which relate to our service, and be for our Interest; Promising on our Royal Word, that we will approve and ratify, and put intirely into execution whatever the said Baron Görtz shall so transact and conclude.'[35]

It was largely for these reasons that Görtz now displayed a new interest in Jacobite plans. Even before his departure from Sweden 'we were already on our side disposed to this expedition,' he now told them. All that was needed immediately were transports to carry the troops and, of course, money to purchase the former. Towards the end of December 1716 he returned to Paris, made one last attempt to obtain the capital there, and, having failed, turned to embrace the Jacobite cause. In early January he met with General Dillon and a plan was executed. The agreement reached was that 'Robertson [the Pretender] [is] to give Saxby [the King of Sweden] or Longford [Görtz] a million French [livres] and Saxby [the King of Sweden] is to transport into England by the twentieth of April or sooner eight thousand foot, five hundred horse mounted, and three thousand five hundred horsemen, with their accoutrements ready to mount, thirty thousand arms, a train of artillery. . .'[36]

Such was the verbal agreement between Sweden and the Jacobites. It had now to be executed. For his part, the Pretender had assurances of £30,000 but probably had no more than about £18,000 in his actual possession. Of this about £15,000 was surrendered to Görtz – only about half of the sum he required for immediate use and less than half of the full amount agreed upon. The remainder had to be obtained with all speed, for the men-of-war, obtained through the services of the Swedish banker at Paris, Antoine Hogguer, were waiting to be procured.[37] Görtz pressed Gyllenborg to secure this remainder; the English Jacobites responded with a guarantee of £10,000 and Gyllenborg began to make preparations to leave England for Holland. From the court at Avignon an express order was sent to Atterbury urging him to make all haste in fulfilling their part of the treaty. 'For God's sake take care

35 HLRO, Records 1716/1717, item 249, 8 Jan. 1717, Görtz to Gyllenborg
36 *Stuart MSS*, III, 481
37 Baron Hogguer, a French banker of Swedish origin, had aided both Louis XIV and the regent. He also promoted the interests of Charles XII. After the battle of Poltava, while Charles XII was still in Turkey, he had supplied the money to pay the Swedish troops holding Stralsund. J. Mathorez, *Les Etrangers en France sous l'ancien régime* (Paris 1921), II, 357-8

the musseline trade goes on,' wrote the Pretender, 'for without that nothing can be done, and that alone can set all hands to work.'[38] On 16 January George Jerningham, the Pretender's agent at The Hague, was sent full powers to negotiate and conclude a formal treaty with Görtz on the basis of the earlier verbal one. The only persons the Jacobites believed to be a party to their plans were the Pretender, the king of Sweden, Ormonde, Mar, Dillon, Görtz, Sparre, and Jerningham. To their list they should have added the names of the leading English ministers – Stanhope, Sunderland, Townshend, and Walpole. Ten days after Jerningham had been named as official negotiator for a formal treaty, and on the very eve of the departure of Count Gyllenborg for Holland with the money and a detailed plan for an invasion attempt, the English ministers took the decision to inform the Jacobites that they, too, had been fully aware of their plans and secrets for some time.

38 *Stuart MSS*, III, 526

2

The ministerial response

Where an enemy of George I existed, there the Jacobites found their warm-est support for any restoration attempt. Of this truism the English ministers were well aware and much of the energy of ministers at home and at foreign courts was exhausted in an effort to keep as fully informed as possible of Ja-cobite dealings with all foreign powers, particularly those who were un-friendly towards Britain. Horace Walpole, Robert Walpole's brother, ex-pressed this fear for all the ministers when he declared: 'The greatest danger we could be in comes from those Princes who favour the Pretender and are in a condition to send him over upon us with a force at least sufficient with the ill-affected to create us trouble and give us disquiet.'[1] From early Sep-tember 1716 the leading English ministers – Charles Spencer, 3rd earl of Sun-derland; James, 1st Earl Stanhope; Charles, 2nd Viscount Townshend; and Robert Walpole – were fully conscious of the revived Jacobite hopes both in England and at Avignon. Their intelligence system was sufficiently keen to assure them that the Jacobites expected foreign assistance for their next en-deavour, but they were still uncertain from whence it would come. They could, for the moment at least, breathe easy with respect to possible French support for the Jacobites, since the death of Louis XIV had brought to the French throne the infant Louis XV with the duc d'Orléans acting as regent. In the event of the young king's death Orléans would succeed to the title, providing the king of Spain, Philip V (Louis XIV's grandson), held to his ear-lier pledge to renounce, as part of his Spanish inheritance, any right to the French throne. Certainly neither Orléans nor his chief minister, the Abbé

1 HMC, *Polwarth MSS*, IV, 81

Dubois, trusted Philip to keep his word; therefore, they had secured the support of Britain and in return had agreed to withdraw all support for the Jacobites.

Since no aid was forthcoming from France, the most obvious quarter seemed to be Sweden as here George I, in his capacity as elector of Hanover, was most closely involved. George I's quarrel with Charles XII of Sweden was with respect to two of his German possessions, Bremen and Verden. In 1715 Frederick IV of Denmark had sold these to George I for the sum of £150,000, plus the support of the British fleet against Sweden. Although James Stanhope was convinced of Sweden's pro-Jacobite sympathy, he was at the same time uncertain just 'how far his [Charles XII's] passion may carry him towards pouring a body of forces into Scotland, or the North of England from Gottenburg, especially considering that he may hope by such a diversion to put it out of his Majesty's power to interpose any longer in the affairs of the north.'[2] Quite obviously, therefore, the correspondence of the Swedish ambassador in London, Count Gyllenborg, had not gone unnoticed by a vigilant ministry concerned with bringing to light any Jacobite intrigue. Gyllenborg's correspondence was intercepted as early as September 1716 and, after careful copies of the seals had been made, it was opened, copied, and then sent on. So successful was the government that on 23 September Townshend was able to inform James Stanhope that the king of Sweden was 'treating with the Jacobites in order to join with the Pretender.' On 12 October he related to him further details but was still uncertain of the extent to which Charles would participate. He did feel, however, the situation was a gravely serious one for 'the weak and low condition to which the Danes are reduced, and the present views and behaviour of the Czar may . . . make him [Charles XII] think that he has now an opportunity of indulging what seems to be his darling passion, revenge upon the King.'[3]

At the beginning of November Townshend summoned a meeting of the Cabinet Council and communicated to the duke of Devonshire, Lord Cowper, the duke of Bolton, Lord Orford, and Lord Parker copies of the correspondence between Gyllenborg and Görtz, the king of Sweden's envoy at The Hague. They unanimously agreed that 'it is of the utmost consequence to the safety of the nation, that all possible precautions should be taken both at Hanover and in England, to put it out of the power of Sweden to execute the design framed by Count Gyllenborg and the Jacobites.'[4] They felt this could best be achieved by keeping the Swedish forces occupied at home and

2 BM, Add.MSS, 28,145, Sept. 15, 1716, Stanhope to Norris
3 William Coxe, *Memoirs of the Life and Administration of Sir Robert Walpole* II, 114
4 Ibid., II, 121

to accomplish this they should seriously entertain the czar's suggestion for a simultaneous descent on Finland and Schonen in the spring. 'This will in the opinion of the Lords,' said Townshend, 'give the King of Sweden his hands full of business, and put him out of a condition to spare any forces towards supporting the cause of the Pretender.' Orders should be given immediately to send a squadron of men-of-war into the Baltic in readiness for the attack in the spring. The other members of the cabinet shared Townshend's fears and, despite clamours that would be raised against it, the decision was taken to continue 'the whole force both at sea and land which is now on foot.' By early November a real fear had gripped the ministers and they did not need the pensionary of Holland to warn them 'to be on their guard' against the activities of Count Gyllenborg. They were too well aware of what the consequence of his union with the Jacobites might bring.

At this critical juncture a split occurred within the Whig ministry. George I left on the first of his many trips to Hanover in July 1716. He was accompanied there by James Stanhope, secretary of state for the Northern Department. During the king's absence his son was to act as guardian of the realm and Charles Townshend, secretary of state for the Southern Department, and Robert Walpole were to serve as his advisers. Over the next several months George I's jealousy towards his son mounted, Sunderland's growing dissatisfaction with his own position in the ministry grew more acute, and the genuine dispute between Stanhope and Townshend over the conduct of foreign policy reached boiling point. On 12 December 1716 Townshend was dismissed from his office and given the inferior one of lord lieutenant of Ireland. The following April he was dismissed from all office and his brother-in-law, Robert Walpole, and several other Whigs resigned their posts and went into opposition. Despite the strident opposition of Walpole, Townshend, and their supporters to government policy over the next three years (until their reconcilation with the ministry in 1720), they did not at any point attack the ministry for its anti-Jacobite campaign.[5] Nor did the change in the ministry in any way affect the vigilance of the government in watching the situation closely. Stanhope, to whom copies of all intercepted letters had been communicated, advised Paul Methuen, the new acting secretary of state, to continue 'the method my Lord Townshend had taken in relation to this secret correspondence.'[6]

On the return of George I from Hanover the pace quickened and it was agreed more decisive action must be taken. This decision was determined by

5 See below, 33, 39.
6 Coxe, *Walpole*, II, 155

the interception of a letter from Gustavus Gyllenborg, Görtz's secretary, to Count Gyllenborg in which he told him Görtz would be in Holland on 29 January and that he expected he would be there with the money from England.[7] On 29 January 1717 James Stanhope laid the most recent news of the conspiracy before the Privy Council assembled at the Cockpit in Whitehall and the final decision was made to arrest Count Gyllenborg and to seize all his papers. Immediately following the meeting Stanhope issued a warrant to Major-General Wade for carrying this out. The warrant stated that 'his Majesty hath certain information that Count Gyllenborg is carrying on a treasonable correspondence against His Majesty's government, and hath endeavoured to engage several of his Majesty's liege subjects to execute and stir up a rebellion, towards the support of which he had promised them foreign assistance.'[8] With the greatest degree of exactitude and speed Major-General Wade, together with Lieutenant-Colonel Blakeney and a detachment of foot-guards numbering between thirty-five and forty, surrounded the home of the Swedish ambassador at eleven o'clock the same evening. At midnight Wade and Blakeney entered the house, informed Gyllenborg of their purpose, and seized those papers which were loose upon the table. Despite protests from the ambassador's wife, the locked desk was broken open and the papers within removed and sealed. Having secured these a guard of no fewer than twenty soldiers and officers was stationed in his house, for Gyllenborg was to be allowed to speak to no one, not even his own secretary, except in public. Even though the ambassador or his secretary had managed to burn some of the dispatches, Wade took with him some three cart loads of the ambassador's papers and these he conveyed post-haste to Secretary Methuen for scrutiny.[9]

Numerous other arrests followed. Earlier the same evening the ministers had arrested Sir Jacob Bankes, the former member of parliament for Minehead. Of Swedish birth, Bankes had been responsible for what became known as the 'Minehead Doctrine' which in essence declared that kings were accountable only to God and a subject's first duty was to obey them under any conditions. Major Boyle Smith was next arrested in the early morning of 30 January – a former Irish officer and one of the Jacobite agents in England, he was taken completely by surprise, having the previous eve-

7 PRO, SP 78/161, f 5

8 PRO, SP 35/8, f 43

9 [D. Defoe] *Mercurius Politicus: Being Monthly Observations on the Affairs of Great Britain; with a Collection of all the Most Material Occurrences in Europe. For the Month of February, 1717* (London 1717), 65

ning been playing cards in the apartments at St James's palace.[10] Charles Caesar, former under-treasurer of the navy during the Harley administration, had entertained Count Gyllenborg on several occasions during the previous summer, and in the early morning of the 30th, while both he and Mrs Caesar were still in their bedroom, the messengers arrived to effect his arrest. Caesar requested his wife be made a close prisoner with him but Stanhope refused. Later the same morning the two secretaries arrived to search his papers, only to find they had forgotten the keys with which they had locked the rooms containing them; Mrs Caesar ordered the servants 'to break open the doors' and, according to her account: 'The doors being opened I bid them go on telling him [Stanhope] I was sure Mr. Caesar would be at liberty as soon as that was over. I pressing them to finish the other [room] they told me if they did he could not be examined that night so promised to come the next morning.'[11] Accordingly, Methuen arrived without Stanhope to complete their work. Although he expressed a certain uneasiness, since the warrant for the arrest and search had been signed only by Stanhope, after some four hours of rummaging in Caesar's papers he finished his task. His rewards were slight, however, since he found nothing of great moment save a list of the army and 'collections out of the English History in Mr. Caesar's hand.'[12]

The ministers were fully cognizant of the extraordinary action they had taken in arresting Count Gyllenborg and no doubt anticipated at least some of the repercussions that followed. They had already suspected Charles XII would retaliate by seizing their minister and had given him early warning to leave Stockholm. Shocked at the government's arrest of Gyllenborg, most of the ambassadors resident in London absented themselves from the court pending an explanation. It was soon forthcoming. On 1 February the two secretaries sent letters to all the foreign ministers informing them of the reasons for their action and this seemed to satisfy most of them. The marquis de Monteleone, the Spanish ambassador, was one of the exceptions. In a letter to Methuen he expressed extreme dissatisfaction that another method could not have been found for 'preserving the peace and tranquility of His Majesty's dominions.'[13]

Further consternation arose over the arrest of Gyllenborg's chief accom-

10 N. Tindal, *The History of England, by Mr. Rapin de Thoyras Continued from the Revolution to the Accession of King George II* (London 1746), XXVI, 362; Abel Boyer, *The Political State of Great Britain* (London 1717), XIII, 147

11 Caesar Journals, Book I

12 Ibid.

13 Boyer, *Political State*, XIII, 153-4

plice, Baron Görtz, the Swedish envoy at The Hague. On 4 February Mr Leathes, the British representative at The Hague, received his orders to have Görtz and his two secretaries, Mr Stambke and Gustavus Gyllenborg, secured. For this purpose the aid of the governor at Amsterdam was sought and on the 9th the States of Holland passed a resolution to aid the ministers in their request. The previous day Görtz had arrived at The Hague. One of his secretaries was arrested but Görtz and the other managed to escape to Amsterdam. Pursuit was given and on 10 February both were taken up.

Within less than a fortnight, then, Count Gyllenborg, Baron Görtz, Charles Caesar, Sir Jacob Bankes, and Major Boyle Smith had been arrested on suspicion of engaging in a plot to restore the Pretender. The interrogations followed. Despite the appeals of both Smith and Bankes, demanding to know the reasons for their arrests, they were held in custody, together with Charles Caesar, until 7 February.[14] James Stanhope had failed to find confirmation for his suspicions and fears among their papers and had hoped, no doubt, to be able to implicate them legally through the rigorous and frequent interrogations he had held already of Count Gyllenborg; failing to do so, he was finally forced to bring them before a committee of the Lords. Each was examined separately and each in turn refused to answer questions. Charles Caesar reminded them strongly that 'no Englishman was obliged to accuse himself.' He was finally bailed at £10,000 and Smith and Bankes at £5,000 each.[15]

The slightest hints or whispers of evidence were sufficient for the ministers to undertake further arrests and the letter of an informer occasioned a spate of them on 12 February.[16] Jonanthan Derbyshire, one Cookson, one Dugar, one Jerningham, a banker and goldsmith in Covent Garden, and one Hollman were taken up to be examined. All were later released save Dugar and Derbyshire who were committed to Newgate. This particular series of arrests shows clearly the problem the ministers faced, since it taught them from first-hand experience the devious and scheming ways of conspirators. No one needed to tell them that persons like Hollman and Cookson were but middlemen for the more important persons involved. With the full knowledge that some £20,000 had been remitted from England to support the Pretender, the government had hoped by these arrests to gain some hint of

14 PRO, SP 35/8, ff 55, 75
15 Caesar Journals, Book I
16 PRO, SP 35/8, f 11. The letter was from an 'anonymous' informer but it appears he was a wine merchant on Tower Hill who gained his information from Cookson, servant to Lady Bland. Those who were arrested on 12 February are the ones mentioned in this letter.

who was supplying the money. Lord Polwarth expressed the interrogative that must have been in the minds of all the ministers when he asked: 'Where the devil do they get it to throw it away in that fashion?'

By this time the public was fully aroused and awaited further news of the threatened invasion. The government extended its defensive measures, including orders for the fitting out of such men-of-war as were already in pay and warrants for manning them. By 10 February there were five ships ready with orders to cruise in the waters to the north. At the same time seventeen additional men-of-war were commissioned and an embargo was placed on all outward shipping to ease the task of securing men for these extra ships. Admiral Byng sailed for the North Sea and Admiral Littleton cruised off the coasts of Scotland. 'A great diligence was used,' said Defoe, 'to find seamen, and rummage them out of their lurking holes, to which they generally have recourse on all such occasions.'[17]

A state of readiness prevailed at home as well. Officers were ordered to their posts, general officers were dispatched to await orders to draw troops together at a moment's notice, Lieutenant-General Willes and other officers were sent to the north of England, Lieutenant-General Carpenter went immediately into Scotland, Lieutenant-General Wade hurried to the West Country. Fearing an attack on London, the government first determined on a camp in Hyde Park but 'the number of troops designed to encamp being too many for the park, it was resolved to appoint a camp at Blackheath . . . to consist of 12,000 men.'[18] Of these precautions the French ambassador in London reported: 'Tout cela, qu'on ne craint rien ici de la part de la Suède.'[19] However, when news was received from a merchant ship that thirty Swedish men-of-war were approaching via Yarmouth, a near panic resulted among the ministers. Ships were immediately dispatched to secure intelligence, only to find that the fear had no real basis for the supposed Swedish fleet bringing the Pretender was a Dutch merchant fleet.[20]

But having undertaken these measures, the English ministers stood ready to meet the intended invasion on behalf of the Pretender. All had been prepared, too, for the meeting of parliament. The ministers were aware of the political advantages this situation provided them. At the opening of parliament on 20 February, James Stanhope placed copies of the correspondence of Gyllenborg and Görtz before both houses. Much time and endless effort had gone into the preparation of these documents – translators, copiers, de-

17 [D. Defoe] *Mercurius Politicus*, 73
18 Ibid., 74-5
19 Arch.Aff.Etr.Corr.Pol.Angl., vol. 292, f 32
20 [D. Defoe] *Mercurius Politicus*, 73-4; HMC, *Stuart MSS*, IV, 110

cipherers, and printers had all been called in to assist in the selection of relevant extracts from the mass of correspondence which had been seized and intercepted. This happy discovery of the plot had for the ministers its desired effect. Both houses expressed their indignation, the necessary supplies were granted, and the army was continued. Sir John Brownlow denounced Sweden's efforts on behalf of the Pretender in no uncertain terms: 'We had no need of the King of Sweden to maintain the English liberties and support the Church of England.'[21]

Additional copies of the Görtz-Gyllenborg correspondence were given to the foreign ministers in London to deliver to their respective courts, and British ministers abroad were also supplied with them. At the French court, Crawfurd, the English secretary, claimed he made good use of his 'by setting forth the malignancy of so wicked a conspiracy so clearly and happily discovered.'

Charles XII continued to remain non-committal on the action of Gyllenborg and Görtz, and, with no further proofs forthcoming, both were eventually released. The sudden panic of the ministers began to abate: the embargo laid on shipping was removed, the forced enlistment of seamen stopped, officials who had been ordered to their posts were given more time, the encampment was delayed, the stocks began to rise. 'All things,' wrote Defoe, 'seem to fall in their former course.'

But the army remained in readiness, the ships fitted out rested at anchor ready to sail at the first order, generals and admirals waited commands, and the British representatives abroad were ordered to relax in no way their efforts to gain any knowledge of the Pretender's activities. The Jacobite camps in France and Flanders were watched even more carefully and each suspicious move was noted and in turn reported to London. At The Hague Secretary Leathes poured some £300 from his own pocket to secure intelligence, while at home 'dutiful citizens' continued to render up the remotest of trivia to a government bent on learning as much as it could of each and every Jacobite move.[22] For the moment the fear generated by the ministers and the resulting action seemed to have struck a blow to Jacobitism. Sweden's role as champion of the Stuart cause was temporarily at an end, but in no sense did the ministers relax their vigilance.

21 Richard Chandler, *The History and Proceedings of the House of Commons from the Restoration to the Present Time* (London 1742), VI, 109
22 PRO, SP 84/255, ff 212-13

3

The exploitation of fear

Whenever the ministers gave public expression to their deep inner fears of Jacobitism, cries of 'sham-plot,' 'frightful bogy,' 'political bugbear,' and 'scarecrow' went up from the opposition forces. The charge was a valid one, for the manner in which the ministers reacted to Jacobitism – and to the Jacobite plots in particular – reveals, in addition to the basic motivating force of genuine fear, an acute awareness of the political advantages to be gained from a careful exploitation of those fears. At the same time, they knew the nature of the political gamble that was involved because once public expression was given to their apprehensions they were faced with the necessity of proving the conspiracy to parliament and the nation. Failure to do so, as Townshend declared, could be ruinous since it would 'fall heavy on their own character, and give foreign powers, as well as their own partisans at home but a very mean idea of their judgment and understanding, as well as expose to the world the weakness of their own Government.'[1] Neither Stanhope nor Sunderland could afford in these years to make public plots that were but a figment of their imaginations, but what they could do, were they prepared to accept the risks, was to magnify out of all proportion an ill-grounded conspiracy for the purpose of securing certain political ends. Their handling of the Görtz-Gyllenborg plot brought them immeasurable political gains.

George I had left for Hanover on 18 July 1716 and when he returned a severe political crisis faced the Hanoverian dynasty and its Whig supporters. To be sure, when he arrived on 19 January 1717 an overwhelming display of enthusiasm and rejoicing greeted him, but it had been carefully staged. For

1 RA, Stuart, 60/98

weeks previously subscriptions had been enlisted, some as high as £50, and elaborate preparations undertaken to ensure a strong pro-Hanoverian and an equally violent anti-Jacobite demonstration. Effigies of the Pretender, the pope, the duke of Ormonde, a Jesuit, and Cardinal Gualterio were carefully executed to be carried in mock procession through the streets of London. Accompanied by crowds, estimated at upwards of a thousand, the procession wound its way to Charing Cross.[2] While the appropriate huzzas were cried up for King George, equally mounting and vociferous ones were throated against the Pretender as the effigies were cast one by one into a massive bonfire. Solid public support seemed to welcome the return of the lawful king, the defender of English liberties and the Protestant succession. Yet Stanhope and Sunderland took little encouragement from such a display. They were too acutely aware of the real nature of the situation, for in that six months' interval between the king's departure and return a crisis had developed that would tax to the full their skill and ingenuity.

This political crisis was largely the product of the single-minded and Hanoverian-centred foreign policy of George I.[3] Since 1714 he had worked, as elector of Hanover, to involve the resources of Britain in a war with Sweden which was not only of no benefit to Britain but was decidedly detrimental to her trading and commercial interests in the Baltic.

Even before his first arrival in England, George I had set in motion the series of events that culminated in the crisis of early 1717. One of his life-long ambitions had been to annex Bremen and Verden and thereby provide his electorate with an outlet to the sea. By the Treaty of Westphalia these duchies had been granted to Sweden, only to be wrested from her control by Denmark in 1712. In November 1714 George I concluded a treaty with Prussia and in May 1715, an alliance with Denmark whereby, drawing for the first time on the resources of Britain, he promised Denmark £150,000 plus support of the British fleet in return for Bremen and Verden. England was not at war with Sweden; George I as elector of Hanover was.[4] His aim was now to dispatch a fleet to the Baltic. Had its real purpose been known to parliament and the nation, the situation in which James Stanhope and Sunderland found themselves in early 1717 might have been predated by two years and a storm of protest and opposition would have been summoned forth.

---

2 Arch.Aff.Etr.Corr.Pol.Angl., vol. 297, ff 40, 52, 60
3 I am indebted to two studies for the foreign policy of this period: Wolfgang Michael, *England under George I: The Beginnings of the Hanoverian Dynasty* (London 1936), and J.F. Chance, *George I and the Northern War* (London 1909).
4 By October 1715 George I was at war with Sweden. So, too, was Russia through the conclusion of a treaty with Hanover in this same year.

Many would have recalled the protective clause of the Act of Settlement which declared: 'That in case the crown and imperial dignity of this realm shall hereafter come to any person, not being a native of this kingdom of England, this nation be not obliged to engage in any war for the defence of any dominions or territories which do not belong to the crown of England, without the consent of parliament.'[5] Such a situation was averted, however, on the grounds of the necessity to protect British trading and commercial interests in the Baltic. 'The first step,' said Friedrich Bonet, the Prussian resident in London, 'was to make the merchants claim protection for their trade' – a justification which had some basis. In early January 1715 Robert Jackson, the British minister in Sweden, had entered a demand for reparations to the amount of £65,000 for some twenty-four English merchant ships and cargoes that had been seized. Charles XII's answer had been the issuance of an Ordinance of Privateers, which allowed for no ship to enter the Baltic without risk of being taken, and by May of that year some thirty-two English and Dutch vessels had been added to the lists of Charles' captured ships. The merchants, particularly those of the British Company, were demanding satisfaction for their losses.[6]

Admiral Norris with twenty-one war ships sailed for the Baltic on 29 May 1715. His instructions were straightforward: to convoy merchant ships to and from the ports to which they were destined in the north and to demand of Charles reparation for the ships and goods already confiscated. Townshend informed Captain James Jefferyes that ' . . . our proceedings are upon a fair and honest foot. We have received repeated injuries contrary to all treatys, our commerce is interrupted, our merchants are ruined, and no redress can be obtained by all the representations which have been made. These circumstances obliged the King to send a fleet into the Baltick to secure trade, protect his subjects, and procure them a just reparation for their losses.'[7] But for George I there was a far stronger obligation necessitating the use of the fleet – a contractual one with the other allies in the war against Sweden. Baron von Bernstorff, his Hanoverian minister, supplemented the instructions given to Norris with secret and verbal commands for the British fleet to assist Denmark and Prussia in the attack on Stralsund and Rügen.[8]

5 E.N. Williams, ed., *The Eighteenth Century Constitution: Documents and Commentary* (Cambridge 1960), 59

6 J.F. Chance, ed. *British Diplomatic Instructions, 1689-1789. I: Sweden, 1689-1727* (London 1922), xxi-xxii

7 Ibid., 77

8 The general plan of the Northern Allies for 1715 was to leave Sweden with Wismar as her only operational base in Germany. Hence the necessity to wrest from her control Stralsund and Rügen.

The seeming failure of Norris to fulfil these latter instructions brought growing pressure from Denmark and Prussia, and, against the wishes of the English ministers, Norris was requested on 2 August 1715 to return to home waters but to leave a sufficient number of ships that, together with the Danish fleet, they would be able 'to compell the Swedes to make reparation for the damage done to his Majesty's subjects and to revoke the unjustifiable edict lately published.'[9] Fortunately for the English ministers, the fleet did not engage directly in battle but its mere presence went a long way in producing the desired result. Stralsund and Rügen fell to the allies and, in October 1715, Bremen and Verden were handed over by Denmark to George I.

The action taken thus far aroused considerable comment in England and the transfer of these two territories, though not completed until 1733, increased unease still further since many began to feel this had been the real purpose of the dispatch of fleets to the Baltic. Fearing further criticism and suspicion, the English ministers refused Denmark's request that the eight men-of-war should remain in the Baltic. However, despite their fear of the potential opposition against George I's northern policy, Denmark was reassured by the promise of the dispatch of a fleet in the spring of 1716. Accordingly, Norris sailed on 25 May with twenty-one men-of-war and seventeen of-the-line. His instructions were almost identical to the ones of the previous year, save he was now 'to insist on a solemn promise and engagement that Our said brother, the King of Sweden, will not directly or indirectly give any assistance countenance or reception to the Pretender to Our Crown . . .'[10] In this way the ministers gave their first public expression to their fears of invasion by the Pretender with foreign aid, and Jefferyes' memorial to Charles XII expressing this demand was printed and circulated publicly. Yet the 'trouble and disquiet' Horace Walpole feared from such a prospect was to a great extent already there.

At the close of the session of parliament on 26 June 1716 the king claimed that the suppression of the late rebellion and 'the numerous instances of mercy which I have shown' had had no other effect than 'to encourage the faction of the Pretender, to renew their insults upon my authority, and the laws of the Kingdom.'[11] By late 1716 informed opinion in town and country was mounting against government foreign policy and the commercial classes in particular looked with increasing suspicion on the close alliance between George I and the czar. They viewed trade competition from the growing

9 Chance, ed., *British Diplomatic Instructions*, I, 81

10 Ibid., 83

11 William Cobbett, *The Parliamentary History of England from the Earliest Period to the Year 1803* (London 1806-12), VII, col. 386

power of Russia as one of the chief threats to their position in the Baltic. Indeed, had Charles XII made the concessions demanded of him by this powerful class, he might well have secured their support.

Into this charged atmosphere stepped Count Gyllenborg and initiated a pamphlet warfare that ended only with his arrest in January 1717.[12] One essay in particular, published in September of 1716, struck a severe blow at the government by laying open the real nature of affairs as he saw them.[13] 'This pamphlet,' said one observer, 'was industriously dispersed in penny-post letters' and 'handed about by persons of figure.' 'It gained credit every day both with the well-intentioned and disaffected part of the nation.'[14] Though his argument was indirect, it exposed in a glaring way the motives underlying the government's policy over the last two years. Why demand reparations of such a paltry sum when Sweden now has equally as great claims against England? Could it be for the purpose of forcing her into a war with Sweden? Why the fitting out of so large a fleet at such expense? This, he claimed 'makes everybody expect its being sent upon an errand of greatest consequence; and no doubt it is so. People even of common sense cannot think so many men of war were intended only to convoy some merchant ships.' He played on the growing Russophobia among the merchant class by pointing out that Sweden's defeat would have for them but one consequence: 'the surrendering the whole trade in the Baltic to the Muscovites.' He described the growing strength of the czar and the hindrance this had already caused to British commerce in the area, and warned: 'This is but a prelude to the dance he [the czar] is like to lead us, when Sweden's ruin puts him in a condition to accomplish his vast projects.' If England has any sense of her treaty obligations to Sweden, of the protection of her commercial interests in the Baltic, of 'justice,' then her last wish should be war with Sweden. Why, he demanded, this 'tenderness' for the Danes? Not commerce, not religion, not property – could it be the ambition of George I? Could the British fleet and resources be solely for the purpose of increasing 'his Dominions in GERMANY at the expense of BRITISH blood and treasure, by involving these nations in foreign quarrels?'

The potential crisis of late 1715 was full upon the ministry by September 1716. So heightened was the agitation against George I's northern policy that Townshend for one was convinced 'if the northern affairs were brought into

12 Evidence of the vast number he undertook in this period is to be found in PRO, SP 107/1B.
13 *An English Merchant's Remarks Upon a Scandalous Jacobite Paper Published the 19th of July Last, in the Post-Boy, Under the Name of a Memorial Presented to the Chancery of Sweden by the Resident of Great Britain.*
14 *Observations on Count Gyllenborg's Remarks upon Mr Jackson's Memorial*

parliament by his majesty's order upon the foot they now stand, his majesty would be so far from obtaining any assistance on that head, that there would be great danger from such a step of ruining his credit and influence in both houses.' Added to this was a serious breach within the ministry itself.[15] A month after Townshend made his observation he was relieved of his post and offered the inferior one of lord lieutenant of Ireland and, in all likelihood, the gap would be widened even further by the resignation of his brother-in-law, Robert Walpole. This division overjoyed the opposition forces, particularly the Jacobites. 'The Jacobites now,' wrote Defoe, 'thought their deliverance at hand, and the time come, when the breaches in the harmony at court should be made wide enough for mischiefs of many kinds to break in.'[16] But Defoe did not, at this point, know what the English ministers knew, for some months earlier 'mischiefs' had already broken in. A plan, they learned, was well under way to restore the Pretender with Swedish help and, fearing the consequences of this, they had already taken certain precautions. The decision had been made to continue the army at its present strength and to dispatch a fleet to the Baltic in the spring. This would put a stop, they hoped, to Sweden's endeavours on behalf of the Pretender. Their fear of the possible consequences had led them to undertake these measures despite their knowledge of the growing opposition against both the standing army and the dispatch of fleets to the Baltic.

Thus, the escalating agitation against the northern policy, the schism in the ministry, their growing fears of invasion of England by the Pretender – all these factors gave Stanhope and Sunderland little reason to be encouraged by the outburst of enthusiasm at the arrival of George I. And the king returned fully determined to send a fleet into the Baltic in the spring to attack Sweden openly.

'It will be every honest man's wish,' declared Defoe, that the joy of the growing opposition against the government might in some way be 'eclipsed.'[17] This desire was at least partially achieved on 29 January 1717 by a second pro-Hanoverian and anti-Jacobite demonstration that resulted in the arrest of Count Gyllenborg and the subsequent disclosure of a Jacobite plot to restore the Pretender. The opposition cried out against this action, thereby challenging the government's sincerity. Many saw it as an artifice to involve Britain in an open war with Sweden and to obtain from parliament

15 For further details see J.H. Plumb, *Sir Robert Walpole: The Making of a Statesman* (London 1956), 243-8.
16 [D. Defoe] *An Impartial Enquiry into the Conduct of the Right Honourable Charles Lord Viscount Townshend* (London 1717), 73
17 Ibid.

the necessary sums for fitting out the fleet, while others viewed it as a ruse to keep the army at its present strength. But the pro-Hanoverians, like the English ministers, were convinced that the arrest of Count Gyllenborg was the surest guarantee against an invasion by Sweden in favour of the Pretender.

Most historians who have discussed the reasons for the government's decision to act in this manner have supported the opposition claims.[18] They, too, view the resolve of Stanhope and Sunderland to apprehend Count Gyllenborg as part of a well-calculated plan to unite the nation at a critical juncture, but the evidence they present is not convincing. They contend that Gyllenborg was engaged in nothing more than floating a loan from the Jacobites. 'Why did the English government interrupt Geortz,' asks one historian, 'when he was conveniently bleeding the Jacobites white?'[19] This allows to the English ministers more knowledge of the situation than they actually possessed. They did not have the historians' advantage of hindsight.

On the basis of the evidence at their disposal in late January 1717 there is good reason to assume that the motivating force for their action was, to a large degree, conditioned by real fear and apprehension. All along the ministers had expressed fear as to how far Charles XII would enter into the project and by 29 December 1716 this was resolved for them through the interception of a letter from Görtz to Gyllenborg in which he declared: 'I am now authorized to enter into the affair which you know of, and that I am allowed the liberty to do in it whatever I shall think convenient.'[20] He enclosed a full copy of his powers from Charles XII and in the same letter informed Gyllenborg of certain plans for an invasion attempt that would include the transport of twelve thousand men, a train of artillery, arms for ten or twelve thousand more, and requisite stores of ammunition. '*Aut nunc aut numquam*, now or never, as well for our friends as for ourselves,' declared Görtz. This much the government knew by early January 1717, and any action on their part was delayed because they also knew that one major problem had to be overcome by the Jacobites before the plan could become a reality – the collection of the necessary sums of money. They were aware by 2 January that the Jacobites at Avignon had handed over a large amount but the money from England was yet to come. This Görtz considered absolutely essential for the success of the project. In one of the intercepted letters he

18 For examples see J.F. Chance, 'The "Swedish Plot" of 1716-7,' *English Historical Review*, XVIII, 1903, 81-106; G.H. Jones, *The Main Stream of Jacobitism* (Cambridge, Mass. 1954), 127-9; J.J. Murray, *George I, the Baltic and the Whig Split* (London 1969).

19 Jones, *The Main Stream of Jacobitism*, 128

20 HLRO, Records 1716/17, item 249

claimed: 'I cannot take the least step in relation to the ships . . . for carrying on the enterprise, before I am in possession of that whole sum; for if I should begin, and the money afterwards should not come in, the sum employed upon this occasion would be lost . . .'[21] When the money was ready from England, Gyllenborg was to bring it to Holland together with 'all the information tending to the execution of our design.' On 12 January Gyllenborg informed Görtz that he would have the required sum in his possession by the end of the following week. On 27 January the government intercepted another letter from Gustavus Gyllenborg to Count Gyllenborg telling him that Görtz was leaving for Holland on 29 January and he hoped he would be there with the money from England.[22]

This is what the English ministers knew and this, it would seem, was the major factor in their decision to arrest Count Gyllenborg. Not only would they put a stop to the project by seizing him *en route* with the money, so necessary to complete the project, but also would be provided with a scheme for the invasion and some indication perhaps of the persons in England who were involved in it. Charles Whitworth demanded that the intercepted letters of Görtz be sent forward as soon as possible 'for 'till we either find out what Jacobites at home have been engaged in so villanous a design, or how a plan was laid for the landing and the junction of the rebels, I shall think the discovery but half made.'[23] It was not so much a combination of 'fear and curiosity,' as one historian has argued,[24] that drove the ministers to this action as fear and determination to come at Jacobite plans and secrets. In the light of the risks involved it is most unlikely that 'curiosity' alone would have played any significant role in the government's action. The numerous arrests of others at the same time and the endless search for evidence lend but added weight to the argument that real fear and apprehension was the prime motivating force for the measures taken by the government. Even after the supplies had been granted by parliament, the government did not relax its efforts to make further discoveries concerning the plot. Defoe records that 'the jealousies of the Swedes continuing for some time, people were taken up, as is usual in times of public apprehensions, on slighter occasions, than at other times, and upon due examination were dismissed again.'[25] The arrest of Görtz as well as Gyllenborg provided them with the added oppor-

---

21 Ibid., item 249
22 PRO, SP 78/161, f 5
23 HMC, *Polwarth MSS*, I, 193
24 J.J. Murray, 'An Eighteenth-Century Whitebook,' *Huntingdon Library Quarterly*, XIII, 1950, 380
25 [D. Defoe] *Mercurius Politicus*, 245-6

tunity to lay bare certain further aspects of the plot and might possibly provide them with some idea of the strength of the European side of the Jacobite movement. Certainly by late 1716 James Stanhope had not the least notion of the value such a situation might provide in forwarding the northern policy of George I. At that time he felt parliament could best be convinced and won over by reference to Cromwell's programme and to Dutch activity in the Baltic:

If I mistake not Cromwell, who understood very well the interest of England with respect to foreign powers, [he] fitted out more than one fleet to the Baltick, with no other view than to secure, that in the treaties of peace to be made betwixt these northern potentates a freedom of trade to the Baltick should be preserved to all nations. He frequently offered considerable summs of money to the King of Sweden for Bremen. The Dutch have likewise heretofore thought themselves very much concerned that a balance of power should be maintained in those seas . . .[26]

Once the decision had been made to act in this manner, however, both from necessity and an awareness of the political advantages to be gained, Stanhope and Sunderland made the most of their fears. They may also have seen in the arrest of Gyllenborg the removal of one of the chief agitators in the coming crisis before parliament, for they knew of his intentions through an intercepted letter. 'I intend,' Gyllenborg declared, 'to have several pieces ready against the meeting of Parliament, and to publish them a little at a time.' With his removal from the scene the ministers would be spared such an embarrassment and the opposition denied one of its strongest supporters outside of parliament. In addition, Stanhope and Sunderland may well have viewed their step as a temporary measure in preventing a further split in the ministry at this critical juncture, for all the ministers shared one thing in common – an almost instinctive fear of Jacobitism. 'The subduing and eradicating of this evil is what ought principally to be aimed at and intended,' urged Townshend. They differed only on the means to achieve this end. Townshend desired 'constant, steady, and uniform application in every branch of the administration' as the surest guarantee against the forces of Jacobitism, and was strongly opposed to violent measures as they proved to be 'always dangerous and often fatal.' In January 1717 Stanhope and Sunderland decided to pursue the latter course and none better than they knew the risks involved. They must have anticipated the nature of the protests that would be raised by their action even before they announced the news of

26 William Coxe, *Memoirs of the Life and Administration of Sir Robert Walpole*, II, 109

the plot to the nation. Although they were convinced of the rightness of their extraordinary procedure in arresting Gyllenborg on the grounds of his involvement in a hideous Jacobite conspiracy, the public and parliament had yet to share that conviction. In the event of success they stood to gain much: a united nation, a weakened opposition, and funds from parliament to allow George I to prosecute his designs in the north. Once the plot was made public they exploited well their own fears to achieve these ends.

Certainly, no step would have been taken had the king not been present. No success, they felt, could possibly attend their efforts 'without the invigorating influence of his majesty's presence and inspection, to quicken the timorous, to strengthen the hands of his servants, and to damp the hopes and expectations of his enemies.'[27] The necessity to be sure of the safety of the monarch, both as a rallying point for the pro-government forces and as the central focus for the ensuing struggle, was an all-important consideration. Once assured of this they proceeded with all speed and resolution 'to prove the plot.' Decipherers and translators were called in to aid them in drawing upon the vast bulk of papers that had been taken with Count Gyllenborg. Warrants were issued and other persons suspected of complicity in the plot were taken up and examined. Their own writers and pamphleteers were summoned forth. 'Everything was done both public and private,' wrote Defoe, 'that might provoke the people against the King of Sweden.' Defoe himself contributed, among other pieces, a pamphlet entitled, *What if the Swedes Should Come?* Another produced a rebuttal to Gyllenborg's attacks on George I's northern policy in a pamphlet called *Observations on Count Gyllenborg's Remarks Upon Mr. Jackson's Memorial.* Another edition of *An Account of Sweden* by the bishop of London, Dr John Robinson, was printed. Yet another supplied the ministers with *The Narrative of the Life and Death of John Rhindolt, Count Patkul, a Nobleman of Livonia, Who was Broke Upon the Wheel in Poland in 1707.* This latter piece was published expressly 'for the information of Count Gyllenborg's friends.' To these were added the almost daily published lists to show the losses English merchants had suffered in the Baltic.[28] The ministers' staff

27 Ibid., 52-3
28 These lists were numerous and often took the form of a petition. On 15 February, five days before the meeting of parliament, the following petition was printed and widely circulated:
'To the King's Most Excellent Majesty: The Humble Petition of the Muscovia Company, Sheweth,
'The company having humbly presented to your Majesty, in their petition of the 28th of October, 1714, the great losses sustained by the Swedes taking and condemning their ships and goods, to the value of near seventy thousand pounds. . .

proceeded apace in the preparation of the report to be laid before parliament. On 15 February Jean Robethon, George I's private secretary, announced that he was about 'to arrange . . . more than sixty letters from Görtz to Gyllenborg and replies' for presentation to parliament.

At the opening of the session on 20 February the king informed the house of the conclusion of the Triple Alliance, the removal of the Pretender beyond the Alps, and then declared: 'Such is the obstinate and inveterate Rancour of a Faction amongst us, that it has again prompted them to animate and stir up foreign Powers, to disturb the Peace of their native Country: They will choose rather to make Britain a scene of Blood and Confusion, and to venture even the putting this Kingdom under a foreign Yoke than give over their darling Design of imposing a Popish Pretender.'[29] Bearing in mind the pressure for the reduction in size of the standing army, the king claimed that 'the preparations which are making abroad to invade us' would prevent such a measure being taken at present. Stanhope then read the intercepted letters to and from Count Gyllenborg. The reaction of the house to these was such that one member, Mr Hungerford, immediately called for a declaration of war against Sweden. On 22 February loyal addresses were forthcoming from both the Lords and the Commons. The latter renounced in very strong terms 'the Popish Pretender' and reaffirmed its determination to support and maintain 'the present happy establishment in the Protestant succession.'

But the final test was yet to come. On 3 April the Commons was requested to grant the necessary supplies not only for the purpose of securing the kingdom against the present danger from Sweden but to prevent, as far as possible, the like apprehension from that quarter for the future.[30] The following day Stanhope moved for the granting of the necessary supply and the opposition reacted accordingly. William Shippen, a prominent parliamentary Jacobite, attacked the request on the grounds that it was unparlia-

'That notwithstanding Your Majesty's demands for them, by your minister at Stockholm, they have had no relief; but have still been exposed to the violence of the Swedes, who have since taken and condemned their ships and goods, to the value of forty five thousand six hundred and ninety eight pounds fourteen shillings and eightpence. . .

'Your Petitioners therefore most humbly beseech your Majesty to take their care into your Royal Consideration, that satisfaction may be obtained for them in such method as Your Majesty in your great wisdom shall seem fit.

'Total of the whole damage . . . by the Swedes interrupting our Trade – £114722-17-5.'

29 Richard Chandler, *The History and Proceedings of the House of Commons from the Restoration to the Present Time* (London 1742), VI, 108

30 Cholmondeley (Houghton) MSS, 65/15 (Lists). Extracts of Commons Proceedings

mentary and unprecedented because neither the sum nor its intended purpose had been given. He was supported by many others of the opposition, among them Mr Hungerford, Mr Lawson, and Mr Grimston. James Stanhope made his appeal on the grounds of apprehension from Sweden and of the absolute necessity to check any invasion attempt for the future. Sir Gilbert Heathcote, an alderman of the city of London, refreshed the memory of the house with respect to the losses sustained by British subjects through the seizure by Sweden of their ships and goods. Craggs pressed the need for new alliances against Sweden owing to the 'doubtful' conduct of the czar.[31] The government capitalized to the full on their fears of invasion of England by the Pretender with Swedish support.

The success or failure of their efforts was tested on 8 April when the motion for the granting of the supply passed by a bare majority of four votes. Had Walpole and Townshend whole-heartedly supported the opposition at this point the verdict would most certainly have been otherwise, but two considerations decided them to support Stanhope and Sunderland. They were genuinely convinced of the Swedish-Jacobite intrigue, but even had they not been it is doubtful they would have failed to support them on this issue. The indelible labels of anti-Hanoverian and pro-Jacobite might well have been placed upon them. In matters involving Jacobitism, Stanhope, Sunderland, Walpole, and Townshend spoke with one voice in their opposition. 'All smaller events are drowned in the noise of approaching dangers,' wrote Defoe, and 'however the great men might have had some remote and opposite views. . .yet as this great affair took up the eyes and ears of all men for some time, either those designs were wholly laid aside, or at least they were no more spoken of at present.'[32] Earlier Townshend had warned Stanhope of the great opposition there would be to George I's northern policy in parliament and had told him that to expect money to carry on a war with Sweden was a 'mere delusion.' The support he and Walpole gave them at this critical moment – a support based on fear of Jacobitism – enabled Stanhope's delusion to become a reality. Parliament voted £250,000 'to allow his Majesty to concert such measures with foreign princes and states, as may prevent any charge or apprehensions of designs from Sweden for the future.'[33]

The political gains made by Stanhope and Sunderland had been largely

---

31 The czar had supported Hanover and Denmark against Sweden but the sudden appearance of Russian troops in Mecklenburg gave the government reason to fear a possible union between Sweden and Russia.
32 [Defoe], *Mercurius Politicus*, 78
33 Chandler, *House of Commons*, VI, 125

the result of the careful exploitation of their fears of an imminent Jacobite invasion from Sweden. The army was continued at its present strength and the arguments traditionally used by those opposed to a standing army – its threat to a free and constitutional government, the burden it placed on the economy – seemed to pale into insignificance in the light of a threatened invasion. The government was able to pursue George I's northern policy reasonably assured that the necessary supplies would be granted by parliament. The fleet was dispatched even earlier than those of 1715 and 1716 had been. In March 1717 Admiral Byng had set sail for the Baltic and this time his instructions were not of a 'dual' nature; he was now commanded 'to burn, sink, destroy, or take all such ships belonging to Sweden as may come your way.'[34]

34 Chance, ed., *British Diplomatic Instructions*, I, 98

4

The Spanish-Jacobite conspiracy of 1719

Despite the interruption of their plans by the British government, the Jacobites on the continent continued to believe that an invasion of England by Charles XII to place the Pretender 'on the throne of his ancestors' would proceed on schedule. With renewed assurances from Sparre, and in accordance with the agreement reached with Görtz, they prepared for the glorious event of 9 April 1717.[1] Even though the Pretender had been forced by the terms of the Triple Alliance[2] to leave the papal territory of Avignon, and by mid-February was on the other side of the Alps, they viewed this as no major handicap. He would proceed quietly to Genoa and there wait in readiness to embark at a moment's notice. Ormonde, whose original intention had been to go north to Danzig and thence to Sweden to join Charles XII, would now hasten instead to Liège and from there proceed via France or Flanders to meet the king of Sweden in England. Nor were the English Jacobites less sanguine of their immediate prospects. The only requirement, according to Oxford, was to change the points of landing, inform them when the attempt was to be executed, and they, for their part, would have 'people in readiness to march that way quickly.' The ministry, he stated, were still 'much in the dark' and 'frightened at their own shadows.'[3] They must come, he said, with blank commissions and a vast number of declara-

---

1 HMC, *Stuart MSS*, IV, 92-3, 98; HMC, *Polwarth MSS*, I, 187
2 Triple Alliance: formed by the accession of Holland to the earlier treaty between France and England. At the preliminaries Stanhope had insisted with respect to the Jacobites (1) that the Pretender should be forced to cross the Alps and (2) that well-known Jacobites should be refused asylum in France.
3 *Stuart MSS*, V, 538

tions. With respect to the latter, one had already been penned for the Pretender by Father Lewis Innes. Despite the efforts of 'the Usurper' to render a restoration impossible by forcing 'His Majesty' to retire beyond the Alps, they were to no avail, the declaration claimed, for now 'Divine Providence' had 'raised up a powerful prince in the pursuit of his own right, against the Usurper of Ours; Our ancient ally, the brave and generous King of Sweden, whose principles, cause, and nation can never raise any jealousy in Britain.'[4]

All was in readiness for Charles XII to make his descent on England, and as the zero hour approached Jacobite circles buzzed with excitement over 'the great and weighty project.' The arrival of a courier from England was sufficient for the invention of a rumour that the event was a *fait accompli*. From The Hague and Paris reports flowed into the British government and all spoke of the same matter: the Pretender's party were 'in motion' for 'some design' and, on the very eve of the event, while, as Mar claimed, they were 'gaping with expectation,' a manifesto, purported to be from Charles XII, was circulated in Paris. [5] But April 9th came and went and nothing happened. By mid-April the Jacobites were still waiting for the king of Sweden's project 'to break out.' In this instance they failed to realize, as did certain non-Jacobites,[6] that their conviction of an immediate invasion attempt ceased to have any significance once the British government had exposed the plot and thereby extracted the potentially serious quality from their endeavours.

By late April, however, the Jacobites had expanded their plans to include the czar of Russia. The visit of Peter the Great to Paris on 27 April provided what appeared to them as an even more certain programme for a restoration. Even though Charles XII's 'great project' no longer seemed imminent, a far broader prospect appeared on the horizon. 'Things are far from being desperate,' declared Mar, 'for if the King of S[wede]n be so wise for himself as well as for us [as] to make up with the C[za]r, which the last is not only, I believe, desirous of, but by what we hear, would be willing to enter conjuntly with him into measures with us, it may soon come about again, and with greater probability of success, nay even almost to a certainty.'[7] A scheme for the formation of a 'confederacy' of Sweden, Russia, and the Pretender now became their central preoccupation. 'We are doing all we can to compass this,' wrote Mar.

This Jacobite desire for a Triple Alliance was not a new idea, for during

4 Ibid., IV, 129
5 For examples see PRO SP 78/161, ff 39, 157; SP 84/255, ff 188, 208.
6 Whitworth, for example, reported to Sunderland on 18 April that 'it was visible the scheme laid by the Swedes is still on foot.' PRO, SP 84/256, f 462
7 *Stuart MSS*, IV, 257

the earlier negotiations with Sparre, Gyllenborg, and Görtz it had been discussed. Görtz had strongly desired to meet with Dr Erskine, a cousin of Mar's, who was chief physician to the czar, to attempt to secure some accommodation between his master and Peter the Great.[8] Even the Jacobites in England had looked with great favour on such a project. Although Görtz failed to meet Erskine, Mar, in his instructions to Jerningham for a formal treaty with Görtz, had ordered him 'to make it his business' at the same time to bring Erskine and Görtz together for meetings. Again this had proved impossible, but this time it was due to no fault of the Jacobites but to the obstruction of their plans by the British government.

By early May, however, the project for 'the Confederacy' was revived. Dr Erskine expressed to Mar the czar's wish to meet him and proposed that the Duke of Ormonde should undertake a special mission to Charles XII.[9] Although the regent, Orléans, requested the czar to have nothing to do with either Ormonde or Dillon, they were encouraged to proceed with the scheme. Since the British government was about to reduce its standing army, it was deemed undesirable that one of Ormonde's stature should venture forth on such a mission because it would give pretence to the government to maintain the army at its present strength. For this reason, therefore, and the possibility, no doubt, that Ormonde might be flatly refused admittance to the court of Charles XII, a lesser figure was chosen to precede him. George Jerningham was selected to pave the way for Ormonde's entrance as the great mediator in a peace between Charles XII and Peter the Great. The arrival of news at this point of Charles XII's rejection of an earlier set of proposals, conveyed to him by General Poniatowski on behalf of the czar, made no dint in Jacobite plans, for the benefits to be reaped by success in such a venture loomed too large. 'Were the confederacy once made betwixt his Czarian Majesty, the rightful King of Britain and his Majesty of Sweden,' declared Mar, 'many other princes would be glad to join with them, and George would necessarily fall a sacrifice to them.'[10] Accordingly, Jerningham was issued with full instructions to proceed to Sweden to herald the arrival of Ormonde, who would bring with him commissions from both the Pretender and the czar. He was also provided with a set of orders enjoining him, in the event he should meet with a blank refusal by Charles XII for mediation, to endeavour to secure the alternative – a 'dual alliance' of the Pretender and the king of Sweden.

Once again the essential bargaining power which the Pretender would

8 'Letters and Documents Relating to Robert Erskine, Physician to Peter the Great,' *Miscellany of the Scottish History Society* (Edinburgh 1904), 420-2
9 *Stuart MSS*, IV, 234
10 Ibid., IV, 295

require, to become a party to such an alliance, would be money. Once again he requested the English Jacobites to provide it. In early August Dillon communicated to Atterbury and Oxford the details of their present situation and requested them to begin in earnest to collect, but this time a new procedure was urged for carrying on 'the muslin trade.' Instead of a general collection, they were now to seek out twenty leading Jacobites and from each obtain £5000 to be repaid at the restoration with interest. Such a method would avoid the earlier problems they had encountered of 'indiscretion' and 'treachery.'[11]

In reply Atterbury sent one of his first letters to the Pretender, and thus initiated a correspondence that was ultimately to lead to his banishment from England at the hands of Robert Walpole. He wrote: 'My heart is better known to you, Sir, than my hand, and my actions, I hope, have spoken for me better than any letters could do; and to these actions I shall always appeal. . .I have for many years past neglected no opportunity (and particularly no advantage my station afforded me) towards promoting the service.'[12] Three days later Oxford, not to be outdone, sent his expressions of devotion. But here, as on previous occasions, agreement between the two heads of the English Jacobite movement ended. The petty bickering and the struggle for position and place went on, especially after Oxford's release from the Tower on 1 July 1717. Two years earlier Oxford and several other leading Tories – Bolingbroke, Ormonde, and Strafford – had been impeached for their part in the Treaty of Utrecht by the new Whig government bent on retaliation. As a result of these proceedings Oxford was committed a prisoner to the Tower of London and was not acquitted by his fellow peers until the Commons failed to put in an appearance against him two years later.

At some stage between the date of Oxford's release and the end of September a split occurred in the English Jacobite party and two groups emerged: the Oxford 'set' and the Atterbury 'set.' Among the more prominent persons in the former group were Lords Poulett, Foley, Dartmouth, Mansell, Bingley; Auditors Foley and Harley; and the bishop of Hereford.[13] Atterbury's supporters listed Lord North and Grey, the earl of Arran, the duke of Norfolk, the earl of Orrery, Sir William Wyndham, William Shippen, and Charles Caesar. No end of complaints against the former set flowed in from Atterbury: of Oxford's failure to advise him when messen-

---

11 Ibid., IV, 521
12 *Letters of Francis Atterbury, Bishop of Rochester, to the Chevalier St. George and Some of the Adherents of House of Stuart*, ed. J.H. Glover (London 1847), I, 1
13 Probably the earl of Nottingham as well. Oxford, although a bitter enemy of his, had at least approached him.

gers were leaving for the continent, of the withholding of information from him, of duplicity on Oxford's and Mar's part to separate Ormonde from the centre of influence at the Pretender's court by sending him on his mission to Sweden, and of Menzies' dishonesty with respect to money matters.[14] The Pretender accurately summed up the English Jacobite contribution during these months when he described their sole achievements as 'diversity of opinions,' 'endless disputes,' and a 'multiplicity of useless letters.'

By early 1718 the possibility of obtaining the required £100,000 from among leading Jacobites in England seemed very remote since Atterbury had refused to have anything more to do with 'the money affair' and had placed the full onus for its collection on Oxford. Nor did the arrival of Francia the Jew with promises of £60,000 come to anything because he had asked so many questions about 'the King's affairs' that the Jacobites were convinced his offers were 'intended for a plot.'[15] In the spring of the previous year the Pretender had journeyed to Rome and received from the pope, Clement XI, assurances of his willingness to provide him with a sum of money equal to that which had been offered to Sweden for his restoration. Acting through Cardinals Imperiali and Gualterio, he now called on them to exert their influence for the fulfilment of the pope's promise of £80,000. He told Imperiali:

I do not ask for the money to be put into my own hands, provided I am assured in writing that it is ready whenever I shall ask for it, on informing his Holiness of the use for which it will be employed, and that I then can receive it promptly and secretly . . . The importance of my demand is clear, my all is at stake, and the advantage to Europe, Italy and above all religion would derive from my restoration is too plain . . . What glory for the Pope to have contributed to it with so little expense.'[16]

The Pretender realized that his prospects from this quarter, too, were slight, for about two weeks earlier he had decided on an additional course of action. A memorial was drawn up and duly forwarded to Cardinal Gualterio for consideration. It was then passed on to Cardinal Aquaviva, the Spanish representative in Rome, to be forwarded to his government. By this circuitous route it eventually reached the hands of the figure who was to come forth at the end of this year as the champion of the Stuart cause – Cardinal Giulio Alberoni, Philip V's chief minister.

14 By this time Atterbury had taken James Murray as his go-between and had dropped Menzies, who was now attached to Oxford's group.
15 *Stuart MSS*, V, 210
16 Ibid., V, 444

In their quest for foreign support the Jacobites had sought in vain to win Spain. Throughout 1715-16 letters had passed to and fro between the Pretender's court and Sir Patrick Lawless, his agent in Madrid. It had been hoped to find refuge in the king of Spain's territory for the Pretender and his court but Alberoni had been strongly against it. When he was approached on this matter he was not only 'amazed' but had told Lawless that 'such a thing would, if assented unto, put this Court in an impossibility of ever being useful to his Majesty hereafter, and ruin at the same time the present system of their own affairs.'[17]

Alberoni and his queen, Elizabeth Farnese, had two things in common: both were Italians and both shared the singular driving ambition to recover the Spanish dominions in Italy which had been ceded to the emperor by the Treaty of Utrecht. For the moment, the Pretender had been precluded from participating in that mission. An Anglo-Spanish alliance had just been concluded by a commercial treaty on 9 January 1717 and many of the difficulties resulting from the Asiento Treaty of 1713 for regulating trade were being worked out.[18] Alberoni, on the surface at least, was opposed, therefore, to any liaison with the exiled Stuarts. Temporarily his ears were closed to Jacobite pleas for money, a place of refuge for the Pretender, and the use of the vast number of Irish troops in the Spanish service.[19]

As Alberoni was obviously 'biassed another way,' Lawless had urged the Pretender to use his influence to make Father Daubenton, Philip v's Jesuit confessor, 'sensible' that he would 'favour him with his good offices with Mr. Druot [the Pope] . . . provided he renders him service with Mr. Allin [the King of Spain].'[20] By mid-August Father Daubenton's services had been secured, and through him the same requests that had reached Alberoni's ears were now voiced to Philip v. They were deafly received for it was quite obvious, even to the Jacobites, that Alberoni, without whose concurrence nothing was undertaken, had first to be won over.

By 1718, however, there was good reason for the Jacobites to feel that his disposition towards them might have changed. The Pretender's earlier visit to Rome, as already pointed out, had been to secure money from the pope. But his journey served another purpose, for he had used all his persuasive

17 Ibid., II, 120

18 Jean O. McLachlan, *Trade and Peace with Old Spain, 1667-1750* (Cambridge 1940), 69-72

19 There is some evidence, however, that Alberoni was assisting with money. By early 1717 the Spanish ambassador in Paris, Cellamare, was conveying money to Avignon. Lawless says in one of his letters: '. . . more of Le Maire [money] than you mention must be arrived before now at Pussole [Avignon] . . . I shall see Janson [Alberoni] to-morrow and thank him for what he has sent and press him to send more.' *Stuart MSS*, III, 398

20 *Stuart MSS*, II, 296

powers to convince Clement XI of the necessity of raising Alberoni to the Cardinalate. Success had attended his efforts and Alberoni was given the red hat on 1 July 1717. 'Only the advantage which might result to your Majesty could have made up for the trouble it has caused us,' Clement XI wrote to the Pretender afterwards, and it was to be hoped, therefore, that Alberoni's gratitude would be shown the next time he was called upon.

In his memorial to Cardinal Aquaviva in January 1718 which he was to forward to the king of Spain the Pretender outlined the present state of his affairs and then let him into 'the secret of the North.' Sweden and Russia, he told him, were backing his restoration but one major difficulty had to be overcome for 'these two princes united in favour of his Britannic Majesty, and resolving to undertake his Restoration, find themselves destitute of an essential article, which is the only thing they want, to put that work in execution, and that is, money.'[21] As the failure on his part to provide the requisite sum of money at the exact moment would undoubtedly 'weaken the good dispositions of those potentates,' he requested that Philip V 'give or order to be given in writing an assurance to the King of England that he has such a sum in his hands ready to be given him, whenever these northern powers shall require it . . . His Majesty does not ask to touch the money, but after he shall have informed his Catholic Majesty of the project in hand and of the use that is to be made of it, and, if he desires it, the interested powers shall not know from whence this succour comes originally.' The benefits to be derived by rendering him such service would be immense for

His Catholic Majesty will be delivered thereby of an enemy who is so by principle and so, having nothing to fear from England, he'll be at liberty to prosecute his just designs without opposition. He'll place thereby on the throne of Great Britain one who will be his friend and ally not only by his interest and by inclination, but also by gratitude, he'll gain for ever the goodwill of the nation which he will have delivered from a cruel slavery, and which cannot after that refuse anything to their King, when it is to do a pleasure to a common benefactor.[22]

Alberoni was not yet prepared, however, to effuse gratitude to the extent of £100,000. In reply to the Pretender's appeal he begged him to be patient and in the near future measures would undoubtedly be taken for his service.

During the next few months Jacobite hopes mounted because Alberoni's

21 Ibid., V, 619
22 Ibid., V, 619-20. No specific mention was made of restoring Gibraltar to Spain but it is certain that the Pretender had it in mind. The reason he did not, he told Gualterio, was because it was not in his power to do so.

actions seemed to make his adoption of their cause a near certainty. According to him, the peace settlement of 1713 had left in its wake the seeds of endless war,[23] and in the summer previous to the Pretender's memorial he had begun to nurture those seeds by an attack on the emperor's island of Sardinia. By mid-1718 the seedlings were subjected to hothouse conditions and in July of that year he poured some 35,000 Spanish troops into Sicily. In August, by the accession of the emperor, the former Triple Alliance of Britain, France, and Holland was expanded into the Quadruple Alliance and the machinery was set in motion to attempt to mediate a peace between the emperor and Spain. Alberoni refused their demands. Even before mediation had failed, however, Admiral Byng, the commander of the British fleet, had attacked and utterly defeated the Spanish fleet off Cape Passaro. Sunderland, first lord of the treasury and chancellor of the exchequer, was quite convinced Byng's victory would have a decisive effect. 'There is now an end put to the Cardinal's projects,' he wrote to Newcastle.[24] In mid-September Stair, the British ambassador in Paris, congratulated Byng on his victory and told him: 'It's possible the Spaniards will now open their eyes and accede to our Treaty, when they are convinced by experience, that they are unable to struggle against the Powers who have united themselves to settle peace in Europe.'[25] But by October those hopes were no longer widely shared. The Spanish ambassador in London, Monteleone, had received his letters of recall and awaited only a fair wind to return to Spain. Towards the end of this month it became obvious that Alberoni had no 'sincere desire of settling peace in Europe' since he had adopted the northern policy of the Jacobites and a second Quadruple Alliance seemed imminent: Spain, Sweden, Russia, and the Pretender.[26] In late October Ormonde was invited by Alberoni to come to Spain to discuss plans for an invasion of England.

Ormonde, as already pointed out, had gone on a mission to the north in the autumn of 1717 to act as mediator in a peace between Sweden and Peter the Great. He was refused entry at both places and by mid-1718 had returned to Paris. Once Alberoni's invitation was received he dashed a letter

---

23 *Lettres intimes de J.M. Alberoni adressées au Comte I. Rocca,* ed. E. Bourgeois (Paris 1892), 306. The Utrecht Settlement satisfied neither Spain nor the emperor. Charles VI still regarded himself as the rightful king of Spain while Spain continued to resent the loss, by that treaty, of her dominions in Italy.

24 BM, Add. MSS, 32, 686, f 120

25 PRO, SP 78/162, f 134

26 Peter the Great played no major role in this aspect of the 1719 invasion attempt. It was reported that eight warships were to be acquired from him but the mission of Baron de St Hilaire for this purpose seems to have ended in failure. *Polwarth MSS,* II, x

off to the Pretender to announce his immediate departure for Spain.[27] Unknown to Ormonde, Alberoni had earlier dispatched Sir Patrick Lawless to Sweden to inform Charles XII of his plan and the same day as Ormonde left Paris an envoy arrived from Sweden and communicated to Cellamare, the Spanish ambassador in Paris, a memorial from Charles XII in which he expressed his desire to form an alliance with Spain for an invasion of England on behalf of the Pretender.[28]

In late November Ormonde arrived in Madrid and with great enthusiasm Alberoni announced to him his decision to champion the Stuart cause. At his request General Dillon was instructed to hasten with all speed to Madrid where 'he shall have a commission of captain general, the pay whereof is 2,000 pistoles a year as also a government and commandery.'[29] During the course of two further meetings the details for the invasion attempt were worked out. Success could only attend their efforts, felt Ormonde, if Alberoni was prepared to send some 7000-8000 men into England and 15,000 in arms and ammunition. Threatened himself with invasion from France and with troops occupied in Sicily, Alberoni felt it would be impossible to spare a man, but at their second meeting he reversed his opinion and told Ormonde that they 'would give 5,000 men, of which 4,000 are to be foot, 1,000 troopers, of which 300 with their horses, the rest with their arms and accoutrements, and two months' pay for them, 10 field pieces and 1,000 barrels of powder and 15,000 arms for foot with everything necessary to convoy them.'[30] In addition, George Keith, the Earl Marischal, was ordered to come immediately to Spain to spearhead a separate invasion into the north of Scotland.

All that remained was to make the plan a reality. Towards this end, and with what was thought to be great secrecy, the expedition fitted out at Cadiz. Ormonde proceeded to Valladolid, the Pretender left Rome for Madrid, the Keiths made their exit from Paris. In the midst of their preparations the first major setback occurred – receipt of the news of Charles XII's death on 1 December. All prospect of aid from Sweden was at an end. This latter event, however, and the declaration of war by England and France caused Alberoni to waver but slightly in his avowed mission.[31] Ships continued to be fitted out and in late February Alberoni's contribution to the Stuart cause set sail from Cadiz: 5 warships, 22 transports, 5000 troops, and

27 W.K. Dickson, ed., *The Jacobite Attempt of 1719* (Edinburgh, *Scottish History Society*, 1895), XIX, 1-2
28 Arch.Aff.Etr.Corr.Pol.Angl., vol. 322, ff 57, 88, 119, 166
29 *Stuart MSS*, VII, 614
30 Ibid., VII, 644; BM, Stowe MSS, 247, f 78
31 Arch.Aff.Etr.Corr.Pol.Angl., vol. 322, f 26

arms and ammunition for 30,000 more. By this time Ormonde had gone to Corunna to await its arrival but he was destined never to go on board. On 18 March, in a violent storm off Cape Finisterre, the fleet was shattered and in the following weeks the remnants of an expedition that was to have restored the Pretender to the throne of Britain struggled back to Spanish ports. The smaller section of the fleet which had gone north to Scotland was also doomed to failure, for the British government had already taken measures to ensure the result that occurred at Glenshiel on 10 June 1719.

Alberoni and the Jacobites could not have forecast the storm that intervened to ruin the invasion attempt but neither did they predict, it would seem, the reception that awaited them even had their fleet reached England. The English ministers, obsessed with fear of Jacobitism, had left little chance for any degree of success to attend their endeavours.

5

Ministerial vigilance and retaliation

The maintenance by Stanhope and Sunderland of an elaborate and expensive intelligence system provided them with a most sophisticated early-warning system for detecting Jacobite conspiracy. They did more, however, than continue the existing arrangement. They greatly expanded it because the Jacobite threat in these years gave an added stimulus to this branch of government endeavour – a stimulus that was only equalled under wartime conditions.[1] Although they continued to receive intelligence (as earlier administrations had done) through domestic and foreign postal control and an elaborate counter-espionage system, their activity, in these two areas, was far more time-consuming and expensive than at any previous period.

Domestic postal control was carried on through the issuing of warrants by the secretaries of state for the holding, opening, searching, copying, and resealing of mail passing through the general post office. The harsh criticism raised against this aspect of government activity, when the full extent of its involvement in this area was revealed in the 1730s, demonstrates quite clearly that, not only was its control in this area extensive, but that, even by eighteenth-century standards of judgment, it was deemed more than was necessary.[2] Although legally postal clerks should have had written authority for the searching of the mails, secrecy precluded legality in many instances and, more often than not, postal clerks took it upon themselves to inform the

1 P.S. Fritz, 'The Anti-Jacobite Intelligence System of the English Ministers, 1715-1745,' *The Historical Journal*, XVI, 2, 1973, 265-89

2 *Report From the Secret Committee on the Post Office; Together with Appendix* (Ordered, by the House of Commons, to be printed, 5 August, 1844), Parliamentary Papers, Session 1844, XIV, 8

government of what passed through their hands and then awaited further instructions. The chief clerk, John Lefebure, often obliged in this latter respect.[3]

Warrants of both a specific and general nature calling for the detaining of post were issued in great profusion. Indeed, so time-consuming had this side of government activity become that in 1718 Stanhope and Sunderland established a Secret Office or Secret Department for the opening of all foreign correspondence. In addition another activity, that of breaking codes and ciphers, was institutionalized by the setting up of a Deciphering Branch to handle correspondence.[4] This latter department was undoubtedly the most taxed because the bulk of foreign correspondence in these years was in code and cipher. Secrecy and speed were of the essence in its activity for any undue delay would have immediately aroused suspicion in Jacobite and other circles. Stanhope and Sunderland's chief decipherer, Edward Willes, together with his assistants, worked diligently at the exacting and demanding task of breaking ciphers used in Jacobite and other correspondence.[5] The ministers were much indebted to Willes and his department since they provided them with many of the details of the Görtz-Gyllenborg plot. They demonstrated clearly the degree of their indebtedness by increasing his salary and, in 1718, securing his promotion to the rectorship of Barton in Bedfordshire.

Throughout 1718 and 1719 the senior clerks in the Secret Department and the Deciphering Branch flooded the ministry with intercepted and deciphered correspondence. In this manner they were kept reasonably well informed not only of the proposed alliance between Sweden and Spain, and of their intention to support the Pretender, but also, through the interception of several of Cardinal Alberoni's letters (as early as December 1718), they knew something of both the nature and extent of Spanish support for the exiled Stuarts.[6] Information from this channel was further supplemented by reports from foreign postal centres. Although the Hanoverian postal officials, through their central office at Nienburg, often dispatched information, other European postal centres, especially those at Leyden, Danzig, and Genoa, supplied the British government with intercepted post. Indeed, it was to be

3 PRO, SP 35/23, f 171

4 Kenneth Ellis, *The Post Office in the Eighteenth Century: A Study in Administrative History* (London 1958), 65-74

5 Stephen Hyde Cassan, *Lives of the Bishops of Bath and Wells: From the Earliest to the Present Period* (London 1829), II, 166-8

6 PRO, SP 35/17, ff 20-6

in the realm of foreign postal control that Robert Walpole was to make the most dramatic expansions in the government's intelligence network.

All these aspects of anti-Jacobite activity were reinforced by Stanhope and Sunderland through an enormous extension of the espionage network. Neither time nor money was a scarce commodity, for within England and across the continent, at most of the capitals and major foreign ports, stretched its lace-like curtain of counter-espionage. Throughout these years the ministers' spies were busily at work and, although the value of their reports varied, they were often most worthwhile. It was primarily due to the efforts of one of these spies, John Pringle, a Scottish merchant in the confidence of the Jacobites living in Spain, that the main details of the 1719 projected invasion were first revealed.[7] Stanhope also learned much on Jacobite activity from one E. Barton who was paid handsomely for his work. And it must be noted that their vast network was further supplemented by intelligence reports from the host of spy networks maintained by British representatives living on the continent. During these years one of the first duties of a British minister, upon his arrival at a foreign court, was to set up, usually at his own expense, an anti-Jacobite intelligence system and such information as he gathered became but part of his routine dispatches back to Westminster. As early as 1716 all ministers abroad were given instructions not to deal directly with the Jacobites but 'to be very cautious to observe all their motions.'

Mention of but two such systems will demonstrate their value. By far the largest anti-Jacobite spy network (for which evidence remains) was maintained by the earl of Stair, the British ambassador to France. Throughout the years of his embassy, from 1715 to 1720, he was well supplied with details on Jacobite activity in and about Paris and elsewhere through his host of spies – Thomas MacCarty, Edward Acton, J. Rampton, Stephen Lynch, A. Lambert, Neisen, Osmin Rollo, and an even more anonymous list which bore such pseudonyms as 'Le Cleve,' 'A.A.,' 'C.R.,' and 'Renard.' By letters dispatched to him personally and by direct interviews he made the bulk of the discoveries that fill his own letters to Stanhope and Sunderland. Certainly the amount of money he poured into his network is a clear indication of the value he placed upon it.[8] Second only to Stair's system was that of Charles Whitworth, minister plenipotentiary to the United Provinces from 1717 to 1721. His spies, large numbers of whom were stationed in Amsterdam

7 Jean O. McLachlan, *Trade and Peace with Old Spain, 1667-1750* (Cambridge 1940), 212, n118
8 SRO, Stair Muniments GD 135/141, vols. 8, 12, 29

and Rotterdam, kept him apprised of what the Jacobites there were planning.

Yet another technique was employed by one minister, at least, as a means of discovering Jacobite intelligence: Sunderland communicated directly with the earl of Mar, the Pretender's agent, on the pretence that he was sympathetic to their cause. From a correspondence, first initiated in 1717, he was well informed of most Jacobite activity.[9]

Through these various methods the ministers were not taken by surprise, therefore, when Lord Polwarth, through his own spy system, communicated to them as early as 4 October 1718 a great many of the details of the encouragements Sweden and Spain were giving the Pretender.[10] The sudden death of Charles XII brought with it, however, one major question for the British government. Would Cardinal Alberoni endeavour to invade England alone on behalf of the Pretender? This was answered for them in the affirmative by the Abbé Dubois, the French foreign minister. On 5 January 1719 Dubois' intelligence system had gained enough of current Jacobite intrigue to enable him to inform Secretary Craggs that the Pretender was about to leave Rome for Spain to join the duke of Ormonde and from there proceed to Ireland to raise a rebellion. The earl of Stair held several meetings with both Dubois and the regent and communicated still further news of the Jacobite plan.[11]

Any doubt Stanhope and Craggs may have expressed at the accuracy of this information was dispelled on 25 February when Dubois produced for them the details of the invasion attempt. He told Craggs that they had discovered a person who was in on all the Jacobite plans now being made in Spain.[12] He had assured them that the invasion attempt would take place in less than six weeks, that English Jacobites were closely involved, and that the effort from there was directed by Oxford. Spain would supply five or six battalions of Irish troops plus arms and once landed at Bristol they would march on London with the duke of Ormonde at their head. The preparations now being made in Spain, the repeated attempts to purchase arms in Holland, the late movements of the Pretender – these were, Dubois urged, ample proof of a designed invasion well advanced.[13]

But the English ministers had had few, if any, doubts about the intelli-

---

9 BM, Add. MSS, 9,129, ff 40-8

10 HMC, *Polwarth MSS*, I, 618-19; PRO, SP 78/162, ff 245, 257

11 Arch.Aff.Etr.Corr.Pol.Angl., vol. 322, f 45; BM , Stowe MSS, 247, f 78: PRO, SP 78/163, f 17, 22, 163

12 This person was probably Pringle. W.K. Dickson, ed., in *The Jacobite Attempt of 1719* (Edinburgh 1895), suggests another possibility – Blaise Henri de Corte, Baron de Walef, 25.

13 Arch.Aff.Etr.Corr.Pol.Angl., vol. 322, f 260-2; PRO, SP 76/63, f 159-60

gence they had received. They had already taken several precautions because this time the threat was not only an external one – the West Country, in all likelihood, would declare for the Pretender. Four battalions and eighteen squadrons had already been ordered to march to that section. Sir John Norris had been dispatched to Portsmouth 'where there is a squadron ready of seven good ships.' Lord Berkeley was to be prepared to sail shortly to join with Norris or to make up a separate squadron. James Stanhope requested four battalions of the Dutch and Monsieur Pendtenrriedter, the imperial envoy in London, also requested the marquis de Prié, governor of the Austrian Netherlands, 'to hold six more in a readiness to pass over from Ostend.'[14] In the light of these preparations there was little weight in Craggs' claim to both Dubois and the French ministers in London that they were not in the least alarmed by news of the intended invasion. The French representatives in London were convinced, however, that the government was genuinely alarmed about the invasion but did not want to give them the impression they might require aid from France. The government's immediate and major concern was to prevent the Spanish ships from reaching St George's Channel before the arrival of Admiral Norris. To accomplish this, said Jean de Robethon, George I's private secretary, 'our admiralty have manifested an almost incredible diligence.'[15]

The arrival of Dubois' information served only to excite the ministers to further action. Twenty-two companies of infantry and ten of dragoons were raised 'to strengthen the army already on foot' and four battalions were brought over from Ireland. The troops in Ireland and Scotland were ordered to encamp. All officers were instructed to return immediately to their posts. The duke of Bolton left for Ireland to be ready 'in case of necessity' to bring over four or five Dutch battalions and eight imperial battalions from the Low Countries with a thousand dragoons. 'They work incessantly to put all in a state of guarantee against the invasion,' reported Chammorel, the French minister in London.[16]

On 10 March the king came before parliament to inform them that he had received repeated advices from France that an invasion would be suddenly attempted in favour of the Pretender. Following an emergency meeting of the Cabinet Council, Mr Leathes was sent immediately to Ostend with instructions to prepare everything for the embarkation of the imperial battalions already requested. At the same time an officer was dispatched to hire transport to bring over the four Dutch battalions without waiting for

14 Dickson, *The Jacobite Attempt of 1719*, Appendix, 234-5
15 *Polwarth MSS*, II, 91
16 Arch.Aff.Etr.Corr.Pol.Angl., vol. 323, f 77

further orders from Rotterdam. The fitting out of twelve more ships was undertaken. At this same meeting a series of proclamations was issued against persons who had been attainted by the rebellion of 1715 – a £5000 reward was offered for the capture of the duke of Ormonde, £1000 for any attainted lord, and £500 for apprehending any attainted gentleman.[17]

As already noted, the government feared a rising in the West Country and the recent trips there of two noted Jacobites, Sir William Wyndham and Mr Gore, served only to increase their suspicions.[18] Was there in fact an organized plan for an internal rebellion? Had not the Abbé Dubois told them that the Jacobites were confident of being able to raise 26,000 men in the West Country for the march on London? The ministers already had grounds for fearing such a possibility, for arms and powder had been seized *en route* for Bristol. They therefore gave directions to the officers at Bristol to go to Bath and Cirencester to examine all wool packs, barrels, and such for concealed weapons and the officers of the western and southern ports were instructed to watch closely all wagons and carriages for 'arms or war-like' stores.

Each Jacobite attempt in these years was thwarted by the government and, therefore, the reaction of the mass of people in the West Country and in the north, had the Pretender been able to land with a sufficiently large force, was never put to the test. However, it does not appear improbable, given the continued state of discontent, disorder, and disaffection of the years up to about 1722, that a considerable number would have joined the Stuart banner. In 1719 the French ambassador in London reported that:

there is not in all England 10,000 men capable of bearing arms and among them are an infinite number of Jacobites ready to desert on the first occasion, for the fire of the last rebellion still burns beneath the surface, and the punishments and confiscations have much alarmed and increased the heats. If the Duke of Ormonde, whose name is ever dear, came at the head of 6,000 men with arms, ammunition and money, God only knows what would be the outcome in the west of England where there are more than 30,000 workers in mines who pass for Jacobites and a large number of tinners unemployed because of the interruption of commerce.[19]

His reference to unemployment among the tinners was due in large part to the interruption of commerce with Sweden as a result of the Görtz-Gyllenborg plot, and this was not the only group that had been

17 PRO, SP, 35/15, f 194
18 Stowe MSS, 247, f 98
19 Arch.Aff.Etr.Corr.Pol.Angl., vol. 323, f 68-9

affected. In Devonshire, too, it was stated that 'great numbers of clothiers had got together in a very audacious manner and refused to pay any more taxes unless there were a new Parliament, and the prohibition taken off as to the commerce with Sweden, by which they say all their manufactories are ruined. Some troops were sent by the Government against them.'[20] A potential popular uprising in support of an invasion by the Pretender was never far from the government's mind.

To meet this threat in the West Country, the ministers sent Samuel Buckley, the publisher of the London *Gazette*, and William Churchill on a fact-finding mission.[21] On 11 March Buckley informed Craggs that although 'the majority of the common people in the west are judged to be disaffected . . . the King's friends are in good heart.' Nor could they have taken greater encouragement from his letter of 18 March claiming: 'There is no reason to fear from the present disposition of the people of Exeter and Devonshire, that there would be any rising for the Pretender; and there is no ground to believe that the chief Tories of these parts have formed a scheme, and engaged any number of the meaner sort of their laity, for such a purpose.'[22] For the potential was what the ministers feared most – 'the meaner sort of laity.' What would they do? The answer was soon forthcoming. At Bristol Buckley examined several people who were well acquainted with that place and from them was able to inform James Stanhope that, although at present Bristol was 'in good hands,' 'the vulgar in general and the men who form the militia are two parts in three more inclined to the Pretender's cause than to the King.'[23] It was absolutely essential, therefore, to use all precaution to prevent the Pretender from landing, since 'Bristol would not make any resistance.' Brigadier Gore and several officers carefully marked out the Pretender's possible landing points. On leaving the West Country Buckley and Churchill established a correspondence with persons in Dorchester, Exeter, and Bristol 'to have speedy intelligence of any happening.' The fear of being faced not only with an external invasion but an internal revolt from the West Country now seemed obvious to the ministers. For this reason they saw the necessity to maintain five to six thousand troops in readiness in the Bristol region.[24]

All these government measures aroused the public to a great pitch and Roger Kenyon reflected, it would seem, the opinion of many when he

20 HMC, *Stuart MSS*, V, 262
21 Stowe MSS, 247, ff 98-9
22 Ibid., f 117; PRO, SP 35/15 f 233
23 PRO, SP 35/15, f 254
24 *Polwarth MSS*, II, 95

wrote: 'We abound here in reports of, I know not what invasions from Spain. That they are frightened in Exchange Alley is certain, but what projects Cardinal Alberoni may have in his head is [out] of my reach . . . we do well to take our precautions . . . I fancy, as yet nobody is very sure.'[25] Speculation continued to mount: it was rumoured that the king would cancel his trip to Hanover, the Habeas Corpus Act would be suspended, Mr Gore and William Wyndham would be arrested. From Paris, Secretary Crawfurd reported that most people 'have the late Duke of Ormonde and the Pretender already landed and masters of Bristol.'

All was in readiness to meet 'the Cardinal's invasion' but it never materialized for, as already indicated, the Cadiz expedition in favour of the Pretender with its twenty-five to thirty ships and 4500 infantry encountered a storm off Cape Finisterre, several vessels sank, and the rest dispersed. 'God has fought for us,' wrote Robethon to Polwarth upon learning of the disaster.

But such was only partly true, for about this time a small part of the Pretender's expedition had gone north to Scotland and, anticipating this, the government had secured the services of three Dutch and two Swiss battalions.[26] The result was the defeat of the rebels at Glenshiel on 10 June. A week later Major General Wightman, who had engineered the defeat, took a tour 'through all the difficult parts . . . to terrify the Rebells by burning the houses of the Guilty and preserving those of the Honest.'[27]

By late October 1719 rumours again circulated of a new invasion to be made, this time by the duke of Ormonde, and, even though the ministers reckoned his effort would be 'a feeble' one, their own was not. Once again all was put in a state of readiness: orders were sent to the duke of Bolton to remain in Ireland, officers hastened to their posts, troops stood ready for orders, General McCartney went to Ireland, and Generals Carpenter and Wightman north to Scotland. The West Country was placed under the command of Major General Evans. This 'threatened invasion' also came to nothing. The expulsion of Cardinal Alberoni in late 1719 from the Spanish court concluded for the present further Spanish schemes in favour of the Pretender.

25 HMC, *Kenyon MSS*, 463
26 Abel Boyer, *The Political State of Great Britain* (London 1719), XVII, 411
27 Wightman's own account. Quoted in Dickson, ed., *The Jacobite Attempt of 1719*, liii

6

The necessity for a plot

The political gains for the English ministers, through their skilful handling of the Görtz-Gyllenborg plot two years earlier, had been considerable. Not only were they able to continue, against great opposition, George I's northern policy, but they had also exploited Jacobite activity to hold the ministry together at a critical juncture. This latter accomplishment was, however, of a temporary nature. Once the potentially dangerous quality had been extracted from the conspiracy, Townshend and Walpole broke with the ministry. The former's dismissal from office in April 1717 was quickly followed by the resignations of Walpole, Methuen, Orford, Devonshire, and Pulteney. From this point Stanhope and Sunderland were faced with an opposition force strengthened out of all proportion to its earlier effectiveness. From mid-1717, until their return to the ministry in 1720, Walpole and Townshend were to harass the government at each and every opportunity.[1]

Some indication of the nature and strength of the opposition was demonstrated on 8 May 1717, when the government was bitterly attacked with respect to the funds disbursed for the transport of the 6000 Dutch troops employed by George I during the 1715 rebellion. Charged with the embezzlement and the mismanagement of public funds, the ministry was forced into the awkward position of requesting the commissioner of transports to lay the accounts before parliament, and on 4 June the entire issue was hotly debated in a packed house.[2] 'Both parties made their utmost

---

1 For the split in the ministry see pages 22, 33 ff; J.H. Plumb, *Sir Robert Walpole: The Making of a Statesman*, 252-92; A.S. Foord, *His Majesty's Opposition, 1714-1830* (Oxford 1964), 70-82, 92-103.
2 Richard Chandler, *The History and Proceedings of the House of Commons from the Restoration to the Present Time* (London 1742), VI, 129-30, 137-42

efforts,' wrote Joseph Addison, secretary of state for the Southern Department, 'and summoned all their friends that could be got together from every quarter of the nation.' Walpole played no small part in the entire affair. For two hours he railed at the government for the padded accounts it had presented, pointing out demonstratively such loopholes as the charging of identical items of expense under several heads and the insuffficiency of vouchers. At the end of the debate the government was able to secure a majority of only ten votes, a margin not indicative of success by early eighteenth-century standards. As Addison declared to the earl of Stair: 'As this was the utmost efforts of all parties united against the present interest, I believe it is not hard to guesse which of the sides is likely to grow the strongest for it. Those who lost the day are amazed at their ill success, and wonder from whence such a body could be drawn together against 'em, for it was their own and the common opinion of the town that they would carry it by 50 or 60 voices.'[3]

An even earlier issue had adequately forewarned the ministry of their plight. On the question of who should preach to the assembled house, they had opposed a private member's choice of Dr Snape, the champion of the High Church, and in the debate that followed 'Mr. Walpole and his friends, joined their votes with the other side for the first time letting their old friends know what their strength was, if they thought fit to appear against what was to be done.'[4] The government had been defeated by a majority of ten votes and the opposition made the most of it. After the sermon was delivered on 29 May William Wyndham, supported by Shippen and several Whigs, rose in the house and proposed that Dr Snape be heartily thanked for his sermon. The motion had carried by a majority of fifteen votes.

The trial of the earl of Oxford later in the year showed the government the real skill and mastery of the opposition with which they were now forced to contend. Although Walpole avoided taking a very active part, his brother-in-law, Townshend, leagued with the Tories in the Lords, conceived and carried through a scheme which ultimately secured Oxford his freedom – a result which must have been most disheartening to Stanhope and Sunderland. As one writer observed: 'When the Earle of Oxford was acquited, and my Lord High Steward brake his staffe as a determination of his commission, the great number of people that were present shew'd their dislike or approbation in claps and hisses, but I think the claps and huzzas carry'd it by a great majority.'[5] The French ambassador reported that a great many

3 J.M. Graham, ed., *Annals and Correspondence of the Viscount and the First and Second Earls of Stair* (Edinburgh 1875), II, 22
4 [D. Defoe] *Mercurius Politicus*, 299
5 *HMC, Polwarth MSS*, I, 289

(LB   PJ   LW   HSM   AL   BD   FG   HO   IR   file)

PUBLICATION INFORMATION

ISBN: 0-8020- 5308-4   Price: $15.00E

Author: **Paul S. Fritz**

Title: The English Ministers and Jacobitism between the Rebellions of 1715
         and 1745

Series:

Publication Date: December 20, 1975

Discount: 20%

Nationality of Author(s):   Canadian

Domicile of Author(s):   Canada

Country of Original Publisher:
(where applicable)

Printed in: Canada

people were already making predictions that in less than six months the king would be forced to change his ministers.[6] Nor did the split in the Royal Household at the end of the year change this impression.[7] It is small wonder Stanhope lamented to George Bubb, the British envoy at Madrid, that the situation in England would provide him with ample matter for the exercise of his political talents.[8]

The government's prospects of success for the 1717-18 session of parliament looked gloomy indeed and the debate over the supply for the army did little to alter the fortunes of the ministry. Though not in favour of disbanding the army, Walpole attacked the government on its size and organization; his speech was sufficiently cutting to rouse William Shippen to seize the opportunity to cast aspersions on the Hanoverians and their foreign policy which he felt was 'rather calculated for the meridian of Germany, than of Great Britain.'[9] For this he was committed to the Tower, in a sense a triumph for the ministers, but hardly overshadowed by Walpole's success in securing a large reduction on the supplies requested by them.

The situation of instability in parliament was mirrored in the nation. In early October 1717 Addison informed Stair that there was 'an unusual spirit got into the enemies of the Government, which discovers itself in the falsehood and virulence of their discourses, newspapers, and clandestine prints and letters, and would make one think that the malcontents of England and France begin to act in perfect concert with one another.'[10] Throughout this and the next year the government was faced with an increasing number of instances of disaffection. In late July 1717 they seized the distributors of a paper called *The Weekly Pacquet* and pressed into force the necessary measures for turfing out its authors. Nathaniel Mist, printer of *The Weekly Journal*, was arrested for printing treasonous libels. On Restoration Day, 29 May, despite the stationing of soldiers 'in all the great places to keep all things quiet,' there was a good deal of rioting.[11] The magistrates in the city of Hereford imprisoned several persons and had others whipped in public for demonstrations against the Hanoverian succession. The rioting in this and other centres gave Stanhope and Sunderland good cause for anxiety, for they knew how easily a riot of weavers in the North Country or of tinsmiths in the West Country, though sparked off by economic grievances, could be turned

6 Arch.Aff.Etr.Corr.Pol.Angl., vol. 298, f 55
7 For the split in the Royal Household see Plumb, *Sir Robert Walpole: The Making of a Statesman*, 259-61.
8 HMC, *Matcham MSS*, 1
9 Chandler, *House of Commons*, VI, 157
10 Graham, *Annals . . . Earls of Stair*, II, 27
11 HMC, *Stuart MSS*, IV, 356

by the Jacobites against their administration. Disorder, discontent, and disaffection – this was the soil in which Jacobitism flourished best.

Informers had a heyday reporting the slightest signs of unrest to the ministers. One of them, John Dunton, was particularly active in his 'detection of enemies to the illustrious House.'[12] Reports of unrest flowed in from Manchester, Bristol, Liverpool, Leeds, and other cities and in many cases the government was adequately supplied with names as well as occupation. In many of the reports the names of weavers, wig-makers, tailors, tinsmiths, and merchants figure prominently.[13] Nor was the city of London a centre of calm. 'We walk our streets in fear,' ran one letter to Sir James Bateman, the lord mayor of London, 'for whoever kills one of us and swears he cursed King George is esteemed to do the Government good service.'[14] The differences at St James's and 'the fall of guineas' were, according to William Hawson, two very sound reasons for the uneasiness in London.

The government sought the solution to this problem, at least in part, through a rigid policy of repression. From the pages of *The Historical Register* for the years 1717 and 1718 the reader is provided with some indication of the nature of anti-Hanoverian and pro-Jacobite sympathy:[15] Mrs Clarke, a printer, taken into custody for printing a pamphlet entitled *To-day is Ours, To-morrow is Yours'*; the Grand Jury of Middlesex issues orders to the attorney general to prosecute the author, printer, and publisher of a weekly paper called *The Scourge*; James Shepheard, a coach painter's apprentice, arrested for conspiring and imagining the death of the king; William Heathcote and Henry Cheap committed to Newgate for printing and publishing treasonous libels; Richard Banks, watchmaker, arrested for drinking the Pretender's health; Robert Harrison arrested for crying out as he went along the street, 'King James the Third Forever, G- d- all his foes: Who dare oppose King James the Third?'

Despite government action, pamphlets from the opposition continued to pour forth.[16] Criers and hawkers of ballads were hurried off to houses of cor-

---

12 John Dunton (1659-1733): in 1706 he published *Dunton's Whipping-post, or a Satire Upon Everybody*. He was a Whig pamphleteer whose most famous pamphlet, *Neck or Nothing*, was a vitriolic attack on Oxford and Bolingbroke. In 1717 he was working with Daniel Defoe on a weekly paper called *The Hanover Spy*.

13 In one anonymous list of disaffected persons in the cities of Manchester, Bristol, and Liverpool in 1717 are included the names of two merchants, two mercers, one headmaster, one glover, one tailor, one wigmaker, and one physician. PRO, SP 35/10, ff 227-9

14 *Stuart MSS*, IV, 302

15 Only a very small number of examples follow taken from the *The Historical Register* for the years 1717 and 1718.

16 For examples see PRO, SP 35/10, ff 227-9, 232; SP 35/11, ff 26-7, 57-9, 115, 125, 129, 131, 134, 136-7, 201, 206-9, 211-12.

rection only to return with their vocal cords rested and ready to pick up with new vigour. Nor could the forcing of persons to take the oath of allegiance have brought little more than increased resentment against the government. The assembling of about a thousand Middlesex tavern keepers for the purpose of informing them that licences would be refused them if they failed to take the oath can only have infuriated many of them. So, too, the interrupting of the service of Dr Richard Welton, the Jacobite ex-rector of Whitechapel, to administer oaths on the spot can only have increased the suspicions of many that the administration was tyrannical.[17] The Whig 'note-takers' attending High Church sermons in London seemed to return to the government offices with increasingly long lists of sedition preached from the pulpit.[18]

Jacobites and Jacobite sympathizers took on new hope but with one strong reservation: they expected the announcement at any moment by the government of another Jacobite plot. 'A new Swedish plot is trumped up . . . if they think fit,' wrote one of them. Nor did the long-delayed Act of Grace seem to alleviate the situation. By mid-1718 there was a good deal of truth in the report of one Jacobite: 'The universal discontent grows daily. The divisions amongst the family, the divisions in the ministry, the divisions now in Parliament are come to a great height and still increasing but, though they should grow greater, nothing will be attempted here whilst the army is united and obedient . . . '[19]

The English ministers looked to success in their foreign policy as a means 'to strengthen the hands of the administration at home' and the prospects in this area seemed very good in September 1717.[20] A year later, however, their hopes were dashed for they were about to go to war with Spain. The conclusion of the Quadruple Alliance between Great Britain, France, Austria, and Holland obligated the allies to force a settlement between Spain and the emperor.[21] The capture of Sardinia by Spain in the autumn of 1717 made it clear to the British government that this aggressive policy of her chief minister, Cardinal Alberoni, would not end here since, in all likelihood, the attack would be projected to include Naples and Sicily. By the Treaty of Utrecht Britain was duty bound to guarantee the neutrality of Italy and by

17 Dr Richard Welton (1671-1726): rector of Whitechapel from 1697 to 1715. He refused to take the oaths to George I. In 1715 he opened a nonjuring chapel in Whitehall, London. In 1722 he was consecrated a bishop among the nonjurors.
18 J. Doran, *London in Jacobite Times* (London 1877), I, 278
19 *Stuart MSS*, IV, 221
20 PRO, SP 78/161, f 132
21 The emperor refused to recognize Philip V as king of Spain and he in turn refused to accept the acquisition by Austria and Savoy of Spain's Italian possessions.

the Treaty of Westminster was obligated to maintain the integrity of the imperial dominions. To fulfil these she had no other choice but to dispatch Sir George Byng and the British fleet 'to hinder and obstruct' Spain's attempts. Negotiation to reach a peaceful settlement failed and on 11 August 1717 Byng engaged the Spanish fleet off Cape Passaro and defeated it. Spain was given until 2 November 1718 to accept the terms of the allied powers or war would be declared. As the time for the summoning of parliament approached it appeared obvious the latter course would have to be followed and that supplies for this purpose would have to be granted by parliament.

This situation of instability at home and abroad caused the ministry to regard even more closely each and every Jacobite move. The reports of the ambassadors for these years are filled to an unusual degree with reports of Jacobite activities. Polwarth reported that he had received several accounts that preparations were being made by Spain 'more in favour of the Pretender and against our Master than against the Emperor,' while the movements of the Pretender and the duke of Ormonde became an increasing subject for speculation. News of the defeat of the Spanish fleet did not cause the great rejoicing that might have been expected in the city of London.[22]

The English ministers had somehow to unite parliament and the nation once again. One answer was suggested to them in mid-1718 by a pamphleteer who declared the time was now ripe to reveal to the country news of another Jacobite plot.[23] 'Did not the Swedish plot, last spring,' he asked, 'conduct the designs of the court smoothly through both houses?' 'And may not something of the same nature have the same effect this year?' In a satirical vein he claimed their action would be well justified for 'in all ages, plots have been in repute with wise men; and as to the effect, it is of no sort of consequence, in popular governments, whether they be ill or well grounded: For the present plot will always serve the present turn, as well as the real one: The same way that credit will carry a man for some time; through the world, as well as if he had substantial fund: And it is his fault if in that season he do not establish himself for the future.'

The English ministers did not raise the bogy of Jacobitism and there is no evidence to suggest that they even considered it as a remote possibility. Even if they did, they brushed such thoughts aside for they knew the risks would be too great. Their past experience with the Gyllenborg plot had shown them the fury an opposition could raise against such a move. They also knew that once they determined on such a course of action, necessity compelled them to prove it to the satisfaction of parliament and the nation.

22 HMC, *Bath MSS*, III, 456
23 *The Necessity of a Plot: Or, Reasons for a Standing Army. By a Friend to K.G.*

With the opposition now greatly strengthened by Townshend, Walpole, and their supporters, their compliance and support for an anti-Jacobite campaign at this point would only be forthcoming if they could convince them of the authenticity of a plot beyond any doubt. They had no near-conclusive evidence to present. Accounts, rumours, second- and third-hand reports – these were insufficient to convince anybody. They had no seized papers to read before a skeptical House of Commons or to publish before an aroused and questioning public. But perhaps even more relevant, any notion of a Jacobite invasion supported by Spain was very far from the English ministers' minds at this point. Charles Whitworth spoke for both Stanhope and Sunderland when he declared: 'His Majesty was informed of this design some time ago, but it appeared so wild and extravagant that thinking men could hardly believe it to be real or imagine that the Cardinal would hazard a little squadron and a small body of troops in the very midst of his enemies . . .'[24]

In order to secure the support of parliament and the nation, then, Stanhope and Sunderland steered a course that did not include the invention of a Jacobite plot. The line they followed at this juncture is well illustrated in the pamphlets of Daniel Defoe. In one of them he put the case for the necessity of war with Spain:

. . . there is a necessity for Great Britain to exert herself in timely preventing the growing exorbitance of the Spanish power, or to give up from this moment all her pretences to the trade either of the Mediterranean or Mexican seas . . . 'tis a scandalous mistake . . . to say that this war was undertaken to aggrandize the House of Austria, and to make the Emperor the Terror of Europe: But that it is undertaken to prevent Spain making herself the Terror of Great Britain, by ruining our trade, overthrowing our colonies, and destroying the liberty of that commerce, by which our manufactures are extended abroad, and consequently supported at home . . . [25]

When parliament met on 11 November 1718 the king informed its members of the conclusion of the Quadruple Alliance and of the consequences of Spain's refusal to adhere to it even though 'better conditions have been stipulated for that King, than were insisted upon in his behalf even at the Treaty of Utrecht.' He then told them that in order 'to vindicate . . . the faith of our former treaties, as well as to maintain those which we lately made, and to protect and defend the trade of my subjects, which has in ev-

24 *Polwarth MSS*, II, 98
25 [D. Defoe] *The Case of the War in Italy Stated: Being a Serious Enquiry How Far Great-Britain is Engaged to Concern Itself in the Quarrel Between the Emperor and the King of Spain* (London 1718)

ery branch been violently and unjustly oppressed, it became necessary for our naval forces to check their progress.'[26] As all reasonable offers had been made to Spain and subsequently rejected by her, they had no other recourse but to grant to him the necessary supplies 'in this important juncture.' Despite the heated debates which followed over the granting of supplies, the government carried the motion by a majority of sixty-one votes.

Only when the ministers had some definite proof of Jacobite endeavours did they give public expression to their fears. Once they had received 'unquestionable advice' of the invasion attempt of 1719, they lost no time in making the most of it. The march of troops to the West Country, the dispatch of Sir John Norris to Portsmouth and of Stanhope to Holland, the augmenting of the forces already on foot by twenty-two companies of infantry and ten of dragoons, the movement of four battalions from Ireland – all this caused a good deal of alarm and the English ministers knew that alarm and fear in the nation of a Jacobite invasion was a sure way of rallying support and unity from it. The king's address on 10 March, when he appeared before both houses and announced that 'an invasion will suddenly be attempted from Spain against my dominions in favour of the Pretender to my Crown,' could not have been a more dramatic piece of staging. At this point parliament and the nation were firmly behind the government and only Walpole demanded to know if the advices received were 'well grounded.'[27] No one was to be provided with an opportunity to raise the same question in 1722 when the Atterbury plot and the Layer conspiracy were disclosed to the nation.

26 Chandler, *House of Commons*, VI, 183
27 Ibid., 195

7

The English Jacobite plot of 1721

In the five-year period from 1720 to 1725 an unforeseen crisis occurred that provided the Jacobites with the most favourable opportunity to rally support for their cause since the death of Queen Anne. That event was the bursting of the South Sea Bubble in August 1720.[1] In January of that year the earl of Sunderland, first lord of the treasury, had entertained a proposal from the South Sea Company that would have allowed it to take over a large part of the National Debt that then stood at some £51,000,000. An agreement was finally worked out and accepted by parliament whereby the company would incorporate into its own capital some £30,000,000 of the National Debt and would, in addition, pay to the government some £7,000,000 for this privilege. In return the company expected to reap great profits from the sale of shares as well as from its monopoly of all British trade with Spanish America. Over the next several months a surge of stock buying resulted and the price of shares soared to astronomical heights. By late August, however, the craze ended. South Sea stock fell dramatically from 780 to 180 per cent and pandemonium set in as thousands were financially ruined. The Whig ministry now faced its most severe challenge since the accession of George I. On 13 September Thomas Brodrick informed Lord Chancellor Midleton of the plight of the ministry. 'The consternation is inexpressible, the rage beyond expression, and the case so desperate,' he wrote, 'that I do not see any plan or scheme, so much as thought of for averting the blow.'[2] And the rage was

1 For a detailed account of the South Sea Bubble crisis and its impact see J. Carswell, *The South Sea Bubble* (London 1961); J.H. Plumb, *Sir Robert Walpole: The Making of a Statesman* (London 1957), Chapters 8, 9.
2 William Coxe, *Memoirs of the Life and Administration of Sir Robert Walpole* (London 1798), III, 190-1

vented upon the government. According to Arthur Onslow, the future speaker of the House of Commons, 'The rage against the Government was such for having as they thought drawn them into this ruin, that I am almost persuaded, the King being at that time abroad, that could the Pretender then have landed at the Tower, he might have rode to St. James's with very few hands held up against him.'[3]

Despair, consternation, rage, discontentment – these remained the central features to describe the mood of both the parliamentary opposition and the political nation over the next year. In mid-July 1721, only a few weeks before an angry mob stormed the lobbies and corridors of the House of Commons, Colonel Molesworth expressed his strong belief that 'our whole multitude will turn Jacobite in a very few months more.'[4] There was, it would seem, a good deal of truth in the report of John Menzies, one of the Jacobite agents in London, that the nation was 'highly out of humour' and all that was needed was for someone 'to set fire to the train of powder.'[5] John Aislabie, chancellor of the exchequer; Charles Stanhope, secretary of the treasury; James Craggs, one of the postmasters general; his son, James Craggs, secretary of state for the Southern Department; and the earl of Sunderland – all of these ministers, together with the directors of the South Sea Company, were singled out as central agents in bringing about this financial disaster. In the final analysis it was to be the political skill and ingenuity of Robert Walpole that was to save the Whig ministry from total collapse. In the course of the parliamentary enquiry that followed, Aislabie and the South Sea Company directors were censured and the bulk of their property confiscated. Three other ministers died: James Stanhope, while speaking in the House of Lords; the younger James Craggs of small pox; the elder Craggs in all likelihood committed suicide. Charles Stanhope, acquitted by a bare majority of three votes, resigned his office, Sunderland alone escaped censure by a majority of sixty votes.

It was in the midst of this crisis that Jacobite circles buzzed with one major interrogative: should they hazard a restoration attempt without the backing of a major foreign power, placing the ultimate expectation of success almost entirely on 'the good disposition' of their supporters within the kingdoms of England, Ireland, and Scotland? The leading English Jacobites and their associates were to answer this question in the affirmative, while a minority on the continent were to consider it folly and madness to undertake such a venture. But the attitude of the former group prevailed and in

3 HMC, *Onslow MSS*, 504
4 HMC, *Clements MSS*, 318
5 HMC, *Moray MSS*, 198

late 1721 a plan was initiated for raising a rebellion and insurrection in England to be supplemented, if possible, by a minimum of foreign support.[6] The risks were tremendous, as was subsequently revealed, but the Jacobites in England, encouraged and abetted by Dillon in Paris, Ormonde in Spain, and the Pretender in Italy, believed the advantages far outweighed the peril involved.

In the months immediately following the bursting of the South Sea Bubble – from about September until December of 1720 – when the rage against the government was at one of its highest peaks, the Jacobites did little. This event had taken them virtually by surprise. As such a favourable juncture was not anticipated, nothing was ready; they had no arms, no ammunition, no scheme ready and waiting. Their only hope was to prolong the crisis while they prepared to take advantage of it. Towards this end the Pretender came forth with his declaration to be circulated among the disaffected in England. 'The cries of our people' having reached his ears as far away as Italy, he saw it as his duty to sympathize with them in 'the great calamity brought upon them' and to express, at the same time, his great impatience to return to his dominions, 'not so much out of a desire to find justice ourself, as to do it to others, and to have an opportunity to show ourself the father of our people.'[7] The discontent did not abate and the Jacobites in parliament, among them William Shippen and the earl of Orrery, employed all their skill to exaggerate the situation by 'opposing any measures that the English ministry ever propose to remedy 'em.'[8] To keep up the resentments of the people they worked feverishly to turn out pamphlets and broadsheets against the government.

One of the first demands for immediate action came, surprisingly enough, from the pen of Orrery. In early January 1721 he asserted his view to the Pretender that they should hasten to exploit the present situation, for 'there is very little expectation left among us of any relief from our present unhappy State by the management of those that have brought us into it, and therefore . . . our present governors and all their agents grow ev'ry day more and more both into aversion and contempt, and the body of the people seem much better dispos'd than ever to wellcome any assistance that will come to their deliverance.'[9] This marks a significant change in Orrery's attitude because he had always insisted on foreign support on a large scale as

---

6 RA, Stuart, 51/53

7 Ibid., 49/45. A great many of these, together with letters to the archbishops and bishops of England, were stopped at the Post Office. PRO, SP 35/23, f 171

8 RA, Stuart, 51/53

9 Ibid.

the absolute essential. Now, even though he urged the Pretender to continue to solicit aid from both France and Spain, he no longer considered it vital for 'a less assistance is requisite,' he said, 'whilst this disposition lasts.' Three months later Francis Atterbury echoed Orrery's sentiments. He wrote to the Pretender: 'The time is now come, when with a very little assistance from your friends abroad, your way to your friends at home is become safe and easy. The present juncture is so favourable, and will probably continue for so many months to be so, that I cannot think it will pass without a proper use being made of it.'[10]

A host of similar appeals were sent from other English Jacobites and, although they varied in the degree of enthusiasm, in general they all agreed that the time was ripe for an immediate attempt. The earl of Arran, Oxford, Charles Caesar, Sir Henry Goring, the earl of Strafford, and Lord North and Grey spoke with one voice on the necessity to seize on 'the present complications of accidents.' By early October 1721 their views were embodied in a memorial conveyed to the Pretender by Lord Falkland who had made at least two missions to England in 1721 and 1722 and while there had discussed the project with several leading Jacobites, among them Atterbury.[11] After an examination of the nature of the circumstance with which 'providence' had provided them, they requested an enterprise of 'vigour' and 'spirit.' Sir Henry Goring assured the Pretender that once landed in England, one thousand men would join him and in less than a day his support would swell to over five thousand. The one imperative as the English Jacobites saw it was for the Pretender to appear in person at the head of the insurrection, for otherwise it would prove abortive. They declared: 'Your presence alone can animate the whole affair and many who will readily fly to your standard, will not stir from their habitations on any other call, the Prince ever gives life to all undertakings, and causes an emulation in each person to perform somewhat extraordinary when he knows his sovereign is an eyewitness of his action.'[12]

The Pretender now faced a decision of paramount importance. The experience of 1715 had demonstrated the necessity of foreign support for any venture. This was still considered to be desirable, but he now judged the crisis in England to be far too fortunate to allow it to slip away unused. Also, the information at his disposal gave him reason to believe that England awaited him with open arms and the demands that had poured in from that quarter in late 1721 served only to increase that belief. Although he would

10 RA, Stuart, 53/48
11 Lucius Henry (Cary), Viscount Falkland, (1687-1730). RA, Stuart, 55/48; 55/55; 61/151
12 Ibid., 55/55

not relax his efforts to secure the good offices of France, Spain, or Russia, it was quite obvious, he told Charles Caesar, that 'the affection of the generality of the nation' was so much in his favour that even were he to come 'alone,' he would have 'a very fair game of it.'[13]

These petitions, together with the visit to Rome in the summer of two emissaries from England, influenced his decision. Christopher Layer, a Norfolk barrister and imbiber of nonjuring principles, had early worked his way into Jacobite circles through one of their chief agents in London, John Plunket, an Irish Roman Catholic, who had been educated at the Jesuit college in Vienna. Layer and Plunket were but two of the vast number of persons the Pretender referred to as 'the insignificant' but 'trusted' ones. Their mission to Rome was heralded by a letter from Plunket informing him that they would bring with them a list of supporters and, on behalf of the latter, would tell him 'what will be acceptable.'[14] Upon their arrival several meetings were held; Layer duly produced his list naming one hundred and fourteen 'persons of fortune' in the county of Norfolk who were now 'desirous to show their loyalty and affection by joining in any attempt that shall be thought advisable to bring about a speedy and happy restoration,'[15] including Sir Ralph Hare, Sir John Wodehouse, Sir Thomas Robinson, Sir Nicholas L'Estrange, Roger North, Doctor Boys, Robert Monsey, and Mr Lake. A special section was devoted to his potential support in the city of Norwich where Doctor Amyas, Aldermen Benny, Newton, and Harwood were numbered among his adherents. The yearly income of each individual was carefully noted to give the Pretender some indication of the financial support he might reasonably expect from this source.

Before leaving Rome, Layer presented his scheme. Although it differed sharply from the one he was to draw up a year later, he now proposed 'that Mr. Thomas Pitt, now Colonel of the Regiment of horse . . . should enter into an association with those Norfolk gentlemen and upon their taking up arms and proclaiming the King in that county, to join 'em with his Regiment and then take upon him the principal command over all such as shall be there assembled together in the King's favour.'[16] To secure the services of Colonel Pitt, it would be necessary, however, to offer him the prospect of a reward and Layer suggested this could take the form of giving him 'authority to assure Mr. Pitt that he shall be made Earl of Yarmouth after the present Lord's decease.' The Pretender had been impressed with Layer's zeal for

13 Ibid., 55/62
14 Cholmondeley (Houghton) MSS, iii, 69/2 (B23); RA, Stuart, 63/68
15 See Appendix 2.
16 RA, Stuart, 65/11 (The Scheme)

he allowed him, on his return to England, to approach either Lord North and Grey or the earl of Orrery to act as proxy for him as godfather to Layer's newly-born daughter.[17] In this way Layer became at least a partial party to the plans of 'the significant' Jacobites during the course of the next year.

With these numerous encouragements from England, consultations were held with General Dillon, the duke of Ormonde, and Lord Lansdowne and the final decision was taken. The opportunity must be seized and it must be seized quickly. Dillon dispatched an immediate express to Sweden to demand the repayment of the 175,000 livres they had advanced to Görtz some five years earlier since it was now needed for the purchase of arms and ammunition. A small group of Jacobites in France were against any programme for an immediate attempt but their opinion seems to have carried no weight and the plan from the European side was finally drawn up. They felt that the Pretender should not make any move to leave Italy until all preparations were made in England. While this was being done they would use their endeavours 'to get the Czar (the only power who at present appears not in measures with George) to give the assistance of some of his troops from Archangel the beginning of next summer.'[18] Once all was ready from the English side and the signal was given to put the plan into execution, Ormonde would go to England, General Dillon and the Scots abroad to Scotland, and a 'fit person' would hasten to Ireland. If the undertaking were handled in this way it could be carried out before the British government could be 'apprized of their design.'

Their 'reflections' were duly communicated to England and in reply Atterbury directed his amanuensis, the Reverend George Kelly, a nonjuror,[19] to request the Pretender to prepare several commissions for persons in England. With a warm enthusiasm the Pretender thanked Atterbury for his previous letters to General Dillon and also the memorial he had sent. He added: 'It is not easy for me to express the satisfaction I received from those accounts and the deep sense I have of the great share you have had in managing and bringing matters to the length they are arrived at. What I have writ . . . in answer to the Memorial will sufficiently show you how much I approve the proposed project and how solicitous I am to promote it as much

17 R.W. Ketton-Cremer, *A Norfolk Gallery* (London 1948), 135-6
18 RA, Stuart, 65/18 (Considerations by some of the King's Friends in France upon the present state of affairs and what had been lately proposed to His Majesty from England).
19 George Kelly was born in 1688 in county Roscommon, Ireland. In 1718 he went to France where he was involved in Law's Mississippi Scheme. He came to England in 1720. *Memoirs of the Life, Travels, and Transactions of the Reverend Mr. George Kelly, From His Birth to Escape from his Imprisonment out of the Tower of London, October 26, 1736* (London 1736)

as in me lies for I am fully convinced of the dangers of a delay and return to you a thousand thanks for your speaking to me on that head.'[20]

Accordingly, he drew up the necessary commissions to be forwarded to England. They were of both a specific and general nature. The latter ones Atterbury was requested to distribute to 'worthy persons.' By the former, dated 4 January 1722, Lord North and Grey was created commander-in-chief 'of all our forces in and about our City of London and Westminster' and Sir Henry Goring was given a commission as governor of Bristol in order to direct the project formed for seizing that city.[21] At the same time expressions of gratitude for their continued zeal and support for 'the important matter now in agitation' were dispatched to the earl of Strafford, the earl of Arran, the earl of Orrery, Lord Bathurst, Charles Caesar, and the Reverend George Kelly. As money would be necessary for the purchase of arms and ammunition, blank receipts, signed by the Pretender, were forwarded to the earl of Orrery who farmed them out to Christopher Layer and others to be filled up.[22] By mid-April 1722 General Dillon, with funds brought from England via Alderman Barber, was in the process of purchasing some 10,000 arms. The Pretender had already sent £2000 to Ormonde in Spain, with which he was hoping to secure 2000 arms plus the services of some officers. Acting through Admiral Gordon, a prominent Jacobite in the czar's service, the Pretender initiated requests for aid. Now that the czar had concluded a peace he was left, said James, with 'many idle workmen on his hands and a great quantity of materials of all kinds' and he urged Gordon to exert his influence 'to induce him [the czar] to employ part of them in my favour, the rather since he could not but find his own account also in so doing.'[23]

By this time the English Jacobites had drawn up a vast general plan for an insurrection to take place during the elections of 1722.[24] Each county in

20 RA, Stuart, 57/1
21 RA, Stuart, Warrant Book: M20, nos 96, 106
22 Ten of these receipts were given to Layer and were seized with his other papers by Robert Walpole's messengers. The originals are in Cholmondeley (Houghton) MSS, iii, 69/2
23 *Moray MSS*, 159
24 See Appendix 3. This document is undated and unsigned, but it was drawn up before August 1721 because it was received at Albano at that time. From its contents, and the plans following it, the knowledge of several persons seems to have gone into its preparation. I impute this particular draft, however, to Thomas Carte. There is a very similar one to this one (though of a later date) to be found in the French Archives (Arch.Aff.Etr.Mémoires et Documents Angleterre, vol. 76, ff 26-33). Carte was a nonjuror with strong Jacobite connections. He refused to take the oath at the accession of George I. After the arrest of George Kelly, Carte appears to have acted as Atterbury's amanuensis. A warrant was sworn for his arrest but he escaped to France.

England was carefully marked off and a potential 'chief' (commander-in-chief) noted. The persons on whom it was felt they could rely for support in each area were listed and, also, those considered 'dubious.' In the West Country, Cornwall was reckoned to be one of their strongest regions. Twenty-nine were listed as assured, among them Mr Bassett,[25] Thomas Tonkin,[26] Mr Hawes,[27] Mr Collins, Mr Kemp, and Mr Glyn, all of whom were to be under the direction of Lord Lansdowne.[28] Those labelled as 'dubious' included Francis and Henry Scobell and Nicolas Vincent. Devonshire, with its list of twenty-nine, boasted potential support from Sir William Courtenay,[29] Sir Coplestone Bampfylde,[30] and Captain Stafford. Somersetshire, where it was remarked Lord Lansdowne's 'credit' was very great, would also be under his command and among its twenty-one numbered Lord Poulett, Sir William Wyndham,[31] and Lord Stourton.[32] In Gloucestershire Lord Bathurst, as 'chief' of a group of fifteen, was to be assisted by Lords Conway and Tracy. Wiltshire, with its composite list of seventeen, was to be under the dual leadership of Lord Bruce and General Webb.[33] Dorsetshire, Hampshire, and Sussex were to be under the joint command of Lord Digby and Sir Henry Goring. Surrey and Kent, with their nine potential adherents, were to have Lord Winchilsea as commander-in-chief. With respect to Norfolk it is probable that Christopher Layer's knowledge was called upon. Although Townshend's and Walpole's 'interest' was felt to be extremely strong,

25 Romney Sedgwick, *The House of Commons, 1715-1754* (London 1970), I, 443

26 Probably Thomas Tonkin, one of the historians of Cornwall who also held large estates in the area of Penryn. He is described by Courtney as a squire of 'high Tory repute.' William Prideaux Courtney, *The Parliamentary Representation of Cornwall to 1832* (London 1889), 48

27 Probably William Hawes. *Gentleman's Magazine*, XX, 332

28 Lansdowne of Biddeford (1667-1735). Removed as treasurer of the household in 1714, he was committed to the Tower. After his release in February 1717 he retired abroad and joined the Pretender. In 1721/22 he was created duke of Albermarle by the Pretender. Marquis of Ruvigny, *The Jacobite Peerage, Baronetage, Knightage, and Grants of Honour* (Edinburgh 1904)

29 Sedgwick, *House of Commons*, I, 588

30 Ibid., 430-1

31 Ibid., II, 562

32 Thomas Stourton. Educated St Gregory's College, Douai. His nephew, Charles, who inherited the estates, married Catherine, widow of Robert Petre. On the death of her first husband, she was considered as a potential wife for the Pretender. George Edward Cockayne, *The Complete Peerage of England, Scotland, Ireland, Great Britain and the United Kingdom* (London 1910-59); HMC, *Stuart MSS*, I, 348

33 General Webb's house was searched by Walpole's government for arms and ammunition in 1722. Diary of Thomas Smith, Esq., of Shaw House, Melksham, *The Wiltshire Archaeological and Natural History Society Magazine*, XI, 215

nevertheless it was hoped that a large number of 'the fishermen about Yarmouth' and 'the manufacturers of Norwich' might be gained. Cambridgeshire, Huntingdonshire, and Bedfordshire would have Lord North and Grey as commander-in-chief and he would be aided by 'the Cottons in their several branches.'[34] Authority in Hertfordshire, 'filled with honest men and able horses,' was to be delegated to Charles Caesar and Mr Robinson, while Oxfordshire, with its seven worthies, under the command of Sir Robert Jenkinson, was to count heavily on enveloping the university. The earl of Strafford, Mr Isham, and Mr Robinson were put forward as fit figures to direct the insurrection in Northamptonshire. As Warwickshire was deemed to have hardly 'a whig in it,' it was felt that Mr Jennings and Doctor Davis, both nonjurors, would be able to bring considerable influence to bear on the mass of workers in Birmingham. Worcestershire, Staffordshire, Shropshire, and Herefordshire were all noted for their 'perpetual loyalty' and would rally quickly under the hand of Lord Gower.[35] Although Radnorshire, because of its small population, was considered to be of 'no great use,' Montgomeryshire, Pembrokeshire, and Brecknockshire were certainly fit 'to be relyed on.' Flintshire and Denbighshire were also judged to be 'very useful,' and the neighbouring city of Chester, in which a vast number of the militia had refused to take the oath in 1715, would, no doubt, rally again. Lancashire, Derbyshire, and Yorkshire would also be placed under the command of Lord Strafford, while Nottinghamshire would be headed by Lord Middleton. Cumberland, Westmorland, and Northumberland would be roused at the right moment by William Shippen.

Widespread general support was obviously to count for much in such an endeavour and several persons were selected for their ability to influence vast numbers of what the Pretender referred to as 'the generality.' In Warwickshire, for example, Sir John Pakington and Mr Lane would use their influence to rally the iron-workers. Birmingham was to be counted on as a city 'capable of furnishing 12,000 men and arms'; the city of Manchester, '15,000 fighting men.' Cornwall, with its great number of tinners and fishermen, Devonshire, with its numerous manufacturers and clothiers, Wales and the entire north, with their colliers and workers – all these might be raised in support of the Pretender at the time of the elections.

This was the paper plan for an insurrection. The next question was how to put it into execution. A programme was embodied in a further project entitled 'A Scheme for a General Rising in England.' This was communi-

34 Sedgwick, *House of Commons*, I, 584
35 Baron Gower of Stittenham. Since 1718 he had been in contact with the Jacobites on the continent.

cated to General Dillon and then passed on to the Pretender.[36] Once the time for the execution of the plan drew near, the main persons to whom the secret had been confided would pass this intelligence on to the commander-in-chief or chiefs in each county and together they would reach agreement on suitable company generals who would then be given commissions from the Pretender. Each company general, upon retiring to his own district, would 'make choice of first officers for the regiments he is to raise.' It was considered extremely important that those persons selected by the company generals were 'men skilful in military exercises.' The company general would 'fix on the proper persons in power to raise at least troops or dragoons in each county to whom the commander-in-chief will give commissions by virtue of the power given him by the King with a promise of making them good at his arrival.' To facilitate this organization, each potential troop officer would be duly advised in advance to have 'twenty men ready at a call with horses of their own and accoutrements as can be provided without noise and not liable to discovery.' Once the signal was received for the general rising, 'the several commanders-in-chief will appoint a place of rendez-vous for all their troops of horse and dragoons to meet in each district at break of day without failing.' The first few days following the insurrection were crucial, and a 'good use' had to be made of the troops or all would end in failure. Their first targets must be the principal cities, 'especially those placed on the rivers and necessary for communication,' and the securing of the customs houses in order to have money to pay the troops. At the very outset it was imperative to declare for the Pretender in as many public places as possible.

The general rising in the country was to be sparked off by an imaginative coup in the city of London.[37] Following a signal, the arms concealed in the city would be dug up and dispersed to supporters in Southwark, Whitechapel, Wapping, Holborn, and Smithfield. Once completed, a march would be made on the city and when the central points were secured a message, signed by three lords, would be communicated to the lord mayor of London. A declaration from the Pretender would be distributed to the people.

Such were the plans of the English Jacobites for an insurrection to take place at the time of the elections 'when all the Freeholders of England are necessarily assembled together, and when the whole Nation is too apt to be

36 RA, Stuart, 65/60. This document is almost entirely in numerical cipher.
37 *A Report from the Committee Appointed by Order of the House of Commons to Examine Christopher Layer, and Others* (London 1722), BB 2

in a ferment, even in the quietest Times.'[38] It is uncertain just how far beyond this stage preparations went, but they were not advanced far enough
to become operative at the time of the elections. This was probably due to
several factors. As mentioned earlier, the earl of Orrery had been one of the
first to call for immediate action. He seems also to have been one of the first
to change his mind. Some time in early January or February 1722 he refused
to sanction the project and urged another course of action. Entrusted with
the collection of money he wished to apply it, not to the purchase of arms
and ammunition, but to influencing the elections in order 'to secure a right
house of commons.'[39] According to James Hamilton, one of Orrery's 'trusted'
agents, 'the company' rejected his proposal as they were convinced 'the ferment in the nation would not admit of delays.' Also, the state of Atterbury's
health at this point and the death of his wife must have allowed for only the
minimum of activity and advice on his part. Ill-health, characterized by frequent attacks of the gout, seems to have been his most constant companion.
Lord Bathurst, with whom Atterbury had been corresponding, also took the
position that the scheme as it stood was 'likelier to destroy than promote
what is so much desired.'[40] Both Bathurst and Orrery described the project
as 'rash' but declared themselves perfectly willing to go into any other 'reasonable measures.' Lord North and Grey, Lord Strafford, and Sir Henry
Goring appear, however, to have desired to press ahead with it. During the
course of several meetings with Lord North and Grey at his country house
at Epping, Green, a London gunsmith, assured him that five to seven thousand arms would be ready when called for.[41] The host of 'insignificant' persons – Christopher Layer, John Plunket, Dennis Kelly, Reverend George
Kelly, Philip Neynoe – actively pressed ahead with plans. The government
committee that was set up to report on the conspiracy noted that there had
been 'riotous conduct at the Coventry election' and attributed it to the machinations of Thomas Carte, a nonjuring clergyman. During the early
spring Carte made two trips into the West Country, one into Cornwall and
another into Warwickshire, Derbyshire, Nottinghamshire, and Staffordshire.[42] He discussed the project with several persons and in Devon secured
the wholehearted support of Sir William Courtenay, Sir Coplestone
Bampfylde, and Captain Stafford. According to Carte, Major Waldron guaranteed the aid of the militia of Devon were the Pretender landed in England.

38 Ibid., 3
39 RA, Stuart, 63/33
40 RA, Stuart, 61/16
41 Cholmondeley (Houghton) MSS, iii, 69/2 (B 11)
42 Arch.Aff.Etr.Mémoires et Documents Angleterre, vol. 76, ff 26-32

Although many seem to have been prepared to proceed without foreign support, several still considered it as an essential requirement. The Reverend George Kelly had already engaged Philip Neynoe, who was well-informed of the project, to draft a memorial to the regent of France with a request for 5000 troops.

One of the major difficulties was, as always, money. After the opportunity for a revolt at the time of the election had passed, Atterbury pleaded with the Pretender 'to press the Gentlemen concern'd by all manner of ways you can think of to furnish what by being hitherto not supplied has render'd the thing impracticable.'[43] As already pointed out, the Pretender had supplied the earl of Orrery with a number of blank receipts. They read:

I acknowledge to have received from ———————————the sum of ——————————
which I promise to repay, with an interest for it, at the rate of ———————————per
annum.

      (Signed) JAMES R:[44]

The ten Orrery gave to Christopher Layer remained in this blank form as must many of the others.[45] Few would have been prepared to have their names on a document which, if seized, would have gone a long way in convicting them of high treason. Certainly some money was collected (how much is uncertain), but it seems to have been not nearly enough for the purchase of the necessary arms and ammunition, let alone to secure the services of a sufficient number of officers and troops in Spain. In mid-April Ormonde was still demanding 'more money from friends' in England.

By early March, however, plans were either sufficiently far advanced or else a premature decision was taken (probably the latter) to attempt to bring Ormonde over to England, a plan that was carried out with the concurrence of some of the 'significant' Jacobites, including Atterbury.[46] One Captain Halstead of Lancashire was commissioned for the purpose and hired a ship, the *Phineas* of Bristol, at £100 per month which set sail on 2 March 1722 for Bilboa and arrived there about 25 March. The ship returned without Ormonde. William Arnold, master of the ship, who, it seems, was not informed of its real mission until his arrival in Spain, absolutely refused to be a party to the scheme, but even had he agreed to the project it would have been thwarted because Colonel William Stanhope, the British ambassador at Madrid, had secured the co-operation of the Spanish government

43 RA, Stuart, 59/42
44 Cholmondeley (Houghton) MSS, iii, 69/2
45 Hamilton reported in September that only one note for £1000 had been filled up.
46 PRO, SP 35/31, f 48

to prevent Ormonde's departure. 'I have ordered Halstead's ship, that I depended upon,' wrote Ormonde, 'to return to England.' 'It was not proper to make use of it for reasons not necessary to trouble you with.'[47] The reasons were obvious. Once discovery of the ship was made, not only could Ormonde not go on board but neither could the ship be loaded with arms and ammunition to be carried back to England.

The Pretender's requests to the czar for support came to nothing.[48] In April the Jacobites were making earnest appeals to the regent for immediate aid, but instead of complying with their request he decided to inform the British government. It is doubtful what Sunderland's reaction might have been to the news the messenger brought from France on 20 April 1722 had he not been aware of Jacobite plans for some time, but, in any case, he had died the day before. There was, however, little doubt as to the course of action Robert Walpole would pursue. In mid-April Atterbury expressed his disappointment to the Pretender that 'this opportunity' had elapsed but hoped another would offer before the end of the year; when a new 'occasion' presented itself, he assured him, he would not be 'idle.' In hindsight this comment strikes an ironic note, for at this moment Atterbury did not know that his letter had been intercepted and a copy of it was safely in the hands of Robert Walpole. Walpole was to present Atterbury with an 'occasion' and for the next year he was to be anything but idle. He was to be fighting for his life as a result of Walpole's decision to initiate a Jacobite investigation of staggering proportions.

In a letter to Sir Henry Goring in early January 1722, the Pretender had expressed great joy over their project and added:

I desire to have my personal share in it and I hope we shall be able to be ready on all sides at the proper time; for it would be of fatal consequence to let that slip, and therefore it will be of the last importance to prevent by your rising, any design of seizing your persons, although that should even in some measure advance the time prefixed, but yours and your partners' zeal is such that I plainly see [that] it wants no incitement and therefore I have nothing left to desire but that God would give a blessing to your resolutions.[49]

That a blessing was not given to their resolution appears obvious by the events that followed the public announcement of the most recent plot on 8

---

47 It is possible that Ormonde had never intended to come with the ship to England since its real purpose may have been to bring arms to England to have in readiness for the event.

48 Maurice Bruce, 'Jacobite Relations with Peter the Great,' *Slavonic Review*, XIV, 1936, 343

49 RA, Stuart, 57/5

May 1722. What their endeavours over the past year and in the months following did receive, however, was the undivided attention of Robert Walpole. Even though the opportunity had blown over it did not preclude, for the English Jacobites, 'a fatal consequence.' By the end of the year Francis Atterbury, Lord North and Grey, and the earl of Orrery were safely in the Tower of London charged with, or on suspicion of, high treason. A host of their associates and other lesser figures were lodged with messengers. Thomas Carte and John Sample had escaped the clutches of the government by fleeing to the continent. Another, Philip Neynoe, attempted an escape and lost his life in the process. Yet another, Christopher Layer, was awaiting his execution.

Layer's part in the entire conspiracy was not nearly as significant as the government report would seem to indicate. The Layer conspiracy was, in many senses, Layer's alone. As already mentioned, he had been privy to the plans of 'the significant' Jacobites since September 1721. Like Neynoe, who also shared in many of the secrets, their combined testimony provided Walpole with sufficient proof to have two of the principals, Lord North and Grey and the earl of Orrery, committed to the Tower. But beyond the overall project Layer conducted his own programme for a restoration. By early 1722 he had abandoned his scheme for a Norfolk insurrection and concentrated his efforts on fomenting one in the city of London. Even after the government announced its decision to act, he continued to enlist the support of as many disaffected persons in the army as he could. He had managed, it would seem, to have secured the services of some eight serjeants by midsummer. His London scheme, an ingenious and intricately involved piece of planning, displays an almost professional knowledge of military detail. His twenty-one point programme for an insurrection in the city of London demanded machine-like precision for its successful execution: the Tower of London was to be taken in seven stages; the Exchange occupied; the 'great men' arrested; proclamations from the Pretender read at certain key moments; the central points in London and Westminster secured; the mob rallied in support; the king and the prince of Wales seized. All this was to be accomplished with split-second timing. So exacting was Layer's plan that it seemed to defy failure. As a mental exercise it can only be marvelled at. Committed to paper and in the hands of Robert Walpole, it led to his conviction for high treason and his execution in 1723.

8

Walpole's investigation

The bursting of the South Sea Bubble in 1720 had provided the Jacobites with an opportunity more propitious than that offered them in 1714, 1717, or 1719. The English ministers must have expressed astonishment when this situation was not initially seized upon by the Pretender's supporters – that is, all but the earl of Sunderland. From early 1717 when John Erskine, 11th earl of Mar, began corresponding with and visiting the earl of Stair, the British ambassador in Paris, Sunderland had been at least partially informed of Jacobite plans and secrets. Though little intelligence was forthcoming from Mar, the situation did encourage other Jacobites to view Sunderland as sympathetic to their cause. Also, early in 1721 Sunderland, in an effort to strengthen his own political position, had approached a number of the more prominent Jacobite leaders. By early April 1722 he had in his possession certain documents from them.[1] In addition, since at least the beginning of April interceptions of more than routine fashion had been going on at the Post Office, for the previous month the king had warned parliament of those enemies who were 'with the greatest industry [carrying forth] the same wicked acts of calumny and defamation, which have been the constant preludes to public troubles and disorders.'[2]

---

1 RA, Stuart, 59/125, 60/7. The Pretender was highly suspicious of Sunderland's motives. In a letter to Lord Lansdowne he claimed: 'I own I never had any opinion at all of Lord Sunderland's wishing me well.' Ibid., 60/88; For a detailed account of Sunderland's insincere overtures to and manipulation of Jacobite leaders in England in 1721 see G.V. Bennett, 'Jacobitism and the Rise of Walpole,' in *Historical Perspectives: Studies in English Thought and Society in honour of J.H. Plumb*, ed. Neil McKendrick (London 1974), 73 ff.

2 William Cobbett, *The Parliamentary History of England from the Earliest Period to the Year 1803* (London 1806-12), VII, 982

Suddenly on 19 April 1722 Sunderland died. The action taken at this juncture by Lord Townshend, the new secretary of state for the Northern Department, and Robert Walpole, the new chancellor of the exchequer and first lord of the treasury, clearly demonstrates at least some knowledge of Sunderland's dealings with the Jacobites, as their first thoughts were to seize his papers. Unfortunately, the duchess of Marlborough and the executors had sealed the desk containing them. Determination to come at them brought the dispatch of the lord president of the council, Lord Carleton, the Lord Privy Seal, the duke of Kingston, and the two secretaries of state, Lord Carteret and Lord Townshend, to Sunderland's lodgings and upon entry they 'tore off the seals, seized what papers related to public affairs, and carried them away.'[3] A week before his death the earl of Sunderland had told a prominent Jacobite, probably Orrery, that 'it was well for them [the Jacobites] . . . that Townshend and Walpole had not in their hands what he had.'[4] On 21 April Sunderland's papers were firmly in the hands of these two ministers.

On the same day as these papers were examined, a messenger arrived post-haste from France bearing an express from Sir Luke Schaub, the British ambassador in Paris, which contained definite advice from the regent that he had received repeated appeals from the Jacobites for support. Again, on the same day, a letter was intercepted at the Post Office in which 'T. Jones' told 'Mr Chivers' that 'nothing of importance should be trusted to the post . . . the death of Lord Sunderland makes such a caution more indispensably necessary . . . those in power here will now enter into measures of more severity and strictness, and employ all their diligence as well as power on such occasions.'[5] Francis Atterbury's, alias T. Jones', prediction was to prove all too true. These three occurrences of 21 April 1722 set in motion a train of events which, compared to those following the discoveries of 1717 and 1719, may only be described as staggering. 'Measures of severity,' 'strictness,' 'dilligence,' and 'display of power' are most apt characterizations of Walpole's activity over the next year as he fulfilled a new role of interrogator. During this period Walpole's instinctive and internal fear of Jacobitism took external shape in one of the largest 'witch hunts' of British history.

On 23 April, four days after Sunderland's death, a meeting of the Privy Council was summoned to meet at the duke of Devonshire's house, and from this session the first display of power was generated.[6] Instructions were given

3 RA, Stuart, 59/125; HMC, *Sutherland MSS,* 190; *Caesar Journals,* Book I
4 RA, Stuart, 60/26
5 Cholmondeley (Houghton) MSS, iii, 69/4 (Papers Relating to Bishop Atterbury)
6 PRO, SP 35/31, f 72. Present were Lord Macclesfield, Lord Carleton, the duke of Newcastle, the duke of Devonshire, Lord Townshend, Robert Walpole, Lord Carteret.

to the Post Office to open and detain all letters in the French and Flanders mails; all persons going to France or Flanders without passports were to be stopped, searched, and secured if necessary; spies were dispatched to France to gain intelligence of the disposition of troops along the French coast; the Guards immediately encamped; the Tower of London was garrisoned; Lord Cadogan was discoursed on the march of troops; Charles Churchill, nephew of the duke of Marlborough, went to Paris to secure further information; Horace Walpole was sent to The Hague for troops; George I was persuaded to cancel his intended journey to Hanover.

The public was immediately aroused. The sight of the Guards encamping in Hyde Park, the movement of the three regiments of horse and four squadrons of dragoons from the north to take up station on Salisbury Plain, the march of two regiments to encamp on Hounslow Heath, the knowledge of six regiments about to embark from Ireland – this caused a major sensation. Many believed firmly an alliance had been formed between France, Spain, and the czar against Britain. 'People grow in eager expectation of what will come out,' wrote Sir John Vanbrugh, 'and will probably talk one another into greater apprehensions in a few days, if something don't appear to make them easy.'[7] Had Walpole aimed to add a dramatic tone to his undertaking he could not have succeeded better.

But no statement was yet forthcoming to allay the public fears. More interceptions were made at the Post Office and further intelligence was communicated from Davenant, British envoy extraordinary to Genoa, and Sir Luke Schaub at Paris. 'Mr. Walpole's horses feel the weight of a first minister, for they never stand still from morning to night,' wrote Lord Lansdowne to Lord Gower.[8] On 8 May the silence from the government ended. In a letter to Sir Gerard Conyers, the lord mayor of London, Townshend disclosed news of a plot:

His Majesty has commanded me to acquaint your Lordship, that he has received repeated and unquestionable advices, that several of his subjects, forgetting the allegiance they owe to His Majesty, as well as the natural love they ought to bear to their country; have entered into a wicked conspiracy, in concert with traitors abroad, for raising a rebellion in this Kingdom in favour of a Popish Pretender . . . The authors of it neither will be supported; nor even countenanced by any foreign power.[9]

He then called on the lord mayor to exert with 'the utmost care' his author-

7 HMC, *Carlisle MSS*, 38
8 HMC, *Sutherland MSS*, 190
9 PRO, SP 35/31, f 158

ity at 'so important a juncture.' A faithful address from the lord mayor followed and this provided the opportunity for a public profession of the king's
determination 'to support the public credit, to protect the privileges and
properties of this great and indulgent City, and to maintain the Religion,
Laws, and Liberties of this Kingdom.'[10] The same day as this latter proclamation was made public all laws against Roman Catholics and nonjurors
came into operation. Their arms and horses were seized, they were confined
to their houses, they were required to take the oath and declaration.[11] On
10 May orders were sent to the earl of Orkney, governor of Edinburgh Castle, and to the other military centres in Scotland to put all in readiness
against the insurrection that is 'speedily intended within this Kingdom,' and
on the following day a warrant was issued to have troops sent to protect the
Bank of England.[12]

By 8 May the news of a 'horrid conspiracy' had been made public. The
basis for such an announcement had been on the most inconclusive of evidence. A few interceptions at the Post Office, intimations from the regent of
France, Sunderland's papers, and reports from the British representatives in
Paris and Rome – this was all the material Walpole had at his disposal. To a
figure less obsessed with his mission against Jacobitism it would have proved
almost impossible, on the basis of such little proof, to discover the 'authors' of
the plot. But not for one of Walpole's bent of mind. He saw Jacobites everywhere and was convinced that a whisper was conclusive evidence of a deep
scheme afoot. The major task now confronting him would never have been
viewed by Robert Walpole as impossible. He was determined to gain the necessary evidence to bring the yet unknown conspirators into the open. 'The
pursuing of it and the conduct of the whole,' wrote Arthur Onslow, 'were
principally the work of Mr. Walpole whose dexterity and skill in it showed
him to be equal to the ablest minister that ever unravelled the deepest and
darkest contrivance against a State.'[13]

The prime object of Walpole's investigation was a person who went by
the cant names of Illington and Jones. The letters he had intercepted at the
Post Office, copied, and then sent on showed clearly to Walpole that this
was a person of great importance in Jacobite circles and one who was
deeply involved in the mysterious plot. These intercepted letters had not,
however, been allowed to reach their destination without knowledge of who
called for them because one of Walpole's spies had observed closely the

10 Ibid., f 168
11 HMC, *Hodgkin MSS,* 348-9
12 PRO, SP 35/31, f 172, 189
13 HMC, *Onslow MSS,* 513

James, 1st Earl Stanhope

The Right Honble Charles Earl of Sunderland, &c.

Charles, 3rd earl of Sunderland

The Right Hon.ble Charles Lord Viscount Townshend

Charles, 2nd Viscount Townsend

Robert Walpole

The Right Reverend Father in God, Francis
Lord Bishop of Rochester and Dean of Westminster

Francis Atterbury, bishop of Rochester

above and opposite obverse and reverse sides of medal struck in 1723 to celebrate the defeat of the Atterbury plot

Christopher Layer

coffee houses to which they had been directed. In this way he discovered that one George Kelly, alias Johnson, 'distributed them properly.' 'When we found we had no further use of seeing them,' wrote Walpole, 'it was resolved to take up Kelly.'[14] By 19 May the location of his lodgings was established and messengers were sent to arrest him and seize his papers. At this point the first of the major setbacks to his investigation occurred, for Kelly was able to hold Walpole's bloodhounds at bay with his sword while he burned his papers. Infuriated as Walpole was, Kelly's action only increased his conviction that he was on the right track. With an air of resignation he told Horace Walpole: 'We fox hunters know that we do not always find every fox that we crosse upon.' But he added confidently that he was 'in the trace of several things very material.'[15]

And well he might have expressed confidence because his action of 19 May had not gone wholly unrewarded. At the same time as Kelly was arrested, his housekeeper, Mrs Barnes, was also placed in custody and rigorously examined. From the intercepted correspondence Walpole learned that the object of his search, Illington, alias Jones, had received from France a small spotted dog, called Harlequin, whose leg was broken on arrival. The recipient of the dog was disclosed by Mrs Barnes. Such a breakthrough represented for Walpole a major achievement and necessitated a full meeting of the Cabinet Council on 23 May. On this date, in the presence of Archbishop William Wake, Lord Macclesfield, Lord Carleton, the duke of Kingston, the duke of Newcastle, the duke of Grafton, the duke of Devonshire, the earl of Berkeley, Lord Townshend, Lord Carteret, and Robert Walpole, Mrs Barnes revealed full knowledge of the small spotted dog brought from France by Mr Kelly and left with her until its broken leg healed. It was intended, she said, for the bishop of Rochester.[16] Illington and Jones then were none other than the cant names used by Francis Atterbury, bishop of Rochester, in his correspondence with the Jacobites on the continent.

This piece of information became conclusive evidence for Robert Walpole. From this moment Bishop Atterbury became the sole object upon which Walpole's pent up Jacobite fears were expended. This physical embodiment of Jacobitism he pursued with unaltered zeal and he spared neither time nor energy for the conviction of that object. Robert Walpole was now resolved, said Sir Robert Sutton, 'to use all instruments to make his report good.'[17]

14 William Coxe, *Memoirs of the Life and Administration of Sir Robert Walpole*, II, 221
15 Ibid., 223
16 Cholmondeley (Houghton) MSS, iii, 69/5 (E 4)
17 Arch.Aff.Etr.Mémoires et Documents Angleterre, vol. 86, f 14

Walpole needed most of all legal evidence – his own imaginings, his own scanty bits of information and paper proofs were ample for him but would not enable him to convict Atterbury of high treason. He must, therefore, secure more papers. Another spy had been watching closely the coffee houses to which further intercepted letters had been sent. It was learned that one Captain Dennis Kelly called for them.[18] Walpole was already aware of his meetings with other disaffected persons at Lady Wentworth's, but such a basis for taking him up would not have aided him at all in his efforts to secure the necessary evidence against Atterbury and his associates. With Dennis Kelly calling for those letters in which Atterbury was mentioned, he determined that he must be in on the plot. His decision to arrest Kelly was taken on 26 May and to prevent any suspicion on Kelly's part, since he was intending to ship to France, he was granted a passport on 27 May.[19] With vivid impressions of the bungling of George Kelly's arrest a month earlier, Walpole allowed no room for slip-ups this time. Sir Robert Sutton established the location of Kelly's lodgings and on 28 July, early in the morning, messengers hastened there. They seized the entire family – ladies, gentlemen, children, servants – and all that was in the house.[20] Another group of messengers, with about thirty soldiers, arrested the master of the ship on which Kelly was to sail, seized the ship's baggage, and the entire crew. At the same time a warrant had been issued to Captain Parker to secure certain other persons who had intended to embark on Kelly's ship.

One of the strictest investigations then ensued. Kelly himself was frisked and his house was ransacked – baggage, wearing apparel, trunks, and cabinets were torn apart in the search for the slightest shreds of evidence.[21] All goods and parcels on board the ship that belonged to Kelly or any member of his family were brought to the Cockpit in Whitehall.

On 1 August the initial series of interrogations of the host of persons Walpole had taken up were held at the Cockpit. During the course of these examinations threats were used with some, bribes with others. Among Kelly's belongings the ministers found several ciphers and a list of the army, and on the basis of these he was committed to the Tower on a charge of high treason. Kelly's mother, Lady Bellew, and his wife, a niece of Lord Strafford, were discharged the same day they were arrested, owing largely to the intercession on their behalf by Lord Bathurst, also a relative.[22]

18 Since mid-May Walpole had been watching his activities as a result of advice received from Crawfurd at Paris.
19 PRO, SP 35/41, f 79, 81, 83, 85
20 BM, Add. MSS, 32,686, f 227; PRO, SP 35/32, f 81, 85
21 RA, Stuart, 61/75
22 HMC, Townshend MSS, 192

Little is known of the nature of the interrogations at the Cockpit, but they were one of the central instruments employed by Walpole to gain knowledge of the details of the plot. Day after day, hour after hour, in laborious and painstaking fashion, the jury of examiners met at the Cockpit. Only on rare occasions was it a full one. It comprised a triumvirate made up of Walpole, Townshend, and Carteret together with their scribes.[23] Cajolery, bribes, threats, and, in at least one case, brute force established the character of many of the examinations. John Sempill (or Sample) was arrested and brought before the committee of inquisitors on 4 August. He later reported:

I received from every one of the Lords in the Council much harsher usage than should be imagined from persons of their degree. I was threatened with gibbets, racks and fire; an order was given me to read by Lord Townshend whereby I was immediately to be hurried into the dungeon of Newgate, there to be loaded with irons, and to have the greatest severity of that prison inflicted on me, but when I was reputed sufficiently terrified, Lord Townshend made me a proposal of pardon and five hundred pounds a year pension, provided I would swear . . . against Lord Strafford, Lord Cowper, Lord Orrery and one Mr. Smith; . . . Then Lord Townshend returned to his furious temper with frightful oaths and execration; he was seconded by Walpole and Lord Carteret, the latters' violence reached to foaming in the mouth, handling me roughly and giving me a blow in the breast; Lord Cadogan acted a counterpart and thought to gain upon me by soothing words, he advised me in a friendly and compassionate manner to comply with the desires of the Council he promised to make my fortune, and besides what had been proferred me by Lord Townshend, he assured me of a commission in the Army.[24]

Another source of Walpole's information came from informers. He was besieged throughout with offers of intelligence and no doubt as many as possible were followed up. Of the vast numbers who paraded to Walpole's Chelsea house 'by the stable yard . . . from evening till midnight,' none proved to be more potentially valuable than Philip Neynoe.[25] On the same day that Dennis Kelly was arrested, Walpole received a letter from Neynoe offering to make 'considerable' discoveries if he was given sufficient 'encouragement.' He would, he said, be willing to wait on Walpole if a proper ad-

---

23 Cholmondeley (Houghton) MSS, 69/1-3

24 PRO, SP 35/33, ff 313-14. As this is the statement of one of the examinees, and an escaped prisoner, his account is probably overdrawn. This particular Sample escaped only to appear later as one of Walpole's chief spies. It is interesting to note that one Elizabeth Brown wrote Walpole demanding the payment of £50 plus the pension he had offered her for the denunciation of Mr Sample.

25 RA, Stuart, 100/45

vertisement was placed in the *Gazette*. In his own testimony given at the trial of George Kelly the following year, Walpole made it very clear that he was concerned not to allow this opportunity to slip by. He said that Neynoe's offer came on the 28th but it was so late in the day he could not then insert the advertisement in the *Gazette* and had to wait for the next issue.

The resulting meeting of Walpole and Philip Neynoe, alias Walton, the next day initiated a long series of 'conversations' for which Walpole gave him ample 'encouragement' – £350 in all, according to Walpole himself. From the outset Walpole found him 'very willing and free to tell all he knew of the conspiracy, and to explain some fictitious names made use of in the letters intercepted.'[26]

Walpole's assessment of the services rendered by Neynoe was, if anything, an understatement, for it was due largely to the information provided by him that Walpole made several major arrests. And Philip Neynoe was in a good position to make valuable discoveries. An Irishman, who had attended Trinity College Dublin with George Kelly, he had arrived in England in 1718, was soon after ordained by the bishop of Chester and granted a small curacy in that area. Dissatisfied with his lot in this place, he moved up to London where 'he became a sort of hanger-on upon Mr. Kelly and by degrees got the names and characters of some considerable persons.'[27] Here he worked actively on the journal, *The Freeholder*, through which he became acquainted with Thomas Carte, a nonjuring clergyman, and under the auspices of the earl of Orrery was granted the use of the English Library.

Of this background Walpole knew very little but, skilled in the art of handling would-be informers, he put him to the test at their first meeting. He presented him with a list of cipher names and claimed they had been seized in the effects of Dennis Kelly. Neynoe, among others, readily named those used by George Kelly, General Dillon, the Pretender's agent in Paris, and Bishop Atterbury. But, unknown to Neynoe, Walpole had in fact shown him a list of the cipher names gained from the correspondence intercepted at the Post Office.[28] Assured now of the worth of his informer, Walpole pumped him for further evidence. During the course of their conversations, some several hours long, Neynoe told Walpole of George Kelly's correspondence with General Dillon, of the bishop of Rochester's letters via the same channel, of requests made to him by Kelly to draw up memorials to the re-

---

26 *An Historical Narrative of the Tryals of Mr. George Kelly and of Dr. Francis Atterbury, (Late) Lord Bishop of Rochester, etc.* (London 1727), 7-8

27 HMC, *Hare MSS*, 234-5; RA, Stuart, 100/45

28 It must have been such a list for the cant names used by Dillon, Kelly, and Atterbury do not appear in the list of ciphers that had been seized with Captain Dennis Kelly.

gent of France, of Thomas Carte's activities, of the names of officers showing pro-Jacobite leanings, and a myriad of other insights into the conspiracy that to Walpole must have seemed 'most material.'[29]

Acting on information received from Neynoe in early August, Walpole had a warrant sworn for the arrest of Thomas Carte, but owing to a tip-off from a clerk in Lord Townshend's office, Carte had already fled to the continent.[30] Cheated of a prize suspect, Walpole demanded to know from his advisers if he could legally seize Carte's papers 'even though they [the messengers] are not possessed of his person.' Were this impossible then he would have another warrant prepared for 'seizing the owner of the house who is a Papist (as well as Carte).'[31]

Neynoe's evidence, the intercepted correspondence, Mrs Barnes' sworn testimony before a full Cabinet Council, and other advices prompted Walpole to make his first major arrest.[32] On 24 August Bishop Atterbury was seized, brought before a committee of the council, and incarcerated in the Tower on a charge of high treason.

Walpole now faced the monumental task of obtaining sufficient testimony to enable him to secure a conviction against his great adversary. He knew that Neynoe's evidence would be of little use unless he obtained it in writing and had it signed by him before a committee of the council, but what he did not know was that Neynoe was about to double-cross him. Like many informers Neynoe had kept in with both sides: with his Jacobite associates in London to gain information; with Robert Walpole in order 'to wheedle him out of a round sum of money.'[33] And Neynoe, too, must have been conscious that Walpole would demand more than mere 'conversations'

29 RA, Stuart, 100/45
30 The *Gazette* of 14-18 August carried a proclamation offering £1000 for the apprehension of Carte.
31 PRO, SP 35/140, f 3
32 Another deciding factor was undoubtedly the establishment of the identity of the person who used the cant name 'Digby,' for this was the recipient and sender of intercepted letters. The manner in which this was accomplished demonstrates clearly the lengths to which Walpole was prepared to go in discovering the plot. On 25 July 1722 (NS) Crawfurd wrote from Paris to describe how they had discovered 'Digby' to be the cant name used by General Dillon. 'I folded up a paper in the form of a letter, and sealed it, and directed it to Mr. Digby at Paris, then wrapped it up in a piece of waste paper, with a memorandum in it, to be informed of Mr. Waters Banq . . . at what part of Paris Mr. Digby lived: I gave it thus made up, to a sharp boy, who speaks both French and English. . .to open before him the sham letters, and to read his memorandum, and to show him the direction of the letter. . .Waters was not at home, and my man acted his part so well, that Waters's chief book-keeper. . .wrote the direction for him on my sham letter. . .' *House of Commons Report*, 1722 (A 31).

– the arrest of Atterbury made this an obvious fact. Shortly after Atterbury's detention, he attempted to escape to France and in so doing was taken up at Deal. He and his companion, Mr Bingley, were brought back to London, confined to messengers' houses, and closely watched.

From 12 to 27 September followed one of the most intensive examinations of any person who had been arrested – he was examined on at least five separate occasions.[34] Neynoe was to pay dearly for his treachery. He was to learn that Walpole now demanded 'conversations' of a different order. He wanted in writing such evidence as Neynoe had communicated to him during the course of the many evenings he had spent at Chelsea. He was rigorously examined on the 13th, 14th, and 15th and, during the course of these interrogations, some of them eight hours long, he admitted sufficient testimony to implicate Atterbury and many of his fellow accomplices.[35] Under pressure at one such session he produced a paper in his own hand, though significantly unsigned, confirming what he had already related.[36] But this was not good enough – Walpole gave him a week to produce a full and detailed sworn report of all he knew or he would have him committed to Newgate. On 24 September Neynoe wrote from the messenger's house, where he was confined, begging for a private audience. 'The posture of affairs,' he said, 'requires it should be speedy and I am in hopes that with your assistance I shall be able to rectify those fatal mistakes, which have been as prejudicial to the public service as to my own quiet.'[37] Such was the appeal of an informer seeking a way out, but none was forthcoming. On the 27th he was brought once again before the committee and this time it was composed of the duke of Newcastle, the duke of Grafton, the earl of Cadogan, Lord Townshend, and Walpole. He was read a paper drawn up from his previous examinations and notes of Robert Walpole's and acknowledged each item to be true. He was returned to the messenger's house and on the 28th made his bid for freedom. It cost him his life for he was drowned in the Thames.

Neynoe's death, however, deprived Robert Walpole of his principal witness. Upon recovery of the body he was presented with, among other items, one water-soaked piece of paper taken from Neynoe's pocket.[38] Walpole

---

33 *An Historical Narrative of the Tryals of Mr. George Kelly. . .* 7

34 PRO, SP 35/40, f 37

35 Cholmondeley (Houghton) MSS, iii, 69/5 (E 7)

36 This paper in Neynoe's hand appears to be hastily written. The paper found in Neynoe's pocket [Cholmondeley (Houghton) MSS, iii, 69/5 (E 11)] is also in his hand. Both are unsigned and undated. That they are in his hand is verified by a signed letter of his. PRO, SP 35/33, f 170

37 PRO, SP 35/33, f 170

38 Cholmondeley (Houghton) MSS, iii, 69/5 (E 11)

copied it out. It consisted of a list of 'unperformed duties' for his interrogator:

> To write a narrative of all proceedings, that I have been concerned in carrying on against the Government, from the beginning of the last session of Parliament to the present time.
>
> To give an account of the purport of such memorials, as I have been employed to draw, and the several times when.
>
> What instructions and directions I have had, and from whom. . .
>
> What conversations I have had with Mr. Kelly and Mr. Carte, or any other persons principally employed and trusted, concerning the designs that have been carrying on for this last year.
>
> What I know or believe, concerning any persons of High Rank, and who I think had the chief conduct and direction of this whole affair.
>
> To be as particular as possible in times, places, and persons.

These had been Walpole's orders to Neynoe. The fulfilling of them would have implicated Neynoe himself and would have provided Walpole with legal proof against his chief informer. This was the reason for Neynoe's decision not to carry them out but to attempt an escape. The drowning had been accidental. Major General Pepper claimed at the time of the drowning that it had been no accident, because 'Philip Neynoe had no occasion to endeavour to escape, for he was the principal evidence they had.'[39] On the contrary, the fact that he was to have been Walpole's principal witness necessitated an escape in which death had been unforeseen.

This must have been a very bitter blow to Walpole. He had counted much on Neynoe's evidence when the time came. The little he had gained he was to employ but it would be far from sufficient. Not only did the law seem to be against him at this point but the fates as well. The two major setbacks thus far – the bungling of Kelly's arrest and the death of Philip Neynoe – served, however, to cause him to redouble his efforts in his unswerving mission to strike a blow at Jacobitism through exposing this conspiracy.

He already had a new angle to follow up. While under pressure from Walpole, after he had been arrested and brought back to London, Neynoe had informed on one Christopher Layer.[40] On 18 September Walpole had

---

39 PRO, SP 35/33, f 226

40 RA, Stuart, 100/45. The late R.W. Ketton-Cremer in his essay on Christopher Layer (*A Norfolk Gallery*, [London 1948], 143) attributed Layer's arrest to Lynch and Plunkett. I can find no evidence to support this. It would seem the reverse is true – that Layer informed on Lynch and Plunkett. Layer was arrested on 18 September and attempted to escape

him arrested and the following morning he, too, attempted to escape. He did not meet with Neynoe's fate but was retaken and subjected to two gruelling examinations. During the course of these ordeals he admitted he had 'endeavoured to sound the inclinations' of two or three serjeants or common soldiers and named in particular Serjeant Plunkett. He also volunteered the name of one Fountain, alias Lynch. Walpole had both arrested and further depositions and examinations followed. On 21 September Layer was brought before a committee of the lords of the council and there he gave sufficient evidence for a warrant to be sworn for the arrest of the earl of Orrery and his secretary, Mr Swerdferger. They were duly seized with their papers, Swerdferger was confined to a messenger's house and Orrery to the Tower on suspicion of high treason.[41] At this same examination Layer had also implicated Lord North and Grey and, even though he had found a means of warning him, it was too late. Lord North and Grey was seized in the midst of flight to the continent. On Layer's evidence several others were in the process of being hunted down, the most important being John Plunket.

At the time of Neynoe's death, therefore, Walpole could count at least six persons committed to the Tower on charges of high treason: Captain Dennis Kelly, Mr Cochrane, Bishop Atterbury, Christopher Layer, the earl of Orrery, and Lord North and Grey. By the end of October John Plunket, the Reverend George Kelly, and the duke of Norfolk were added to the list. Doubtless, Walpole would have followed up Layer's part in the conspiracy even if Neynoe had lived, but he now had no other choice.

During the several examinations surrounding Layer's arrest witnesses had referred, on several occasions, to a paper Layer had shown them outlining his plans for an insurrection.[42] After 28 September the existence of such a paper became fact for Walpole and the next day he ordered a thorough search of Layer's lodgings and all that was in the house. The result was more than Walpole could have imagined. In the rooms of one of the other

early on the morning of 19 September. After he was retaken he was examined twice on the same day and during the course of the second examination admitted, among other things, that he had made approaches to Serjeant Mathew Plunkett and Fountain, alias Lynch. The evidence of Lynch was given on the day following this examination (20 September) and that of Plunkett on the 21st. See Cholmondeley (Houghton) MSS, iii, 69/2 (B 1-10). That Lynch and Plunkett did not inform on Layer is also supported by another set of documents. In a list of 'Prisoners in custody on January 21' are the names of Lynch and Plunkett. The dates given for their arrests are even later than those established here. PRO, SP 35/41, f 63; RA, Stuart, 66/36

41 *The Official Diary of Lieutenant-General Adam Williamson: Deputy-Lieutenant of the Tower of London, 1722-1747*, ed. J.C. Fox, Camden Society, 3rd series, XXII (London 1912), 165
42 Cholmondeley (Houghton) MSS, iii, 69/2, (B 1-10)

occupants the messengers discovered a trunk containing two bundles of papers left there by Layer for safe-keeping. Besides the detailed plan for an insurrection, written in Layer's hand, Walpole now possessed blank receipts for money, signed by the Pretender, and lists pertaining to the military personnel and persons in London. For Walpole this was an achievement of the greatest magnitude in his long and exhausting pursuit of Jacobite activity. Only on one other occasion had a full committee of His Majesty's Most Honourable Privy Council been present at an examination – the examination of Jane Barnes who implicated Atterbury in the conspiracy. A second one met on 1 October. The papers were presented and Layer made a full discovery of what he knew of the conspiracy. Adam Williamson, deputy-lieutenant of the Tower, was given explicit and strict orders to slap him into irons for his security was of 'the greatest importance to the safety of His Majesty's person and the peace of his realms.' John Plunket, his fellow conspirator, was seized soon afterwards.

Parliament met on 9 October. Bishop Atterbury, the chief object of Walpole's investigation, must have anticipated the first demand Walpole would make at the opening of the session – the suspension of the Habeas Corpus Act. A month earlier he had been brought to the Old Bailey on his application to be bailed or brought to trial notwithstanding the possible suspension of this act and his request had been circumvented only through a legal technicality.[43] With conclusive legal proof in his hands against only Layer, Walpole considered the suspension of the Habeas Corpus Act vital. More evidence might be found and no one now in custody should have recourse to this act and as a result be bailed. None of the conspirators must be provided with the opportunity to destroy any further evidence that might exist. On 10 October the suspension of the Habeas Corpus Act passed the House of Lords and, after much debate, the House of Commons on the 16th.[44] From 17 October the conspirators now lodged in the Tower were at the mercy of Walpole, for the act declared that 'every person that is in prison upon the 10th day of October, 1722, or after, by Warrant of the Privy Council, signed by six of the said Privy Council, for High Treason, suspicion of High Treason, or Treasonable practices, or by warrant signed by any of the Secretaries of State, for such causes, may be detained in custody without bail, until the 24th of October 1723 . . .'[45]

43 It was ruled that the judges of the commission to deliver the gaol of Newgate could not bail prisoners in the Tower.
44 *The Parliamentary Diary of Sir Edward Knatchbull, 1722-1730*, ed. A.N. Newman, Camden Society, 3rd series, XCIV (London 1963), 2-3
45 Ebenezer Timberland, *The History and Proceedings of the House of Lords from the Restoration in 1660 to the Present Time* (London 1742-3), III, 247

After the discovery of Layer's papers, Walpole's single goal became that of securing convictions against those in the Tower. After taking stock of his evidence for this purpose, he was certain only of the sufficiency of his proof with respect to Christopher Layer. This explains in large part not only the suspension of the Habeas Corpus Act but also the rigid measures against the prisoners in the Tower. An especially close watch was maintained on all Atterbury's activities. Pope wrote: 'Even pigeon pies and hogs puddings are thought dangerous by our governors, for those that have been sent to the Bishop of Rochester are opened and profanely pried into at the Tower. It is the first time that dead pigeons have been suspected of carrying intelligence.'[46]

No further discovery of papers was forthcoming. Christopher Layer was brought again and again before his jury of examiners – Walpole, Townshend, and Carteret – but he added nothing to what they already knew. Finally, on 31 October, he was presented in irons before the bar of the Court of King's Bench to plead to his indictment for high treason. He pleaded 'not guilty.' On 21 November his trial took place. The most incriminating piece of evidence, called 'The Scheme,' unfolded for the jury his detailed plans for an insurrection: the seizure of the Tower of London and the Bank of England; the taking of 'some great men . . . at their houses'; the rousing and arming of the Westminster mob; the capture of the prince of Wales; and the apprehending of the king 'under a pretence of securing the King's person from the insults of the mob.' After an adjournment of only half-an-hour a verdict of 'guilty' was brought in. On 27 November the lord justice read the sentence of the court 'that he shall be led back again to the place when he came, and from thence shall be drawn upon a hurdle to the place of execution and there shall be hanged by the neck, and then shall be cut down alive; and his entrails and privy members shall be cut from his body and burned in his sight, and his head shall be cut off and his body shall be divided in four parts and shall be disposed at the King's pleasure.' With this horrid spectacle dancing before his eyes, Layer wrote to Walpole from the Tower pleading for mercy.[47] He did so on the grounds that Walpole had given him assurances that nothing he had said at his examination before the full committee on 1 October would be used in evidence against him. But he did not know Walpole. Two secretaries had taken full minutes and Walpole did use them in evidence. A reprieve was granted to Layer, from no sense of compassion on Walpole's part, but rather from a feeling that Layer might

46 *The Official Diary of Lieutenant-General Adam Williamson*, 41
47 Cholmondeley (Houghton) MSS, 989

still make some valuable disclosures. Seven times he was granted a reprieve and as many times interrogated before the committee. He was finally delivered over for execution on 17 May 1723.

By early January 1723 Walpole had to face the plain yet bitter fact that he did not have enough evidence to secure the conviction of his prisoners by the usual legal process. The reality of the situation gave him but resort to the use of bills of pains and penalties. The highest court in the land – parliament – must now be called on for 'the courts below could not reach people that were grown so artful in plots as to do everything that was really treason but not within the strict rules of the law.'[48]

But once he had at least partially accepted this limitation, his drive to achieve success went unslackened. If the law denied him the death penalty against Atterbury, this external object of his deep inner fear of Jacobitism, then he must settle for his banishment from England. Much had yet to be done to encompass that desire, including the preparation of a full report for parliament's consideration. Careful lists were prepared of all the queries and points to be established in order to guarantee the carrying of these bills against Atterbury and the other conspirators.[49] Throughout January and February work went ahead on the preparation of the necessary material to be given to the committee appointed to prepare the report on the conspiracy. The committee, chaired by William Pulteney, met from nine in the morning often until ten at night, and Walpole's staff worked diligently and quickly to provide them with the necessary papers. A host of persons of all degree and character – lodgers, landlords, landladies, servants, a tailor, a butcher, king's messengers – were brought in to be examined or to swear to points that needed to be clarified. Clerks from the Post Office attested to having intercepted and copied correspondence. By the end of January the papers relating to Bishop Atterbury, the Reverend George Kelly, Christopher Layer, and John Plunket had been submitted to the committee. On 24 January Poyntz, Townshend's secretary, wrote: 'Our committee who are great devourers of paper have finished the reading of all those you gave them, and expect a fresh supply against nine o'clock.'[50] The following morning they had the papers for Captain Dennis Kelly and John Sample before them. Rarely did the committee come into direct contact with the suppliers of their material, but on one occasion they spent the day together deciding on methods of presentation. The reason for this surface impression of impartiality was to prevent, as one of them said, the idea that they were a 'club.'

48 *The Parliamentary Diary of Sir Edward Knatchbull, 1722-1730*, 15
49 PRO, SP 35/34, f 340
50 PRO, SP 35/41, f 105

On 1 March William Pulteney came before the House of Commons with the report on the conspiracy and a large trunk, locked and sealed, containing the original papers accompanied him. Ten months of Walpole's effort was spun out in six hours as Pulteney read the report to a full house. Accordingly, bills of pains and penalties were brought in against John Plunket, George Kelly, and Bishop Atterbury.

On 29 April the bill against John Plunket passed the House of Lords, whereby he was to forfeit his estates and be kept a prisoner in the Tower during the king's pleasure. A similar fate was met by his co-conspirator, George Kelly, but unlike Plunket who died in the Tower in 1738, Kelly escaped to return in 1745 with the Young Pretender.

On Monday, 6 May Bishop Atterbury was brought to the bar of the House of Lords charged with 'being principally concerned in forming, directing, and carrying on the said wicked, and detestable plot.' The main evidence Walpole had against him rested on the interceptions made at the Post Office and Atterbury's counsel contested most strongly the legality of such evidence. Atterbury's speech in his own defence was skilful – appeals to sympathy by expounding on the harsh treatment he had received in the Tower, his ill health, the lack of major witnesses against him, and letters admitted in evidence which had no legal basis. But it was all to little avail. Late on the evening of 15 May the bill of pains and penalties was carried by a vote of eighty-three to forty-three. Walpole had engineered and directed matters too well for the verdict to have gone otherwise. He had used all methods and means at his disposal to produce this result at least. Indeed, his zealousness might well have produced another set-back for on 4 April he had ordered Williamson to seize certain seals he knew to be on Atterbury's person. He did so without a warrant. Atterbury had protested to the House of Lords and a crisis was only narrowly averted by Townshend, who drew up a warrant and pre-dated it.[51] The earl of Orrery, Lord North and Grey, and the duke of Norfolk were released on bail and never brought to trial.

For the majority of persons the banishment of Atterbury concluded a long and gruelling effort to bring conspiracy into the open, but Robert Walpole did not share the view of the majority. He must have been disappointed at the result for he knew that as long as Atterbury lived the spectre of Jacobitism would be there to haunt him. For this reason he was to pursue him until his death in 1732. In this sense, therefore, there was no finality for Walpole in the event that occurred on 18 June when Atterbury left for Brussels. He was convinced that, once on the continent, Atterbury would become

51 PRO, SP 35/43, f 283

the focus for new plotting and new conspiracies. For Walpole, the Atterbury plot would not even end with the death of Atterbury himself.

On 22 April 1732, when Atterbury's body was brought back to London for private burial, Walpole, once again, made every endeavour to secure that concrete affirmation of Atterbury's guilt he had so eagerly sought after in the years 1722 and 1723. An elaborate set of instructions was given to the messengers. Among other things, the sloop bearing the body was to be discovered and stopped before it reached England; Morice, Atterbury's son-in-law, 'in case he should be on board with the corpse,' was to be arrested and searched; the containers holding the dead bishop's last remains were to be opened and examined for those ever elusive papers.[52].

Fully aware of Walpole's obsession in this area, Atterbury's friends in Paris had carefully packed the body to resemble a bale of cloth. This did not, however, deceive Walpole's bloodhounds, for once discovered, the cloth wrapping was removed and the wooden crate containing the body was 'wrenched open.' Then the lead casing around the body was cut down the middle, across the back, and folded back. According to the report, 'the officer thrust his hand in every way and was sure there was no papers.'[53] But the messengers pressed on: the lead case containing Atterbury's heart and the other one containing his entrails were opened. Again no papers. As a last resort the servant, who was accompanying the body to England, was seized and subjected to a rigorous examination typical of those that had taken place at the Cockpit some ten years earlier. Among the questions hurled at the man were the following: Did you know of any papers or letters written or received by the late bishop of Rochester during his time in France? If so, what has become of them? What proceedings were carried on in France following the bishop's death relating to his papers? Were you aware of the parcels of papers that were seized to-gether with the bishop's body on board the ship? Did any person or persons enquire after papers following the bishop's death? If so, who were they? As with Walpole's earlier investigations, this one too, it would seem, proved fruitless.

The magnitude of Walpole's investigations of 1722-3 illustrates clearly his fear of Jacobitism. For him the threat was a very personal one. He had grown up amidst sporadic outbursts of disorder and instability, all of which he identified with Jacobitism and all aimed at the overthrow of the established order. By 1722 he saw himself as part of that order and, with the death of Sunderland, the possibility of being at its head. For this reason he struck

52 BM, Add. MSS, 32,686, f 447
53 PRO, SP 36/26, f 306-10

out at Jacobitism with a vengeance that only he seemed able to muster. The conspiracy of 1722 differed from the many others in that he saw this one as directed at himself and, in the event of its success, his banishment. His failure to secure the convictions he so earnestly sought in 1722 served, however, only to increase his fear and apprehension of Jacobitism.

9

Walpole's political gain

Although the majority of the Jacobites had backed the restoration attempt of 1721, a significant minority on the continent had argued against it for two reasons. Firstly, they considered foreign support as the absolute *sine qua non* for the success of any venture and in the years 1720 and 1721 such aid was not forthcoming. Secondly, they were convinced that their candidate, James III, would not be allowed to cross either France or the emperor's dominions in order to head an invasion attempt. They had urged him to await another opportunity rather than hazard a move at this stage because they felt that any 'stirring' on his part would cause the British government to 'put themselves in a posture of defence, by suspending the Habeas Corpus Law, imprisoning all those suspected to be the King's friends, and calling in foreign forces, besides taking all the other advantages they have ever done from an ill-concerted undertaking.'[1] This advice had been given to the Pretender on 15 October 1721 and, as already demonstrated, seven months later this anticipated reaction and much more was undertaken by Robert Walpole when news of a Jacobite conspiracy was communicated to the public. Unlike his predecessors, however, Walpole pursued the plot to the end. Where Stanhope and Sunderland had feared to tread, he entered with all the ruthless skill he could muster. Two factors drove him forward in the years 1722 and 1723. One of these, his fear of Jacobitism, has already been examined in the previous chapter; the other was his acute awareness of the political gains to be made from success in such an action. That the affair of Atterbury and company did not bring 'the blood and confusion' the king had referred to in his speech to

1 RA, Stuart, 65/18

parliament on 9 October 1722 was due to the detection of a widespread conspiracy by Robert Walpole. That he profited immeasurably was due to his skill as a politician. The death of his closest rival, Sunderland, and the discovery of a Jacobite plot provided him with an unforeseen opportunity. He seized it and made the most of it.

Upon the discovery of the conspiracy he could have done as Stanhope and Sunderland did in 1717: arrest a few, examine them, play it up before parliament and the nation, and then drop it. But, whereas Stanhope and Sunderland showed a wariness in giving public expression to their deep inner fears of Jacobitism, Walpole displayed in these two years an overpowering zeal to share his with the public. The course he chose in 1722-3 was more rigid, more expensive, and more time-consuming than either Stanhope or Sunderland could have imagined and Robert Walpole brooked no barrier, large or small, to come to the bottom of the conspiracy he knew was there. This was especially true once he discovered Bishop Atterbury was at the head of it. The seemingly endless interviews with informers, the interminable inquisitions at the Cockpit, the multitude of arrests, the drudgery of seeking out the necessary legal evidence – all this was not in vain, for the profits went to Robert Walpole. And they were many.

The dramatic tone of his undertaking, which he managed to spin out over the better part of two years, rallied the support of the nation, particularly the city of London, for the Hanoverian succession to a degree that had not been possible since the accession of George I. To no small degree the credit for the firm establishment of the Protestant succession in the House of Hanover must be given to Robert Walpole. He managed successfully to make his own fear of and desire to hunt down Jacobitism the mission of the public as well. 'The public is engaged,' wrote Onslow, 'in an enquiry after the deepest conspiracy that has ever been carried on in any age against His Majesty's person and Government, and you may easily imagine the zeal and industry to defend those miscreants and an art to inflame and raise disputes between the two Houses to prevent any further punishment.'[2]

The tactic he adopted from the death of Sunderland until the disclosure of the plot to the public on 8 May was a skilful manœuvre because it secured for him, at the very outset, the support of the nation. He deliberately allowed fears to mount. 'There has been a good deal of whispering [for] some time,' said Sir John Vanbrugh to Lord Carlisle, 'and now the sending away Horace Walpole, Col. Churchill etc. and the King's deferring his voyage till after the Birthday, with several other circumstances increase the talk

2 HMC, *Clements MSS*, 357

and fear very much that there is an alliance formed or forming between Spain, France, and the Czar, which may regard us.'[3] The public had long expected a Jacobite attempt might be made, but nothing official was forthcoming from the government either to confirm or reject their suspicions. The rumours were allowed to mount, the speculations to issue forth, and still Walpole did nothing to alleviate the growing fears among the public of possible invasion from France, Spain, or Russia on behalf of the Pretender. The only government activity – the camping of troops, the dispatch of officials – continued to raise the desired interrogative: why these elaborate precautions? Walpole must have known the psychological effect the withholding of any information of a plot would have on the public. The growing apprehension and expectancy, particularly in London, created 'a diffidence, and a jealousy of every shadow' and the more mysterious everything was kept, the more apprehension was produced since 'people are generally most afraid in the dark.'[4] As a consequence, the people focused their attention to an increasing extent on the government. They waited for it to confirm or reject their suspicions; to allay their fears; and, above all, in the event their fears were well grounded, to protect them. With Sunderland, Craggs, and Stanhope now dead, they naturally looked to Walpole and Townshend as their deliverers, and on 8 May 1722 these two accepted this inferred mandate when Lord Townshend announced the discovery of a wicked Jacobite conspiracy in an open letter to Sir Gerard Coyners, the lord mayor of London.

The first of the political gains for Robert Walpole followed the next day when the formerly recalcitrant city of London hastened forth with a very loyal address.[5] In glowing terms the city, through an address from the Court of Aldermen, declared its 'most humble and unfeigned thanks' for the 'indulgent' regard of His Majesty for 'his faithful and dutiful subjects of this city.' They assured him of their 'steady and Unalterable affection and zeal. . .for the continuance of the Protestant succession' and concluded:

As Englishmen that value our liberties, as honest men that have sworn allegiance to your Majesty, and who have abjured and renounced the Pretender, and as real friends to our excellent constitution in church and state, (with a Protestant Prince at the head of it) we beg leave in the most solemn manner to declare to Your Majesty that as we are bound in gratitude, we will exert ourselves in our several stations,

3 Arch.Aff.Etr.Corr.Pol.Angl., vol. 341, ff 78-9; HMC, *Carlisle MSS*, 38

4 RA, Stuart, 61/93

5 For the city of London in this period see A.J. Henderson, *London and the National Government 1721-1742* (Durham, NC 1945); C.B. Realey, *The Early Opposition to Sir Robert Walpole 1720-1727* (Kansas 1931).

with the utmost care and vigilance, for the preservation of the public peace and tranquility, and for the restoring of publick credit; and that we will use our sincere and hearty endeavours, for the firm support of Your Majesty upon the throne, and for the making your reign easy and happy.[6]

Such tender expressions of compliance represented a complete volte-face for the city of London. Only a few months earlier, acting in its traditional manner, it had opposed the government in the parliamentary elections and out of the heated contests that had ensued only one of the four elected candidates, Peter Gregory, was a government supporter.[7] In addition, the earlier debates in parliament on the Quarantine Act had gone a long way to alienate the sympathies of the powerful merchant community in the city. On 8 December 1721 the lord mayor, Sir William Stewart, the alderman and commons of the city had petitioned the government with respect to this act, claiming that certain clauses of it not only affected 'the Rights, Privileges, and Immunities,' but also 'the Trade, Safety, and Prosperity of the city of London.'[8] The House of Lords had refused to consider the petition and the opposition among them had pounced on the opportunity, pointing out that its rejection would only 'widen the unhappy differences that have arisen and increase the disaffection to the government, which hath already too much prevailed in this kingdom.'[9]

The 'unhappy differences' referred to included Walpole's handling of the South Sea crisis. Throughout 1721 some of the strongest opposition came from the city and his popularity there seemed to decrease as the year ad-

6 Abel Boyer, *The Political State of Great Britain* (London 1722), XXIII, 528-30. The letter of Lord Townshend was also printed in the *Gazette* and even the French ambassador in London remarked that the address of the city of London was a 'most lively' one.

7 Henderson, *London and the National Government*, 59-66

8 The petition of the city of London was occasioned by a request in the king's speech on 9 October 1721 for all possible measures to be taken on account of the plague then raging in Europe, particularly in France, by preventing 'the abomindable practice of running of goods' (Richard Chandler, *The History and Proceedings of the House of Commons from the Restoration to the Present Time* (London 1742), VI, 264). On 25 January of this same year an act had been passed, The Quarantine Act, which repealed all previous ones in existence and stated new rules governing ships, persons, and goods coming into Britain. Many merchants, feeling the restrictions to be harsh, had evaded the conditions set down in the act.

9 William Cobbett, *The Parliamentary History of England from the Earliest Period to the Year 1803* (London 1806-12), VII, col. 931. With respect to this petition Hamilton reported that the ministry rejected it 'with great indignation, and Lord Townshend . . . called the Petitioners a Mutinous and Seditious pack in a speech against receiving the Petition.' RA, Stuart, 58/38

vanced. The acquittal of Charles Stanhope by only three votes 'putt the towne in a flame' and 'the whole kingdome are enraged against the South Sea Scheme, and not less so against those who support their abettors,' claimed Thomas Brodrick who, although a bitter enemy of Walpole's, nevertheless spoke a good deal of truth.[10] The conviction of John Aislabie gave the city an opportunity for great rejoicing and the lighting of bonfires as he was spirited away to the Tower. In August 1721 the mob had actually entered the lobby and corridors of the House of Commons. One observer wrote: 'The multitude were particularly rude to Mr. Comptroller, tearing part of his coat as he passed by; upon which the House being informed, that a crowd of people were got together in a tumultuous and riotous manner, in the lobby and passages to this House, it was ordered, "That the Justices of [the] Peace for the City of Westminster, do immediately attend the House, and bring the constables with them." '[11] Accordingly, four justices of the peace and five or six constables arrived to handle the situation. Only after the Riot Act was read twice and threats of imprisonment made, should it be necessary to read it a third time, did the angry mob disperse. The petition they had brought with them was refused by Walpole. It was quite clear that Walpole's engraftment 'scheme'[12] had created a good deal of unrest and dissension in the city. A ballot was held in London in December 1721 and by a majority of 178 votes the city had registered its disapproval of the scheme. This latter result had been achieved even though 'no means, no arts were omitted to have turned it on the other side.'[13]

In these and other matters[14] the government had been faced with a constant and ever increasing opposition from the city of London. In March 1722 it did not appear as though it could look forward to much change in its attitude. For Robert Walpole, who was aware of the weight the city carried throughout the country, this was not a happy state of affairs. His careful exploiting of the situation in London, prior to the disclosure of the Jacobite plot, brought him the first show of enthusiasm and support since the bursting of the South Sea Bubble, and through this and the next two years the city remained firmly behind him. In 1724 Lord Townshend reported to the

---

10 William Coxe, *Memoirs of the Life and Administration of Sir Robert Walpole*, (London 1798) II, 209

11 Cobbett, *History of England*, VII, cols. 903-4

12 For Walpole's engraftment scheme as a solution to settling the financial crisis arising out of the South Sea Bubble see J.H. Plumb, *Sir Robert Walpole: The Making of a Statesman*, 329-32, 336-7, 338.

13 HMC, *Portland MSS*, VII, 310

14 The city had also bitterly opposed the Westminster Bridge bill.

king that 'a very great change has been wrought in favour of Your Majesty, in the City of London, whose influence and example is of so great a consequence to the whole nation.'[15] This change was due in no small part to Walpole's skilful exploitation of his fear of Jacobitism. London, as one opponent of Walpole's put it, had been 'handsomely bit' and, with London supporting him, Walpole then proceeded apace 'to spirit up the corporations in the country to address in imitation of the City of London.'[16] The trumpeting of his fears had the desired effect in this respect as well – addresses flowed in from the Tower-Hamlets, the city of Edinburgh, the county of Worcester, the corporation of Shrewsbury, the borough of Tewkesbury, the county of Derby, the borough of Portsmouth, the town of Monmouth, the borough of St Albans, and elsewhere. All of them were equally strong in their denunciation of 'the Popish Pretender' and in their zeal and firm support for the Hanoverian succession.

This securing of whole-hearted devotion and submission from the city of London and the country was not the only result of Walpole's witch-hunt. During the better part of two years the central preoccupation of both parliament and the nation was with 'the Plot.' The public was bombarded almost ceaselessly with news 'of plots, conspiracies, and goals [and] scarcely an hour passes but what some one or other is taken up and running reports [circulated] of more that are to be seized.'[17] With this as their steady diet, a great many of the earlier prejudices against George I and his family were swept away. The king's pursuit of a northern policy contrary to the interests of England, his seemingly strong preference for his German dominions, the aloofness and icy quality of his manner, the bitterness aroused over his placing of too much confidence in his German ministers – these paled into insignificance as the government and the nation turned their attention in those years to contemplating the horrible thought of the alternative, a 'popish' Pretender.[18]

15 Coxe, *Walpole*, II, 297
16 PRO, SP 35/31, f 324
17 PRO, SP 35/32, f 255. This playing on the fear and apprehension of the public, through the failure to inform them, had another very important result as well. When the announcement of the plot was made public, in actual fact Walpole knew very few of the details. His actions after 8 May, and the further fear that was struck into the public by the character of his proceedings, secured for him some of his most valuable information. There was a good deal of truth in the comment of one observer that 'the whiggs say there is a hellish conspiracy tho' they can tell no more of it than the others.' PRO, SP 35/31, f 324
18 HMC, *Onslow MSS*, 513. A great many criticisms of the Royal family proceeded from the discontents arising out of the South Sea crisis. One particular pamphlet, published early

The successful prosecution of the Atterbury plot had for Walpole another more personal gain. In the words of Speaker Onslow: 'It fixed him with the King.' Since his resignation in 1717 his relations with the king had not been the most cordial and this was especially true after the split in the Royal Household when, to an increasing extent, he had become associated with the Leicester house opposition. Even when he returned to the ministry in 1720, and it became obvious to all that either Walpole or Sunderland would emerge supreme, George I was still determined that 'Mr. Walpole shall not govern.'[19] The death of Sunderland removed his only serious rival other than Carteret, but the zeal and determination with which Walpole handled the Atterbury plot made his popularity with the king a certainty.[20] It must be remembered that his activity throughout 1722-3 was not only anti-Jacobite; it was an equally pro-Hanoverian demonstration and in this period none had shown more devotion to the Hanoverian succession than Robert Walpole. His execution of the plot gave to King George 'fresh proofs of his abilities and usefulness as a Minister.'[21] When the king conferred the Order of the Garter on him in 1726 there was little surprise expressed for he was, according to de Saussure, 'the King's favourite.'[22]

Fears aroused of a Jacobite invasion and their association with Roman Catholics secured for Walpole a considerable increase in the revenue. One hundred thousand pounds was to be gained from the imposition of a tax on the estates of Roman Catholics. This, he claimed, would 'make up what was deficient' in the way of supply. He saw the measure as a perfectly just one in the light of 'the ill use they make of the saving out of their incomes, which most of them laid out in maintaining the Pretender and his adherents abroad, and fomenting discord and rebellion at home.'[23]

in 1722, aired most of the major criticisms. It was entitled: *An Historical Account of the Advantages that Have Accru'd to England. By the Succession of the Illustrious House of Hanover*. In it the author claims that George I came to England 'purely to advance his own interests abroad.'

19 BM, Add. MSS, 32,686, f 193

20 Immediately after the death of Sunderland the French ambassador reported that the king 'hated' and 'feared' both Walpole and Townshend. *Arch.Aff.Etr.Corr.Pol.Angl.*, vol. 341, f 92

21 *Onslow MSS*, 462

22 César de Saussure, *A Foreign View of England in Reigns of George I and George II*, translated by Madame van Muyden (London 1902), 175

23 Chandler, *House of Commons*, VI, 292. By 1726 less than 60 per cent of the money had come in. On this issue Walpole was forced to include the nonjurors as well as the Catholics. Onslow reported that as it required the taking of the oath of allegiance, people came 'crowding to give a testimony of their allegiance to a Government, and cursing it at the same time for giving them the trouble of so doing.' HMC, Onslow MSS, 463

In addition, this exploitation of his fears went a long way towards accomplishing one of his most cherished ambitions – to render the opposition in parliament ineffective. Not only did the banishment of Atterbury remove one of his most powerful opponents from the opposition force in the House of Lords, but the voice of Lord North and Grey, whose name had appeared almost as often as Atterbury's on the protest sheets, was also silenced. He had succeeded in placing on any element that might be called opposition the label of 'Jacobite.' 'He always aimed at the uniting of the Whigs against the Tories as Jacobites . . . ' said Onslow, 'and making therefore combinations between them and any body of Whigs to be impracticable.'[24] In achieving this end Walpole sounded the death blow to parliamentary Jacobitism. Never again was it to gain the strength it had in the years 1717-21. Less than a month after Atterbury's banishment, several of the leading opposition members – Kinnoull, Bathurst, Wyndham, and Gower – expressed their desire to concert measures with the government as they 'wished to rid themselves of the disagreeable situation they were in by renouncing Jacobitism.'[25] Fully confident of this political gain, Walpole remained aloof, considering for the moment at least that 'all sorts of negotiations with the Tories' was not only 'dangerous' but 'useless.' The relative calm of the next two sessions of parliament is ample proof of the effect of Walpole's witch-hunt on the opposition in parliament. With his newly-won success he could on one occasion at least even 'make merry' about it. Spotting a knot of opposition members standing together, he was reported to have said that 'he did not like to have the House accustomed to pains and penalties for fear of being found in plots.' He then turned to Charles Caesar, a noted Jacobite, and said: 'Here's one we came very near.'[26]

The Jacobite movement itself had been dealt a crushing setback. The earl of Orrery in late 1723 reported on the state of their affairs to the Pretender and despaired completely of any immediate hopes or prospects for their cause as the power of the government was now 'too great not to be feared.' 'They have,' he wrote, 'a large army well paid, well clothed, and well provided for in all respects; ammunition and magazines of all kinds [and] a large fleet and the officers of it are generally, I believe, devoted to them.'[27]

By mid-1724 England was experiencing a flourishing condition at home both in trade and public credit, an uninterrupted tranquility abroad, and a

24 *Onslow MSS*, 462
25 BM, Stowe MSS 251, f 14
26 Caesar MSS, Book II
27 RA, Stuart, 70/46

period of calm and stability the like of which had not been seen since George I's accession. That such a state was achieved owes a great deal to Walpole's public expression and ruthless exploitation of his fears of Jacobitism during the course of the years 1722 and 1723.

From 1724 the Jacobites laboured under a major handicap. During the course of the two previous years they had witnessed the limits to which Walpole was prepared to go in seeking them out. Not only had they been terrified by his 'strange proceedings' but now that he 'ruled the roost' he was fully capable, if he so desired it, 'to have another plot.'[28] Walpole did not have another plot but he was prepared to do so if the need arose. In 1725-6, when Britain seemed on the point of tumbling into the abyss of war, he informed Townshend that if it was unavoidable then it was absolutely essential that 'this nation may think, an invasion by a foreign power, or an evident design of such an invasion, the support of the Pretender, and the cause of the Protestant Succession, are the chief and principal motives that obliged us to part with that peace and tranquility, and the happy consequences thereof, which we now enjoy.'[29]

The length, the proportion, the ruthlessness of Walpole's Jacobite witch-hunt of 1722-3 had struck fear not only into the Jacobites but the nation as well. Any discontent, any disorder, any disaffection, Robert Walpole identified with Jacobitism. He made no distinction and following his actions of these two years, the nation knew this as well. As he said at a later point:

Most of the discontents and uneasiness that appear among the people, proceed originally from disaffection. No man of common prudence will profess himself openly a Jacobite; by so doing he not only may injure his private fortune, but he must render himself less able to do any effectual service to the cause he has embraced; therefore there are but few such men in the Kingdom. Your right Jacobite, Sir, disguises his true sentiments; he roars out for revolution principles; he pretends to be a great friend to liberty, and a great admirer of our ancient constitution; and under this pretence there are numbers who every day endeavour to sow discontents among the people, by persuading them that the constitution is in danger, and that they are unnecessarily loaded with many and heavy taxes. These men know that discontent and disaffection are like wit and madness: they are separated by thin partitions; and therefore they hope, that if they can once render the people thoroughly discontented, it will be easy to render them disaffected.[30]

28 RA, Stuart, 68/66; 70/129
29 Coxe, *Walpole*, II, 486
30 Cobbett, *History of England*, X, cols. 400-1

As already pointed out, the ferment he raised during the course of the Atterbury plot was both anti-Jacobite and pro-Hanoverian. All the English ministers in these years operated on this principle and when they applied it in public they differed only in the degree to which they utilized it. By comparison to Walpole's efforts, Stanhope and Sunderland seem to have barely scratched the surface. Walpole pressed deep and the result was enduring, for the fear of Jacobitism generated by Robert Walpole in 1722 and 1723 established the Hanoverian succession. But Walpole did not believe for a moment that Jacobitism was dead. His frame of reference was far too broad to make it even a remote possibility. When Dr William Stratford, canon of Christ Church, Oxford, remarked to Harley that there was 'somewhat more than party' in Walpole's proceedings during the course of the Atterbury plot, he was quite right.[31] There was much more. For Robert Walpole there was the hideous force of Jacobitism. 'I am not at all ashamed to say I am in fear of the Pretender,' he declared. 'It is a danger I shall never be ashamed to say I am afraid of; because it is a danger we shall always be more or less exposed to.'[32] And in that danger Walpole saw the greatest threat to the situation of 'peace' and 'tranquility' in the Protestant succession he so much desired.

31 *Portland MSS*, VII, 351
32 Cobbett, *History of England*, X, col. 401

10

Walpole's intelligence system

By his action in the years 1722 and 1723 Walpole must have realized that he had struck a serious blow to Jacobitism, especially in England, but just how serious he could not be certain and he made every effort, therefore, in the years to come, to keep an even closer watch on Jacobite activity. This he achieved through the maintenance of his own elaborate and expensive intelligence system. An examination of it provides further evidence and concrete expression of his deep inner fear of Jacobitism.

In the areas of domestic and foreign postal control Walpole continued and expanded the efforts of his predecessors, Stanhope and Sunderland. Although warrants for searching the mails continued to be issued, they became more frequent in number and more general in nature. For Walpole, the slightest hint from an informer or spy was deemed sufficient for the issuing of a warrant to search the mails. In 1722 one was issued to Edward Carteret and Galfridus Walpole, the postmasters general, to open and detain all letters in the French and Flanders mails and 'to transmit immediately' all copies to the government.[1] By 1726 fear of possible European support for the Pretender also determined Walpole and Townshend to issue one instructing the postmasters 'to open and detain all letters directed to persons believed to be carrying on treasonable correspondence.' A list of ninety-five names followed. Listed among them were the emperor; the Austrian minister in London, Count Palm; the Austrian diplomat, Georg Ludwig von Sinzendorff; the French diplomat, Comte de Morville; and the imperial diplomat, Count Königsegg.[2] In short, Walpole seems to have judged but few European states

1 PRO, SP 35/31
2 PRO, SP 35/62

to be free from pro-Jacobite activity. In 1731 not even a list was included with the warrant to the postmasters general as it simply gave orders to open all 'suspected treasonable correspondence with France and Flanders.'[3]

At the same time as it was involved in searching out Jacobite activity via the post, the government was provided with an excellent method of keeping a close eye on the affairs of opposition members. 'Sir Robert will see everything I write to you,' wrote Pulteney to a friend.[4] When a complaint was raised against this in the House of Commons in 1735, Walpole agreed to the appointment of a committee of investigation only on the understanding it should not 'inquire into anything that might tend to discover the secrets of the government.' Earlier in 1730 criticism had been raised against the apparent liberties that were taken by the government in searching the mails without a warrant when the duke of Newcastle sent explicit instructions to the postmasters general ordering them to open nothing without authority from one of the secretaries of state.[5]

The personnel of the two departments – the Secret Office and the Deciphering Branch – set up earlier by Stanhope and Sunderland were not only retained but augmented by Robert Walpole. The secret committee set up in 1742 to investigate Walpole's administration revealed that in that year the first of these departments, paid directly by the crown, was staffed by one senior and four minor clerks.[6] Devotion to the cause of the government in its

3 PRO, SP 36/23
4 Quoted in Edward Raymond Turner, 'The Secrecy of the Post,' *English Historical Review*, XXXIII, 321
5 PRO, SP 36/19
6 *A Report from the Committee of Secrecy Appointed to Enquire into the Conduct of Robert, Earl of Orford; During the Last Ten Years of His Being First Commissioner of the Treasury and Chancellor and Under-Treasurer of His Majesty's Exchequer* [delivered the 30th of June, 1742] (London 1742). The report of this committee listed the staff of each of these departments and their salaries as follows:
Secret Department
Mr Lefebure, chief clerk £650 pa
Mr Bode £300 pa
Mr Thouvois £300 pa
Mr Clarke £300 pa
Mr Hemmitt £300 pa
Mr Day, comptroller £60 pa
the doorkeeper £40 pa

Deciphering Branch
Rev. Ed. Willes and son, chief decipherer £1000 pa
Mr Corbière, second decipherer £800 pa
Mr Lampe, third decipherer £500 pa
Mr Zolman, fourth decipherer £200 pa

anti-Jacobite campaign and skill in their profession were still among the prime prerequisites for members of this office. Within the confines of this department, to which were admitted only the postmasters general and the clerks, John Lefebure, the chief clerk, continued to supervise the work of opening, copying, translating, and resealing of correspondence. John David Barbutt, who gave evidence before the secret committee in 1742, claimed Lefebure's was 'a very troublesome post, it being necessary he should always be present at the going out and coming in of the mails.' In order to give the appearance of normality to postal operations, the utmost speed was required in carrying out these varied operations and by 1722 Lefebure had at least two other assistants, Peter Thouvois and Robert Clarke, to aid him in his task. Secrecy was of the greatest importance and the government took the added precaution of paying a doorkeeper, whose duty it was to give adequate warning of any attempts by the uninitiated to enter their sacrosanct precincts.

Jonathan Swift was bitterly critical of Walpole's Deciphering Branch. He described it as being composed of 'a Set of Artists, very dextrous in finding out the mysterious Meanings of Words, Syllables and Letters.' 'For instance,' he said, 'they can decypher a Close-stool to signify a Privy-Council; a Flock of Geese, a Senate; a lame Dog, an Invader; the Plague, a standing Army; a Buzard, a Minister; the Gout, a High Priest; a Gibbet, a Secretary of State; a Chamber pot, a Committee of Grandees; a Sieve, a Court Lady; a Broom, a Revolution; a Mouse-trap, an Employment; a bottomless Pit, the Treasury . . . a running Sore, the Administration . . .' When this method failed, said Swift, they then turned to what 'the Learned among them' called 'Acrosticks and Anagrams.' Finally, they could resort to transposing letters of the alphabet and thereby 'lay open the deepest Designs of a discontented Party.'[7] Critical as Swift was of the nature of their work, Walpole, like his predecessors, considered the decipherer's work as vital for the detection of plots since much of the intercepted material was still in code and cipher.[8] Edward Willes, who had been first employed as chief decipherer by Stanhope, was continued by Walpole. Often his task, and that of his assistants, was a very difficult one. One of the junior decipherers, Anthony Corbière, found it virtually impossible in 1731 to break a code that was being used in correspondence by one of the foreign ministers in London. To better ensure the privacy of his communications the minister in question had switched to a much more difficult code with at least two thousand different

7 Jonathan Swift, *Gulliver's Travels 1726*, ed. Herbert Davis (Oxford 1959), 191
8 For examples see BM, Add. MSS, 32,256 (The Deciphers of Diplomatic Papers). Among them are many codes used by the Jacobites, eg ff 50-1 (the Pretender's cipher); ff 106-7 (cipher of Lord Mar and Grange).

characters. Frustrated by this, Corbière asked Newcastle to send him all the minister's correspondence for his perusal in the hope it might provide him with some new insights in breaking the code.[9] Walpole obviously considered Willes almost indispensable, for in 1724 he was rewarded by being made canon of Westminster with an increase in salary to at least £500 a year.[10] During the Atterbury plot of 1722 it was due largely to the efforts of Willes and the clerks of the Secret Department that Walpole was able to secure even a bill of pains and penalties against Bishop Atterbury. During the course of the proceedings the main evidence against him and his two associates, Kelly and Plunket, came via the Post Office. Both Willes and Anthony Corbière gave evidence during the trial that the letters presented were true copies from the originals which had been 'stopped at the Post Office, and copied, and then sent forward as directed.'[11] Others at the Post Office, Robert Clarke and John Lefebure, also gave sworn testimony.

At Atterbury's trial, Willian Wynne, one of the legal advisers for Bishop Atterbury, did not question the legality of the warrants issued by the secretaries of state but did strike a blow at the very heart of the shaky and dubious means Walpole had resorted to in building the case against his client. He claimed, quite rightly, that there was nothing in the Postal Act of 1711 which allowed copies of letters in the Post Office 'to be received as evidence in the courts of judicature; . . . not only against the writer himself, but against other persons too.' How, he pointed out, could the party have an opportunity to disprove it, if the original has been sent forward and the copy falsely made?[12] Even in the proceedings against Atterbury in the house he was prevented from questioning the decipherers. When the nature of Willes' methods was queried a quick stop was put to such prying when the house resolved in the affirmative that 'it is not consistent with the public safety, to ask the decypherers any questions which may tend to discover the art or mystery of decyphering.'[13]

Walpole was aware that the staff of this office had enabled him to secure Atterbury's banishment and, indeed, that most of the Jacobite intrigues had come to light through interceptions at the Post Office. As pointed out already, the interception of the letters of Görtz and Gyllenborg had brought

9 PRO, SP 36/22
10 Stephen Hyde Cassan, *Lives of the Bishops of Bath and Wells* (London 1829), 166
11 K. Ellis, *The Post Office in the Eighteenth Century* (London 1958), Appendix, 129; J.C. Sainty, *Officials of the Secretaries of State 1660-1782* (London 1973), 51-2. There were two other decipherers as well – Frederick Ashfield and John Lampe. The latter succeeded Ashfield in 1729.
12 *Report from the Secret Committee on the Post Office, 1844*, Appendix LXXX, 108-9
13 Ibid., Appendix LXXIX, 108

early detection of the 1717 plot and, at a meeting of the lords of the council, this correspondence was the chief evidence laid before the members to prove its existence. In the same way Walpole's seemingly insatiable thirst for information during the Atterbury plot was satisfied. 'All the intercepted letters and correspondences carried on it cant allegories, cyphers, and fictitious names,' he wrote to Horace at Paris, 'have hitherto confirmed our other accounts.'[14] Having been warned as early as 1718 of Atterbury's activity, from at least 1721 on a close watch was kept on his correspondence, especially that between him and Lord Bathurst. Indeed, the first knowledge Walpole had of the extent of the Jacobite intrigues of 1722 came through the interception of a letter of Destouches, the French envoy in London, to Dubois. On 31 August 1722 Poyntz told Newcastle that Destouches' report had been confirmed by the efforts of their spies and by certain passages in letters since intercepted. Certain of these letters also served Walpole in the matter of arrests and several were taken up to be examined on the basis of what had been learned from them.[15]

In pursuit of what must often have appeared as the elusive, though ever present, force of Jacobitism, Walpole allowed not the slightest possibility for the success of Atterbury and his fellow conspirators. Throughout this year his own Secret Department was busily at work. Instructions were sent on 16 June to send all letters to his office where there were people more 'dexterous at opening, and closing them again.'[16] Practically all the letters contained in the files presented for the perusal of the Privy Council were based on interceptions at the Post Office. At the same time the Post Office was able to supply him with some indication of public opinion during the course of his investigations of 1722. Even following the banishment of Atterbury, the letters of Morice, his son-in-law, through interception, became part of Walpole's reading matter.[17]

But Jacobite correspondence was not the only area of government interest in matters of conspiracy. The government was aware that a restoration could, in all likelihood, only be achieved with foreign support. Therefore, of vital interest were the dealings of foreign courts with the Jacobites. This resulted in a regular interception of foreign correspondence.[18] The clerks at the Secret Office detained letters to and from foreign representatives in Eng-

14 William Coxe, *Memoirs of the Life and Administration of Sir Robert Walpole* (London 1798), II, 221

15 BM, Add. MSS, 32,686, ff 224, 232

16 PRO, SP 35/31, f 345

17 Cholmondeley (Houghton) MSS. The intercepted letters of Morice are scattered throughout the correspondence. Several of them were intercepted on leaving London and others were passed on to Horace Walpole at Paris by Sempill, Walpole's spy.

land and made full copies, extracts, or translations from the originals. These were then dispatched to the secretaries of state, read, initialled, and sent to other members of the government. After opening, the originals were re-sealed, new ones being applied where necessary, and then allowed to pro-ceed. Throughout the Atterbury plot of 1722 Walpole, fearing early detection as the only guarantee against foreign aid for the Pretender, was liberally supplied with copies of most foreign ministers' letters. Great concern was ex-pressed to find so few from Chammorel, the French resident in London, and the postmasters general were duly instructed to search carefully again the Paris bag in the event he was using a cover name. Mr Lovell, agent for the packet-boat service at Dover, was told to detain the boats while this was carried out.[19]

In the area of foreign postal control Robert Walpole's efforts surpassed those of all the other Whig ministers. The post offices of Danzig, Brussels, Louvain, Leyden, Antwerp, Calais, Hamburg, to mention but some, came under his sway, either directly or through his agent in the city concerned. Some time in 1721 the Danzig Post Office, once again through the machina-tions of Joshua Kenworthy, became part of Walpole's intelligence system. In an attempt to keep as close a watch as possible on Russian and French ac-tivities, after the first leaks of the 1722 plot, Kenworthy undertook to secure copies of the dispatches of Jacques Campredon, the French diplomat, and also those of the czar.[20] He estimated it would cost him the grand sum of £1590 in bribes to the postal officials.[21] The fact that diplomatic relations with Russia had been cut since 1719 was no doubt an added incentive for the advance to him of £500 for this purpose. Even though his information proved of little value, Walpole and his colleagues were provided with the assurance of knowing something of the czar's actions at this all-important juncture of events.

It was mainly, however, after the banishment of Atterbury in 1723, ac-companied as it was by his determination to pursue his Jacobite activities abroad, that Walpole's exertions were directed to foreign postal control on any large scale. Atterbury's decision to reside at Brussels convinced Walpole

18 BM, Add. MSS, 32,258-32,365. Herein are contained the deciphers and dispatches passing be-tween foreign governments and their ministers in England. In this period the govern-ment regularly intercepted mails going to and from the ministers of France, Prussia, Saxony-and-Poland, Sweden, Russia, and Spain.

19 PRO, SP 35/32, f 27

20 D.B. Horn, *The British Diplomatic Service, 1689-1789* (Oxford 1961), 277-8. Kenworthy received £200 pa and approximately £100 more for expenses.

21 PRO, SP 88/21, Poland. Fearing the government would consider this high, he claimed 'the charge must be proportioned to the performances of my agents.'

'all business' would be focused there as 'no design of consequence' would be kept from him. With a good deal of satisfaction, therefore, Walpole wrote to Townshend on 18 October 1723 to say John Macky, one of his spies, had 'sett on foot a correspondence betwixt me and Mons. Jaupain . . . who has engaged to open and send me copies of all letters, that come and go, to the bishop, from all parts of Europe, and whatever else, he may apprehend to be of consequence.'[22] By this method Walpole gained François Jaupain, the postmaster at Brussels. But Jaupain's potential in postal affairs involved much more than control of the Brussels' office. He held the position of director general of postal services in the Austrian Netherlands, having been elected to that office on 23 May 1706. By 1708 he had signed contracts with the Antwerp office at Amsterdam and by 1718 another one with the postmasters at The Hague. He had no fewer than thirty-one offices under his direction. His prospects for rendering 'service of consequence' must have appeared limitless to one with Walpole's tastes for collecting information on Jacobite intrigue.

Late in 1723 he received the first of Jaupain's letters, the beginning of a correspondence that was to last until 1725.[23] Walpole replied personally to Jaupain to thank him for his and also the ones he had enclosed in cipher. He added: 'I beg you will continue your efforts in this useful work and you may be assured of being rewarded to your satisfaction.'[24] Although at the outset Jaupain had set certain conditions for his services, no financial arrangement was arrived at for, as Walpole told Townshend, he would wait and see 'how his service would answer.' But of one thing in connection with this new correspondence Walpole was sure – if it was of consequence Carteret must not be informed since Walpole strongly suspected him of intrigue with the Jacobites. Bonin, one of Horace Walpole's agents, supplied him with information claiming Carteret had betrayed to the Jacobites Walpole's decision in 1722 to publicize the news of a Jacobite conspiracy. It would seem that Horace Walpole considered this information reasonably reliable because he immediately paid him £400 for it and promised him an additional £200 in the near future.[25]

John Macky held frequent and secret meetings with Jaupain, who often communicated to him the information he had secured through postal inter-

22 Coxe, *Walpole*, II, 284

23 Jaupain's letters to Walpole are scattered throughout the Cholmondeley (Houghton) MSS correspondence. The Haus-, Hof- und Staatsarchiv, Vienna, contains a good deal of Jaupain's correspondence for these years but there is not the slightest indication of his association with Walpole.

24 PRO, SP 35/45

25 Coxe, *Walpole*, II, 284; BM, Add. MSS, 9,129

ceptions. Walpole was particularly desirous to learn the names by which Atterbury was written to from England and France. Jaupain agreed to oblige in this respect, but hesitated when it came to opening the bishop's letters to Rome. These latter went in the packet of the papal nuncio and to tamper with this route, according to Jaupain, represented 'a sin against the Holy Ghost.'

To provide intercepted correspondence for Walpole's use Jaupain maintained his own secret office. He was considerably hampered in his endeavours, however, as he had little of the necessary skill required for copying characters and ciphers. Further, his inability in many instances to read the handwriting of the bishop's correspondents prevented him from taking copies. He seems to have been almost constantly plagued with fear of discovery and concentrated much of his time in changing the channels by which he sent his information. In order to avoid detection and keep the appearance of normality in postal operations, he employed four assistants, from time to time, for the purposes of dictation, copying, and comparing copies taken. At one point he claimed a whole hour had been used in opening alone. Early in 1724 the fear of committing a sin against the Holy Ghost seems to have been suppressed, at least temporarily, for Jaupain was intercepting the mails from Rome and transmitting the copies to Walpole. 'Mr. Jaupain and I sett up four nights in the week and spare no pacquet to come to the bottom of the affair,' wrote Macky to Walpole.[26] By February they had discovered the bishop's Rome packets to be received in cipher by a priest at Louvain named Murphy.

But Jaupain did not answer Walpole's expectations and he dispensed with his services sometime during 1724, probably shortly after Atterbury moved to Paris in May of the same year. His need to pursue his activities there was answered by another of his spies, John Sempill, who shared the bishop's confidence. Jaupain had been employed to watch Atterbury and now he was of no further use. Also, Walpole must have been disappointed with the nature of the intelligence Jaupain communicated to him. By no stretch of the imagination would one say Walpole's craving for Jacobite intelligence had been satisfied. And more often than not he desired to have his worst suspicions confirmed. Jaupain did not fill this need; not so much because he allowed the important to escape his notice, but for the simple fact that little seemed to be happening in the Jacobite camp between 1723 and 1725. For Walpole, however, there was no such thing as 'little or no Jacobite activity.'

26 PRO, SP 77/70

Also, by mid-1724 Walpole had grown tired of Jaupain's demands for money, as he must have with many of his spies. He was fully aware of the conditions under which Jaupain had entered his service – in the expectancy of collecting the rewards offered him for his work for an earlier administration. According to Jaupain the duke of Marlborough had pledged him 2000 guineas for his discoveries in the conspiracies of 1704 – a promise confirmed in letters to him by Mr Cardonnel, the secretary-at-war. He had also supplied the government in 1713 with letters of Secretary Torcy showing clearly Louis XIV's plans for supporting the Stuarts.[27] Walpole had, however, employed Jaupain through assurances – assurances he would 'take his arrears into account' and 'reward him for his services.' But at the same time he was only willing to do so if these were of value. The inconsequential nature of his correspondence, the removal to Paris at this time of Atterbury, and the constant parading before him by Jaupain of his financial demands caused Walpole to discontinue his services. Indeed, by 1725 Jaupain himself was fully aware that he had failed to satisfy his employer. He continued to send material but to Delafaye,[28] not Walpole. 'It has been my misfortune to be troublesome to him,' said Jaupain. 'I fear he did not open my letters.'

It was also through Macky that Walpole gained influence over the postmaster at Louvain. The latter was a particularly important centre as it was the focus for the bulk of all mail going and coming from England to Rome. The postmaster worked closely with Macky and provided himself with an assistant to aid him in his endeavours; through him Walpole was kept informed of Irish affairs throughout 1723-4.[29] There is no evidence that Walpole ever came to any financial arrangement, but at one point Macky felt his services to be of such consequence that he informed Walpole he would go to Louvain and offer him money out of his own allowance.

The threatened Jacobite invasion of 1725-6 provided Walpole with new in-

27 Cholmondeley (Houghton) MSS, P 26, 18/1, 'Mémoire Touchant le Sr. Jaupain'
28 Delafaye was one of the most trusted members of the government, especially in all matters relating to Jacobitism. When William Morice's papers were seized, following his father-in-law's death in 1732, Delafaye alone was entrusted to make a thorough search of them. Walpole obviously placed the greatest of confidence in him. In 1718 he had held the confidential post in the secretary of states' office and in 1719 was made secretary to the lords justices of the regency during George I's trip to Hanover. He held this latter post again in 1720. In 1728 he received a post as one of the gentlemen servers to George II. Little is known of his background but it is possible he was the son of Dr Delafaye, a London physician, who died in 1720. His wife's brother was Thomas Colborne. He died 11 December 1762. Cholmondeley (Houghton) MSS, 1193; Sainty, *Officials of the Secretaries of State*, 74-5
29 Cholmondeley (Houghton) MSS, 1038

centives in the realm of foreign postal control. This time the menace seemed to be centred among the Jacobite colony at St Petersburg.[30] No industry must be spared to secure their correspondence and thereby their designs and secrets. Walpole reckoned it very unlikely that they would hazard any such undertaking without first securing strong financial support. Obviously, therefore, they would try to contact their bankers. Acting on this assumption he gained, through Townshend, leave of the French court to have all letters coming to the Paris Post Office and directed to the Jacobite bankers, Hease and Waters, intercepted and copied. On this same reasoning he sought the assistance of the postmaster at Hamburg to search the packets of one H.H. Drusina, a banker in that place. Influence was brought to bear on the Leyden Post Office, also in an attempt to discover the correspondence of one of the principal Jacobites there, John Archdeacon. At Amsterdam action was taken to have the packet boats of Croagh, a merchant and conveyer of Jacobite letters, searched. If these methods failed, Walpole had recourse to still another measure in his grappling efforts to discover their correspondence: he would buy off someone who shared their secrets at St Petersburg. This, he felt, could be accomplished by the employment of one Taylor, 'a kind of secretary' to Sir Henry Stirling, the Pretender's agent there, and through him would be able to secure copies of any letters they wrote.[31]

As circumstances dictated, other postal officials came under the government's influence. The postmaster at Calais was, for Walpole, another source of information. Closely connected with Macky, he frequently supplied him with Jacobite correspondence. Mainly through him Walpole was able to keep a close watch on Francia the Jew who acted as a carrier for Atterbury's letters after his banishment to the continent in 1723.[32]

Although in this period a permanent connection was maintained only with the Hanoverian post office, Walpole's driving zeal to pursue Jacobitism brought several other centres under its sway. The difficulties involved in securing information by this method seems, in hindsight, to have been scarcely worth his effort. The highly recalcitrant nature of the burgomasters

---

30 Coxe, *Walpole*, II, 480-1; Cholmondeley (Houghton) MSS, 1250

31 Cholmondeley (Houghton) MSS, 1250, 1251

32 Cholmondeley (Houghton) MSS, 1023; *Arch.Aff.Etr.Corr.Pol.Angl.*, vol. 323, f 134. The activities of Francia the Jew were of considerable importance to Walpole. After Francia's acquittal on a charge of high treason, he moved to Calais where it was suspected that he was aiding the Jacobites by allowing his name to be used as a cover address for their correspondence. No doubt acting on information from the postmaster at Calais, the government ordered the interception of any letters to him in 1722. Francia had also accompanied Atterbury to Calais.

at Leyden, who owned the offices there, and the bungling efforts of their opener and resealer during those moments when they were willing to co-operate were but two of the many problems encountered. Nevertheless, for one obsessed with fear of Jacobitism, no source was to remain untapped if it might open discovery. Robert Walpole saw foreign postal control as but an-other potential to be explored in his quest of Jacobite intrigue and at the same time it provided an outlet for the more basic and driving force that lay at the base of his activity – fear of a Stuart restoration.

Walpole also established a vast counter-espionage system, for spies were absolutely essential to him. Among other things, his experience of the 1722 plot had taught him the necessity for an all-embracing vigilance where Ja-cobitism was concerned. In the 1722 action even the law seemed to have fav-oured them. He was fully convinced of Atterbury's guilt and yet had failed to secure the death penalty against him. As the only evidence he could build to secure his conviction was circumstantial, he had had to resort to a bill of pains and penalties. By it he knew Atterbury would be banished but he also knew, once on the continent, he would continue his endeavours for the Pre-tender. He must, therefore, be watched at every moment. Indeed, Walpole was quite convinced of Atterbury's importance in Jacobite circles – an im-portance of such magnitude that no action would be undertaken without his knowledge and compliance. For this reason he had secured François Jau-pain to obtain copies of all his letters passing through the general post. For this same reason he now sent one of his chief spies, John Macky, to watch closely Atterbury's every move. From 1723 to 1725 he was one of Walpole's main sources of Jacobite intelligence.[33]

Macky possessed impressive credentials for counter-espionage work. From the reign of William III he had been engaged in such an occupation and had been instrumental in revealing the intended expeditionary plans of France for an invasion on behalf of the Pretender in 1692. For this he had been appointed inspector of the coast from Harwich to Dover. He had also made the discovery of the proposed descent on England in 1696 as part of the assassination plot of Sir George Barclay. In 1708 the preparations for an ar-mament at Dunkirk were conveyed to the government by this spy.

With this background and this time in the guise of a Jacobite, Macky was dispatched by Walpole closely upon the heels of Atterbury. The ar-rangements for his mission were probably finalized at Chelsea and it was of such a secretive nature that not even his own son, Spring Macky, knew his

---

33 Of the letters from spies preserved in the Cholmondeley (Houghton) MSS correspond-ence, Macky's are second only in number to those of John Sempill.

whereabouts on the continent. On 18 October 1723 Walpole informed Town-shend that Macky was 'acting his part so well he has got admittance to the bishop, and into some degree of confidence with him, which he has satisfied me in, by sending me over an original letter from the bishop to him, all in the bishop's own hand writing; and the accounts he gives me, of their con-versations are very natural and probable.'[34] His first letter confirmed one of Walpole's strongest convictions. Macky told him that as soon as Atterbury arrived on the continent 'he had pulled off the mask and declared himself Jacobite.' Through Macky's letters Walpole learned not only of the bishop's activities but of other occurrences in the Jacobite camp as well. By his intel-ligence he gained knowledge of new packet-boat services, especially of one under the direction of Mr Gordon, the Jacobite banker at Paris. Macky's in-formation was often of the most detailed nature: of secret Jacobite corre-spondence being received into coffee houses in and around London, of the machinations of Francia the Jew, of the English who frequented the bishop's residence. Perhaps with no degree of surprise Walpole learned through Macky that Atterbury claimed Sunderland had offered him the bishopric of Winchester.

As already pointed out, the efforts of Macky gained François Jaupain and the postmaster at Louvain. Macky served as the middleman for Wal-pole for several of the transactions that thereby ensued. He frequently en-couraged Jaupain through giving him small gifts. Also, posing as an art dealer, he made missions for Walpole to Antwerp and Ostend.

But Macky hesitated to proffer information on Jacobite activity in other centres. As he wrote to Walpole: 'I doubt not but a minister of your pene-tration and vigilance hath people there [Boulogne] already and must conse-quently know everything that passes amongst them.'[35] Macky was quite right. Walpole did have his spies at Boulogne. He had them everywhere. Among those at Boulogne was one 'de Rowell' who had been his agent for some time and who frequently sent him letters in code and cipher. Walpole's main intelligence in this centre came, however, from another of his spies, William Thomson. The method by which Walpole gained him il-lustrates very clearly the limits to which he would go in his determination to bring conspiracy to the surface.

Thomson had first approached Walpole through his brother in Paris in late 1723 with information he had signed in the form of a letter to him. This advice, merely sent Walpole on a wild goose chase, but, despite this, he did not despair of his services. He wrote him:

34 Coxe, *Walpole*, II, 284
35 Cholmondeley (Houghton) MSS, 1023

As you are a person stranger to me both in person and character, I think fit to explain myself to you in very express terms. I desire you will upon no account say anything that is not strictly true. I hope you will not endeavour to amuse and deceive me, but if you do know anything that concerns the government and are willing to declare it, I am ready to hear it and give you all fitting encouragement, but must insist you will not upon any consideration declare anything that is not unquestionably true and consistent with your own knowledge.[36]

So desperate was Walpole for even the slightest shreds of evidence of Jacobite plots that he was willing, as he told Thomson, 'to make an experiment' of him for once. He desired he would come directly to England for, where spies were concerned, a face-to-face encounter and questioning were, for Walpole, the best means of assessing their worth. He gave him full assurances that he would see he was 'privately' conveyed to London and that he, personally, would 'take great care' to see him 'without being in the least known.' He told him he would even keep him concealed in London if he so desired. Such meetings were not infrequent for Walpole; he met his spies not only in the secrecy of Chelsea. Often, it would seem, he went incognito to a particular tavern or other meeting place suggested to him.[37]

With the death of John Macky in 1726 Walpole lost one of his chief agents. But the loss meant little as he already had an equally important contact planted among the Jacobites – John Sempill or Sample.[38] This spy had been Sir Robert Sutton's butler while he was envoy in France and had been arrested by Walpole's government in 1722 but had managed (no doubt with government connivance) to escape to France. With this background and his seemingly strong Jacobite connections it was most unlikely he would be even the least suspect in Jacobite circles. At least two years before Macky's death John Sempill, on numerous occasions, became Walpole's eyes and ears at Atterbury's dining table. He reported his gleanings to Horace at Paris, who in turn relayed them to Walpole at London. Through Sempill he was dealt out the smallest details of Atterbury's activities: the visits of Sir Patrick Lawless, the Spanish ambassador to France, and Sir Redmond Everard; the slightest moves of Colonel O'Brian and General Dillon, the Pretender's agents; the reactions in the Jacobite camp to Pulteney's attacks on him; the journey of the earl of Orrery to The Hague; and plans for invasion. Sempill corresponded with many of the leading Jacobites and passed such information as they communicated to him on to Walpole.

36 PRO, SP 35/45, f 204
37 Cholmondeley (Houghton) MSS, 1257
38 See Appendix I.

But Sempill shared in common with most of Walpole's spies a sponge-like desire for money. 'He is expensive,' wrote Horace, 'and always wants money' and his letters bear testimony to this craving. By 1729 he was demanding 4000 French livres a year to be paid in quarterly instalments, otherwise he claimed it would be impossible 'to be of service.' Probably with a view to impressing Walpole with the scope of these services, he followed up his demands with a suggestion that there were new plots in the making.

With the death of Atterbury in 1732 Sempill's usefulness to Walpole was finished. Although his letters continued, they became less in content and more demanding in money. Walpole abruptly terminated his services in 1733 after Sempill drew on him for £50. He informed Waldegrave, the ambassador in Paris, that he was to make it clear to Sempill he would pay no more bills. But he added: 'I think he should not quite starve, and if you will let him know you will pay him about £50 p.a. it is but justice, and 'tis wonderful how the fool could think to draw bills upon me by the common post and with his own hand, and not be discovered.'[39] Up to this point Sempill had not been discovered. At Atterbury's death when his son-in-law, William Morice, asked him for any letters the bishop had written to him, Sempill told him he had not preserved them. Little did Morice know that they had in fact been carefully preserved in Robert Walpole's files of Jacobite intelligence.

Walpole's decision to place spies in Atterbury's counsels was based on his belief that any Jacobite plan of consequence would be communicated to him. The obvious place, however, from which these plans would originate was the Pretender's court at Rome. From here Walpole was supplied with intelligence from 1721 by Baron von Stosch, alias John Walton.[40] Stosch, an antiquarian whose fondest dream had been to hold a professorship in history at Cambridge, aided Walpole during the next ten years in his endless pursuit of Jacobitism. His appointment to Rome was made largely through the efforts of Richard Bentley, master of Trinity College, Cambridge, who was a close friend of both Stosch and Carteret. For his services he was to be paid £520 a year in quarterly instalments by Langlois, a Leghorn merchant, who was to be reimbursed by the government.

As a man of considerable fine taste and learning, he was an ideal choice for the position and within the confines of the Vatican carried out his literary researches while at the same time fulfilling undetected, at least at first, his main task of collecting material on Jacobite activity for the government.

---

39 Waldegrave MSS (Chewton House). Box marked 'Letters from Mr. Tilson and the Brothers Walpole 1727-1740.'

Dorothy Mackay Quynn, 'Philipp von Stosch: Collector, Bibliophile, Spy, Thief (1611-1757),' *Catholic Historical Review*, XXVII, 3, Oct. 1941, 332-44

During his earlier stay in Rome he had made many valuable contacts and had in fact been given a pension by Pope Clement XI. This time he soon numbered among his friends Cardinal de Polignac and Count Renato Imperiali. These latter two, quite unknowingly, supplied Stosch with a large part of the information that filled his reports. But even inside the Pretender's household he had his own agents who filtered to him the smallest of happenings from the private chambers.

Until the Pretender's removal to Bologna, and finally Avignon in 1726, Stosch's reports enabled Walpole to follow closely most of his moves. By the time the Pretender returned to Rome at the Pope's command – though, as was generally believed, by Stosch's influence with one of the cardinals – his secret was out. Up to this point he had deceived many into thinking he was working for the czar, but once discovery was made, his value as an agent for Walpole rapidly diminished. On 31 January 1731 Stosch was attacked in his carriage by four masked men and, fearing for his life, he fled Rome. His services to Walpole from that quarter were at an end.

From these and many other centres Walpole's spies channelled their reports to him. His main knowledge of the secret articles of the Treaty of Vienna came through two of his spies in Paris – the Sicilian abbotts, Carracciolo and Platania. Banished from Spain by Elizabeth Farnese, they had taken up residence in Paris and any efforts by Spain to prevent their activities proved fruitless.[41] In Spain, at St Malo and Madrid, Walpole had other spies stationed. One, Richard Hay, had busily collected Jacobite intelligence for him, laying out money from his own pocket for 'the service.' There is little doubt that Walpole read each report carefully. In some cases he initialled them and in others he affixed the sender's name. Each bit of evidence was weighed and anything he judged of importance he communicated to the king.

There were few sources or means that Walpole would not explore to alleviate his dread fear of Jacobitism. There is no evidence of his corresponding directly with any of the leading Jacobites, as Sunderland had done, because Walpole was too well aware of what a direct correspondence with them could mean. Had he himself not secured the banishment of Atterbury on the very basis of such evidence? He had, therefore, to resort to subtler means in his desire to lay naked the conspiracy he knew was there. When once asked why he employed a certain Jacobite, Walpole had replied: 'Who should I employ else? How can I learn Jacobite designs but from

41 Basil Williams, 'The Foreign Office of the First Two Georges,' *Blackwoods Magazine*, CLXXXI, 1907, 103

themselves?'[42] For the purpose of sapping this source Walpole saw highly secretive and personal meetings with them as an excellent way to come at evidence. But even here he did not see the method as foolproof. After a face-to-
face encounter he knew all too well how it might be turned against him, for
the examinee would be 'capable of publishing accounts of any kind.' In the
case of one Mannis, a well-known Jacobite who was interviewed by Walpole
in late 1723, the means to prevent such an occurrence was hit upon. It was
suggested by Townshend, who felt he should be 'put in custody of a messenger, and examined before the council, and if they approve of it, committed
not so much with a view of drawing discoveries from him . . . as to put it out
of his power to do you [Walpole] harm by you publickly disclaiming him.'[43]

The caution Walpole exercised in dealing directly with Jacobites is well
illustrated by his interview of Thomas Carte, the nonjuring clergyman, in
1739. Trapped very carefully into believing Walpole was sympathetic to their
cause, Carte came to England as an emissary of the Pretender for an interview with him. The first meeting was held in the secrecy of Chelsea at nine
o'clock at night. Carte was ushered into a room and there left alone with
Walpole. Fear of what concurring evidence from two witnesses could mean
made this latter precaution vital. Telling Carte that he believed he was a
'well wisher to [his] country and zealous for the Protestant religion,' Walpole then commanded him to reveal any plans or designs of the Pretender.
When Carte refused to do so threats and then bribes were used. According
to Carte: 'He put me in mind that the warrant against me was not called in
but still lay in the messenger's hands, and there were two witnesses who had
deposed that I knew where there were 10,000 arms concealed and ready to be
used in an insurrection.'[44] In the second interview, after more pressure was
exerted, Carte disclosed to Walpole what he knew of the Pretender's plans.
The necessary information gained, Walpole announced that the notion had
never been entertained by him of supporting a Stuart restoration. The interview was at an end.

In his never-ending search to bring Jacobite plot and conspiracy into the
open, Walpole never lacked in offers from informers and would-be spies.
They were as varied as their number was large: William Freke, 'skilled in
the art of futurities'; Henry Pearson, a Roman Catholic doctor; Thomas
Wells, financially destitute; J. Ellis, priest-catcher; John Smith, collector of
treasonable papers; Richard Hay, conveyor of 'strange things and news little

42 Arch.Aff.Etr.Mémoires et Documents, vol. 76, f 79. Journal of the negotiation of Mr Carte
  with Robert Walpole.
43 BM, Stowe MSS, 251, f 56
44 Arch.Aff.Etr.Mémoires et Documents, vol. 76, f 79

thought of'; John Kirman, keeper of Jack's Coffee House in Dover Street. In seemingly infinite number such proposals were paraded before the government. Nor was the nature of the information they proffered as an enticement more uniform: designs for invasion, lists of Catholic priests, plots of assassination, recruitment for the Pretender, popish plots, imminent internal rebellion, drinking of the Pretender's health, and so on. There is little evidence that the government ever seriously entertained many such offers. In 1733 one Edmund Martin, alias Hungate, offered to turn informer if Walpole would send him the wherewithal to make the journey from Paris to London. But Walpole hesitated for, as he told Lord Waldegrave: 'It will not be the first time, that I have been drawn in, under these kind of pretences, to bear the expenses of their [the Jacobite] courriers, both to and from foreign ports.'[45]

45 Waldegrave MSS. Box marked 'Letters from Mr. Tilson and the Brothers Walpole 1727-1740.'

11
The death of English Jacobitism

Robert Walpole's ruthless handling of Jacobite activity in the early years of his administration, together with his careful scrutiny of each and every Jacobite move in the following years, explains, at least in part, the subdued nature of Jacobite activity after 1723. His dragging of conspiracy to the surface in England and his parading of it before the nation dealt the English Jacobite movement a blow from which it was never to recover fully before Walpole's death in 1745. Neither the Pretender, nor his supporters on the continent, received pleas for action from the English side because the penetrating quality of the ministry's investigations of 1722 and 1723 gave Jacobites everywhere good reason to be 'terrified' and 'to boggle at any dealings' for some time to come. The Pretender no longer spoke of sallying forth 'alone' to England, but now declared himself to be 'but too sensible of the difficulties there will be after this of executing any project without foreign help.' Ormonde and Dillon, who had been previously bombarded with the most fulsome accounts of the good disposition of the people of England towards a restoration, were now confronted with silence. 'I find that there is no encouragement from friends in England,' Ormonde reported to Hay, the Pretender's new secretary of state.

Nor did the Pretender continue to press his demands for sums of £50,000, £30,000, or £20,000 from among his supporters in England. 'If last year's affair had not happened,' declared Orrery, 'I should have procured a good sum for you.' That prospect, too, had now vanished and the Pretender told them he would be content with any amount at all. Atterbury also cautioned against undue movement of any kind, for even the most 'ineffectual alarm' would be attended by horrendous consequences which would permanently defeat any end they might deign to encompass. For the present the Pretender shared Atterbury's conviction and urged a programme of inertia as the safest guarantee against Robert Walpole finding 'the least handle of raising a new plot.' Their main concern, he said, should be 'to keep as quiet as we can in appearance,' and 'to be very cautious who we speak freely to or anyway employ with our friends on the other side.' Among this latter group Orrery, now their spokesman, could not recommend enough precaution. Nervousness, irresoluteness, trepidation, hesitation, uneasiness, and despondency – these were to remain the marked features of Jacobite activity during the next several years. In short, the deep inner fear of Jacobitism to which Robert Walpole gave external expression during the years 1722 and 1723 had struck a proportionate amount of fear into the Jacobite movement itself. 'The ministers look me up,' declared Orrery, 'without having the least thing of consequence against me.' They could still speak of 'fair prospects' and 'new hopes' but, temporarily paralyzed with fear, their every movement until 1725 was a guarded one.

Walpole's retaliatory measures of these two years also disrupted the internal structure of the Jacobite party in terms of its personnel. Several of the leading Jacobites, including Atterbury, were convinced that Mar had played no small part in bringing this vengeance upon them by turning informer. Whether guilty or not, Mar became their scapegoat and Atterbury, condemned to exile partly on the strength of intercepted letters Mar had sent him, joined wholeheartedly in the mission to topple him from office. In the course of their own witch-hunt General Dillon's integrity was also seriously questioned and he was severely rebuked by the Pretender for failing to turn Mar's papers over to Atterbury for perusal.

In casting about for foreign support for their cause during the years 1723-5, Atterbury was instructed to use 'cautious solicitations' at the court of France. With the death of the duc d'Orléans they had anticipated aid from this quarter, but by later 1724 it was obvious, even to the Jacobites, that his successor, the duc de Bourbon, was 'fully resolved to stick to his predecessor's engagements to the Elector of Hanover.'[1]

By 1725, however, a number of Jacobites on the continent had recovered a sufficient amount of their former zeal and had begun to regard a new project as imminent. The British government's attempt to disarm the Highland clans and to levy a malt tax on Scotland provided them with a situation of discontent they felt disposed to exploit.[2] Their renewed hopes were mainly

1 RA, Stuart, 62/102; 70/2; 70/25; 70/38; 70/46; 78/128; 79/9; 79/111; 79/136
2 G.S. Pryde, *Scotland From 1603 to the Present* (London 1962), 60-1; *Arch.Aff.Etr.Corr.Pol.Angl.*, vol. 352, f 159

inspired, however, by the European crisis of this and the next year.[3] France and Spain had reached an earlier agreement for an alliance to be based on the marriage of the infanta of Spain to Louis XV. The duc de Bourbon had viewed this as a certain guarantee against the inheritance of the throne by his bitter rival, the younger duc d'Orléans. A sudden illness of Louis XV in February 1725 caused the duc de Bourbon to panic, taking the hasty decision to arrange an immediate marriage if Louis recovered. The infanta, therefore, would be unacceptable.[4] In early March Elizabeth Farnese and Philip V were informed of Bourbon's repudiation of the infanta and the intended marriage of Louis XV to Maria Leszczynska, daughter of the former king of Poland, which took place by proxy in August 1725. Bourbon's action naturally infuriated Elizabeth Farnese.

At about the same time the emperor, Charles VI, had begun to rankle over allowing garrisons to enter the duchies of Parma and Tuscany on behalf of Don Carlos, a son of Elizabeth Farnese. The Congress of Cambrai, called into being to handle this problem in 1722, had created its own problems, did not formally meet for the first time until January 1724, and six months later had made no progress towards solving the dispute between Spain and the emperor. Elizabeth Farnese took matters into her own hands. She dispatched her chief minister, the Duke of Ripperda, to Vienna to secure a treaty with the emperor permitting Don Carlos and the garrisons to enter the duchies in question and also to form an alliance with his imperial majesty through the marriage of her two sons, Don Carlos and Don Philip, to the Archduchess Maria Theresa and her sister. By February 1725 negotiations towards this end had progressed little, but the arrival of the news at this point of the repudiation by France of the infanta brought in its wake instructions to Ripperda to conclude a treaty with the emperor on any terms.

It was this situation of instability which shocked the Jacobites temporarily from their earlier state of fear and trepidation. Atterbury recounted the drama of the crisis to the Pretender and was one of the first to suggest that they apply themselves towards taking advantage of it. He wrote: 'The affair of Spain is now come to a crisis. Sir Patrick Lawless went away yesterday morning at five o'clock and left orders (as he himself said) for Monteleone to follow him . . . The ministers of Spain at Cambrai are ordered to withdraw . . . so that assembly is broken up. The Infanta goes away certainly and soon

---

3 For the general situation in this period see B. Williams, *The Whig Supremacy, 1714-1760* (Oxford 1962); Arthur M. Wilson, *French Foreign Policy During the Administration of Cardinal Fleury 1726-1743* (Cambridge, Mass. 1936).

4 She was born 19 March 1718.

. . . The opportunity is great and should be laid hold of, with all possible dispatch.'[5]

The Pretender, too, entertained the greatest hopes that affairs in Europe would now alter sufficiently to provide him with a new project. It would be most unfortunate, he told Orrery, if 'in this universal posture of affairs it should be possible that all those clouds should blow over and affairs settle into a new calm without anything being undertaken in my favour.' 'It is hard,' he added, 'to imagine that from the present confusion of affairs, some event should not happen which may determine a foreign power to embrace my interest.'[6] The war clouds that loomed forth in these years did eventually blow over, leaving the Pretender without a project, but not before he had made endeavours to secure foreign support. In 1722 he had expended a considerable sum of money on the purchase of arms and ammunition in Holland and now, at Atterbury's request, General Hamilton was sent there to discuss, with the person to whom they had been entrusted, the most effectual means of transporting them to Scotland when it was felt to be necessary.[7] In early June Atterbury was given full power by the Pretender 'to give such orders and directions to all my subjects now residing in France, relating to the present situation of my affairs . . . as you shall think necessary.'[8] At this point the Pretender envisaged himself as the mediator in a peace between France and Spain and towards this end dispatched a memorial to the queen of Spain with an offer of his services. Ormonde was ordered to seek an audience with their Spanish majesties and to assure them that once restored to his throne he would enter into the 'strictest' alliance with them; James Murray, with a similar view in mind, had been granted an audience with the French minister, Cardinal Fleury.[9] It was obvious by June 1725, however, that France would not be a party to any Jacobite scheme. 'It is now put beyond all doubt,' wrote Atterbury to the Pretender, 'that you have nothing to expect from here, while the strict friendship between England and France continues.' The Pretender's letters to Spain remained unanswered.

On 30 April 1725 Spain and the emperor signed treaties of peace, commerce, and alliance. By September Britain, France, and Prussia had signed

5 RA, Stuart, 81/28

6 RA, Stuart, 81/95

7 RA, Stuart, 61/22; 63/108; 81/28

8 RA, Stuart, 83/3

9 RA, Stuart, 81/126; 81/131. Murray had actually requested Fleury to consider an invasion attempt. It could be safely concealed from the notice of the British government, he told him, on the pretence that France and Spain were preparing for war with each other and at the appropriate moment they could unite and invade England.

a counter-alliance at Hanover.[10] Philip, duke of Wharton, who had gone to Vienna in July as the Pretender's plenipoteniary to that court, to promote, if possible, the Pretender's interest, now seized on the Hanover treaty as a fitting opportunity to represent to his imperial majesty the truly evil contents of this counter-alliance. In his representations he pointed out that the treaty had been concluded for no other purpose than 'the aggrandizing [the power] of the Elector of Hanover in the Empire, the supporting the interest of France, the destruction of the Ostend Company and the settling the succession of the Empire in case of failure of issue male in his Present Majesty.'[11] Since this was, according to Wharton, their design, his imperial majesty was, therefore, at liberty 'to take such measures as may effectually defeat the designs of those who have formed an alliance so contrary to his inclinations.' His interest could best be promoted at this point and protected by embracing the Pretender's cause. Wharton was admitted to private conferences with both Ripperda and Count Sinzendorff and on the basis of these meetings the rumour was immediately spread that the Pretender was to be included in the second treaty between the emperor and Spain that was signed in November 1725. Certainly Wharton was quite convinced this would be the product of his efforts and Ripperda seems to have done little to discourage him.

The scare of 1725 resulted from these intrigues and produced one of the best examples of Robert Walpole's deep and educated fear of Jacobitism. From the formal treaty arrangements Walpole knew that the Pretender would find his warmest reception in either Spain, Austria, or from those countries leagued with them – Sweden and Russia. The actual scare came from Russia.

As already demonstrated Walpole had worked, since the banishment of Atterbury, to establish an effective espionage system on the continent and by 1725 had his agents planted in most of the capitals of Europe and in the Pretender's circles. From this network, from European postal control, and from the English representatives abroad, he had hoped to have early warning of any Jacobite conspiracy. Where his intelligence system was strongest he feared the least; where weakest he feared the most. And St Petersburg was in this latter category for he had no reliable agent there whose sole function it was to send reports for his files of Jacobite intrigue.[12]

10 For this period see J.F. Chance, *The Alliance of Hanover* (London 1923).
11 RA, Stuart, 83/88
12 William Coxe, *Memoirs of the Life and Administration of Sir Robert Walpole* (London 1798), II, 485. Thomas Consett, chaplain to the English factory in St Petersburg, had reported earlier on Jacobite activity but was suspect among the Jacobites; he was discharged as chaplain in the autumn of 1725. See Cholmondeley (Houghton) MSS, 1250.

From the early spring of this year Walpole's fear of military preparations in Russia began to mount and the intelligence dispatched to him from Vienna, Madrid, Paris, Copenhagen, Rome, and elsewhere seemed to concentrate to an increasing extent on events taking place there. He was determined to try to tap nearer to the source and in early May sent Captain John Deane to St Petersburg. Acting in the official capacity of consul-general, Deane's main concern was to secure Jacobite intelligence but the mission failed almost before it had been initiated.[13] Before leaving the court at St Petersburg, however, Deane made what was to prove a most valuable contact – Edward O'Connor, a Jacobite, who was soon to become a carrier of Jacobite correspondence.[14]

Despite this failure, information continued to flow and in direct proportion Walpole's alarm continued to rise. The visit of the duke of Wharton, a well-known Jacobite, to Vienna in July made him wary of that court.[15] The mouthings of the duke of Ripperda, the queen of Spain's minister, in favour of the Pretender, and the repeated advice on Jacobite activity from Cardinal Fleury, were, for Walpole, more than ample reason to be on his guard against Spain.[16] By September the meanderings and wanderings of three Russian ships became an increasing object of his attention.[17] These events, coupled with the reports flying in from his own spies on the continent, almost convinced him a mission was well under way for an invasion by the Pretender with the support of Spain, Austria, and Russia. The dispatch to him of three intercepted letters of Jacobites at St Petersburg tipped the balance of Walpole's mind from near certainty to absolute conviction. An invasion by these countries on behalf of the Pretender became at this moment indisputable fact.

Captain Deane, now stationed as an agent in the Jacobite camp at Amsterdam, had received several Jacobite letters from Edward O'Connor just arrived from St Petersburg. These Deane communicated to Lord Townshend at Hanover who immediately sent them to Robert Walpole.[18] Among them was one from Sir Henry Stirling, the Pretender's chief agent at St Petersburg, and, as it was not couched in the usual cant and allegory of most of their correspondence, there was no mistaking its import. Stirling wrote

---

13 Deane was suspected from the moment he arrived in St Petersburg and was given eight days to leave. Chance, *The Alliance of Hanover*, 84
14 Cholmondeley (Houghton) MSS, 1249
15 BM, Add. MSS, 33,199, f 323-4
16 Coxe, *Walpole*, II, 475, 480; BM, Add. MSS, 33,199, f 327
17 Captain Deane on his outward journey to St Petersburg reported passing three Russian men-of-war bound for Cadiz. Poyntz reported that they had stopped off in Scotland.
18 Cholmondeley (Houghton) MSS, 1249; 1250; 1251

and Robert Walpole read: '. . .I hope the three first ships and goods are arrived without damage; there is one more ready to sail, and two preparing . . . I cannot but repeat, that you must not neglect the least time to set all your engines at work, and answer the next season . . . There must be one hundred and twenty thousand pounds sterling at least, ready to be answered where required, to do matters effectually . . . Matters are carried on here with all imaginable discretion.'[19] From this and the other discoveries the entire design was now crystal clear in Walpole's mind. It was quite obvious that the dispositions lately made by the Russian fleet were for no other purpose than to be in readiness to sail simultaneously with the fleet from Spain. Part of it would land forces and supplies in Scotland; the other in the west of England. The forces necessary for the expedition would be supplied by the emperor. The designed invasion of England and Scotland in favour of the Pretender would take place in the spring. All this Walpole unravelled from the previous advices and the three intercepted Jacobite letters – letters which he considered of 'the last importance.' He immediately wrote to Lord Townshend to express these convictions and to request immediate action for 'the apprehensions of some design next spring, obtain so much with me,' he wrote, 'that I think it deserves the greatest attention, and we cannot be too watchful to trace and discover all that can be possibly known.'[20] Such a discovery was of the greatest significance for a mind obsessed with Jacobitism. The safest way to guard against this design would be through 'a sufficient fleet, sent early enough to the Baltick, and another . . . in our own seas . . . and to guard our own coast.' Perhaps even more significant, this event pointed out to Walpole, in a most glaring way, the weak point of his intelligence system. 'We have nobody at Petersburg,' he wrote in desperation to Lord Townshend, and his first thoughts were to remedy that situation. Six months still remained to them and they must make every effort 'to dive into the secret.'

For Walpole the obvious candidate to provide them with a link to the Jacobite design was Edward O'Connor, the Jacobite who had communicated the letters to them. But unknown to Walpole at this point, O'Connor, as his channel of intelligence, was already lost. Hired by the Jacobites as a carrier of letters, he was not entrusted with their plans and secrets, but even of more importance the night before he left St Petersburg he had let slip 'to a whore he kept company with' knowledge of the contents of some of the letters that had been entrusted to him. The following morning a Jacobite, Captain Hease, had been sent hot on his trail to apprehend him.[21]

19 Coxe, *Walpole*, II, 484-5
20 Ibid., II, 487
21 Cholmondeley (Houghton) MSS, 1249

Though disappointed at the loss of this valuable contact, O'Connor was rewarded with money and the grant of a pardon for the services he had already rendered.[22] Walpole pressed on in his search for a reliable agent. He contacted his chief source on affairs at St Petersburg, Sir Nathaniel Gould, the head of the Russia Company, and through him negotiations were started to secure the services of one Taylor, a book-keeper to Mr Wyatt and Company. Taylor was an ideal choice for he also acted as secretary to Sir Henry Stirling.

At the same time Walpole had turned his attention towards opening up new insights into the Jacobite plan through the interception of correspondence. Any further letters to those persons named in the ones O'Connor had turned over to them were to be opened and copied and more intensive searches of the post were carried out at Leyden, Hamburg, Paris, and Amsterdam.[23]

All of these endeavours were undertaken with the greatest of secrecy. Above all Walpole wished to avoid any suspicion among the Jacobites that they had any knowledge of their plans. This, and the desire to prevent any alarm in England, were the two factors governing the taking of military precautions. For this reason he had avoided ordering the dispatch of ships to the West Indies to act as a check on the Spaniards. Orders were given, however, for the commissioners of victualling to contact and provide for 10,000 seamen, 'as in the ordinary course,' for the year 1726. He reckoned this force could be easily raised at the proper moment to 2000 or 3000 more. Still with a view of avoiding any suspicion and alarm, instructions were given to have thirty or forty ships-of-the-line ready to sail by March. Assurances were also gained from France of support in the event that this Jacobite attempt materialized and the king of Prussia, now their ally by the defensive treaty just concluded, was warned of the intelligence they had received.[24] At Madrid, William Stanhope worked diligently and with the greatest secrecy to uncover further information. The rest of Walpole's machine followed suit.

The designed invasion never materialized. It had existed for the most part in the minds of the Jacobites and Walpole and his ministers. The three Russian men-of-war, whose dispositions Walpole had been following, were on nothing more than an 'essai de commerce' and this Stanhope firmly established from information he gained at Madrid.[25] The ships had stopped at Scotland for the purpose of repairs. Walpole had been convinced they were depositing arms. Their mission to Cadiz was to convey naval stores and

22 He was paid £100 and the promise of further reward for any discoveries.
23 Cholmondeley (Houghton) MSS, 1250; 1251
24 Chance, *The Alliance of Hanover*, 143-4
25 Ibid., 149

there reload with salt and oil. Walpole had been sure they were carrying arms and supplies to equip the Spanish fleet. Such was yet a further manifestation of a mind obsessed with fear of invasion of England by the Pretender aided by a foreign power.

Robert Walpole and his fellow ministers continued, however, to fear, at this juncture, possible foreign support for the Pretender and by 1726 their fears seemed confirmed when rumours began to circulate that certain secret articles relating to the Pretender had been included in the second defensive treaty between Charles VI and Philip V. Indeed, the supposed secret articles were disclosed the very next year by Ripperda to Sir Benjamin Keene, the British ambassador at Madrid. He told him that Spain, Russia, and the emperor had agreed to support the Pretender: the czarina would supply 12,000 men and transport; Spain would embark 8000 men from Gallaecia under the command of the duke of Ormonde; the emperor would contribute 6000 men.[26] In return the Pretender, according to Ripperda, had promised to restore Gibraltar and Port Mahon to Spain and to guarantee to the emperor the Imperial East India Company of Ostend.[27] No secret articles to this effect have yet been found and, although it created a sensation when the news was revealed, its reality would seem to have been only in the minds of Ripperda and the Jacobites.[28] Ripperda had earlier expressed his belief to Wharton that he would not have the 'least difficulty' in persuading the emperor to join with Spain in overturning the House of Hanover, but by mid-1726 Ripperda had been dropped from office and at the end of this year the emperor had not yet been 'persuaded.' Each Jacobite solicitation to that court met with the same answer: his imperial majesty cannot espouse the cause of the Pretender while he remains in peace with the elector of Hanover.[29] The emperor did not go to war with George I and the Pretender was without a project. Even had he been able to initiate one, with the aid of the emperor, from the English side he was still faced with the earlier state of fear. He had requested the English Jacobites in parliament to use their utmost endeavours to weaken Walpole's administration but they were still paralyzed with fear. Were they to show even the least signs of disaffection, declared Orrery, it would most certainly 'awaken 'em to their old cruel methods of prosecution.' To ask them to use obstructionist tactics at this stage,

26 Cholmondeley (Houghton) MSS, 1340
27 Ibid., 1289
28 For a discussion of this problem see a review by E. Armstrong of Gabriel Syveton, 'Une Cour et un Aventurier au XVIII siècle: Le Baron de Ripperda,' in *English Historical Review*, XII, 1897, 796-800.
29 RA, Stuart, 101/8

he told the Pretender, was to invite disaster. He declared: "Tis well known the ministry have an absolute power [and] can make judges interpret laws as they please, and can command Parliament as much as a master can command his meanest servant, 'tis well known too that they have shown the extremest rigour against those they do but suspect don't wish well to 'em without any regard to the established rules or methods of justice.'[30]

Nor did the death of George I cause any change in the attitude of the English Jacobites. It was soon obvious that Sir Robert Walpole 'possesses the same power he had in the late reign as to money and to foreign affairs.' Lord Strafford, fearing the Pretender might hazard some ill-designed attempt, pleaded with him not even to consider it for it would have 'the worst consequence.' Charles Caesar, in a like vein, begged him to brush aside any thoughts of a project unless he was absolutely sure of the support of foreign power capable of pouring at least 12,000 troops into England. Without this, his prospects, he told him, were nil. The fear Walpole had struck into the Jacobites in England was operative even at this late date and by 1730 the Pretender himself was convinced their solicitations to the emperor would 'never signify very much.'[31]

For the next fifteen years the Jacobites continued to seek out a champion for their cause but not until the opening of the War of the Austrian Succession in 1740 did it appear even remotely possible that their efforts would pay off. In that decade France championed the cause that ended in the ill-fated 1745 rebellion. In the previous interval, however, their repeated appeals to France, Spain, and Russia came to nought. So, too, their efforts to take advantage of certain internal situations within England proved fruitless. Far too often, as on earlier occasions, the potentially favourable situation seemed to work against them, as happened in the Excise Crisis of 1733, the general election of the following year, and the London Riots of 1736. In each instance Robert Walpole raised the bogy of Jacobitism and thereby attempted to strengthen his own position politically.[32] During the riots[33] his obssessive preoccupation with Jacobitism was clearly articulated. At one point Westminster Hall was shattered by a gun-powder explosion. Referring to the incident in a letter to his brother Horace, he wrote:

---

30 RA, Stuart, 102/68
31 RA, Stuart, 107/97; 108/73; 109/6; 133/60
32 For the first two of these see J.H. Plumb, *Sir Robert Walpole: The King's Minister* (London 1960), 233 ff.
33 For the London Riots see G. Rudé, ' "Mother Gin" and the London Riots of 1736,' *Guildhall Miscellany*, series no 10, Sept. 1959, 53 ff.

Since my coming to town, I have been endeavouring to trace out the authors and managers of that vile transaction, and there is no reason to doubt but the whole was projected and executed by a sett of low Jacobites, who talked of setting fire to the gallery built for the marriage of the princess royall, by a preparation which they call a *phosphorous*, that takes fire from the air. Of this I have had an account from the same fellow that brought me these and many such sort of intelligencies.[34]

Although admitting that many other factors, among them the influx of cheap Irish labour into London, had sparked these riots, he went on to say: 'At the same time there are great endeavours using . . . to inflame the people, and to raise great tumults upon Michaelmas-day, when the ginn-act takes place; and as these lower sorts of Jacobites appear at this time more busy than they have for a great while, they are very industrious, and taking advantage of every thing that offers, to raise tumult and disorders among the people.'[35]

The low point of Jacobite activity in these years occurred in 1732, when the Pretender appealed for support not to Sweden, Spain, France, Russia, or the emperor, but to none other than Robert Walpole. In a mood of despondency the Pretender told him he knew of no one who could contribute so much to his restoration and requested him to do all in his power towards encompassing that end. In canvassing his support, the Pretender betrayed the extent of his desperation, since he knew that Walpole was one of the surest guarantees against the very thing he had requested. His appeal to this quarter was utterly hopeless in view of the obsessive preoccupation of Robert Walpole, like the other English ministers, with fear of Jacobitism. From the moment of their commitment to the Hanoverian succession, they were aware of the nature of their malady. In a sense, they had by their action brought it into being. They knew also the serum they required to counteract it: stability at home and abroad. If this was provided, then 'the Jacobites would not know where to fix their least views or hopes, the party would consequently moulder away, the malcontents in every place would be dispirited.'[36] But the existence of potential foreign support for the Pretender denied them such a situation. The threats of these years served only to convince them that their disease was genuine. The military measures on a grand scale and the harsh retaliatory penalties inflicted were but external expressions of their desire to find that counter-poison.

34 Coxe, *Walpole*, III, 348
35 Ibid., 348-9
36 PRO, SP 84/257, f 26-7

Conclusion

During the years following the Jacobite rebellion of 1715 the most serious internal threat to the British government of a Jacobite uprising occurred at the time of the South Sea Bubble crisis in 1720. The most dangerous external threat did not present itself until 1744 when the Jacobites secured French support. Up to this point few foreign powers found it to their political advantage to promote the Stuart cause. This reveals an acute awareness on the part of the English ministers of the absolute necessity to maintain the status quo in foreign policy. Genuine fear of a Jacobite invasion was a central factor in the shaping of English domestic and foreign policy in this period. As Walpole himself declared to the House of Commons in the late 1730s:

Five or six thousand men may be embarked in such a small number of ships, and so speedily, that it is impossible to guard against it by means of our fleet. Such a number may be landed in some part of the island, before we can hear of their embarkation: and if such a number were landed, with the Pretender at their head, there is no question that they would meet with many, especially the meaner sort, to join them. In such a case, we could not march our whole army against those invaders and their assistants; because, if we should draw all our regular forces away from the other parts of the Kingdom, the disaffected would rise in every county so left destitute of regular troops; and the rebels being thus in possession of many parts of our sea coasts, would be continually receiving supplies, by single ships, from those who had at first invaded us.[1]

---

1 William Cobbett, *The Parliamentary History of England from the Earliest Period to the Year 1803* X, 402-3

For the English ministers the guiding principle in foreign policy had to be the avoidance of near or open conflict with another power. On this hinged not only the securing of the Hanoverian dynasty, but also the best guarantee against the Pretender finding a champion for his cause. This lesson was well demonstrated in the years 1725 and 1726, because when Britain hovered on the brink of war, the Pretender also came close to securing support from Charles VI and Philip V. Had war not been averted the Jacobites would have secured their longed-for objective.

In the period after 1715, the position of France was crucial to the fortunes of both the Jacobites and the British government. The unwillingness of the Stuarts to give up their religion meant that any restoration attempt had to be backed by foreign support on a grand scale, and the only power capable of providing this in the first half of the century was France.[2] Both the Jacobites and the English ministers realized this. For this reason Stanhope in 1717 reversed the traditional Whig policy and formed an alliance with France. For Britain it was an alliance based on self-defence, stemming from her necessity to check the Jacobite threat and thereby maintain the Protestant succession. As long as the alliance lasted, the Jacobites had little prospect of aid from this quarter. None realized this better than Bishop Atterbury who, in 1730, lamented to Sempill:

France gives him [the Pretender] a little encouragement now and then to support a little grandeur, in order to keep him fast to them, and that they may have it in their power either to frighten or assure the ministry of England as they shall require. But they never had nor never will think of doing him real service; knowing while they have such a tool to play with they will always have it in their power to keep the government of England on their side.[3]

Less than fifteen years later, Atterbury's judgment was proved wrong, for France did see it in her interest to consider 'doing him real service.' The British decision for war with Spain in 1739 and the outbreak, a year later, of the War of the Austrian Succession provided a most fortunate opportunity for the Jacobites. The ensuing crisis brought a final break in diplomatic relations between Britain and France in 1744 and at that point the Jacobites secured French support.[4] By this time, however, it was too late. In 1745 the English did not rise in great numbers to support the march south to Derby by

2 D.B. Horn, *Great Britain and Europe in the Eighteenth Century*, 31
3 Cholmondeley (Houghton) MSS, 1720
4 Diplomatic relations had in effect ended in 1740 when France sent her fleet to check British interests in the West Indies. For this period see Horn, *Great Britian and Europe in the Eighteenth Century*.

Prince Charles Edward Stuart.[5] That they did not do so must be attributed to Robert Walpole and his fellow ministers, who had destroyed Jacobitism as an active force in England.

In the light of this fact, much more significance must be attached to a medal that Walpole had struck in 1723 to mark the defeat of the Atterbury plot. On its obverse side is depicted a group of conspirators seated about a table. The presiding figure, a bishop with a mitre firmly on his head, is in the process of circulating a plan for a Jacobite project to his fellow conspirators. Surrounding the relief is the inscription: 'DECRETUM EST, REGNO BRITO RESTITUATUR ABACTUS.'[6] On the reverse side of the medal, the eye of Providence (the British government) hurls glints at the same assembled group. Atterbury's mitre is knocked from his head; one of the plotters, Christopher Layer, is struck dead; and the rest of the party is cast into disarray. The inscription reads: 'CONSPIRATE, APERIT DEUS, ET VOS FULMINE PULSAT.'[7] The simple act of turning this medal from the obverse to the reverse side signifies two years of the most painstaking effort on the part of the British government, while in its entirety the medal represents the successful conclusion of its endeavours. In hindsight, at least, such a medal is far more significant than the one that was struck several years earlier to celebrate the coronation of George I. The latter marks the accession of the Hanoverians, while the former proclaims their establishment at the hands of Robert Walpole.

The accomplishment of this feat had not been easy. The English ministers had been confronted with an almost ceaseless spate of Jacobite intrigue and conspiracy that honeycombed its way throughout Britain and the courts of Europe. Two rebellions, two projected invasions, and a widespread internal plot were but the more concrete evidence indicating the extent of Jacobite intrigue after 1715. Internal disorder, discontent, disaffection, and general instability added yet another dimension to the potential strength of Jacobitism because of the opportunity it provided them for exploitation. And, as demonstrated, the external danger of possible foreign support for the Pretender's cause was never very far from the ministers' minds. The Jacobite intrigue that came to light, either through the employment of spies, domestic and foreign postal interceptions, the offerings of informers, or communications from foreign courts, made the ministers acutely aware that there was no inevitability attached to the succession they supported and with whose fortunes they were inextricably bound up. By their preoccupation with and fear of Jacobitism in these years the English ministers, especially Robert Walpole, demonstrate clearly that the only guarantee for

5 G.H. Jones, *The Main Stream of Jacobitism* (Cambridge, Mass. 1954), 237
6 'It is decreed that the Briton who was taken away will be restored to the Kingdom.'
7 'Unite together! God shows the way and drives you on with his thunder.'

maintaining intact the Hanoverian succession was to watch closely each and every Jacobite move. Only early warning and the detection of Jacobite plots could preclude an invasion of Britain by the Pretender. They also laboured under a handicap in coping with Jacobitism, as they were on the defensive. For this reason, they saw the need to maintain an elaborate and expensive intelligence system, a standing army, and a fully equipped fleet. Throughout the years after 1715, the role of all three was predominantly a defensive one. Once a sufficient amount of Jacobite intrigue was garnered, the ministers could choose, however, to take the offensive, and they did so in 1717, 1719, and 1722. In these instances, they were forced to do so largely by necessity, but they also acted out of an awareness of the political advantages to be gained by a public exploitation of their own fears. Their action in the Görtz-Gyllenborg plot of 1717, the cardinal's invasion of 1719, and the Atterbury plot and Layer conspiracy of 1721-2 displays clearly this two-fold aspect of their endeavours.

In the failure of the Jacobites to take the British government by surprise lay one of the basic weaknesses of Jacobite projects for a restoration. The tense nervousness of the English ministers concerning all matters of Jacobitism denied them such a favourable situation. The deeply educated and instinctive fear of Jacobitism shared by Stanhope, Sunderland, Craggs, Addison, Townshend, Walpole, and the other ministers meant that they were ready, at any moment, to strike with cobra-like precision at any Jacobite project that appeared to be even remotely possible. The deep internal fear of Jacobitism to which Robert Walpole gave public expression in 1722-3 was, for the Jacobites, the most serious threat of all. From it the Jacobite movement, especially in England, never fully recovered. But there was no finality for Robert Walpole in his action of these two years because he knew that only penetration and vigilance could prevent a like occurrence in the future. His actions following the Atterbury plot expose this conviction.

Years later, in 1760, an edition of *Colonel Hooke's Negotiations in Scotland* appeared in the booksellers' shops. In the preface the editor rejoiced at 'the happy coalition of forces' that had sounded the death-blow to Jacobitism. He then enumerated what he considered to be the greatest contributing factors. It had, he felt, been worn out by time, forsaken by persons who saw it as 'useless,' dropped by those who saw it as 'pernicious.' As the primary contributing factor to the defeat of Jacobitism the author should have added the preoccupation of the English ministers, particularly Robert Walpole, with fear of Jacobitism.

APPENDIX 1

John Sempill (Sample),
Walpole's anti-Jacobite spy

Confusion has existed as to which member of the Sempill family acted as Walpole's anti-Jacobite spy. Folkestone Williams, in his *Memoirs and Correspondence of Francis Atterbury, D.D., Bishop of Rochester*, suggested that the Sempill who acted as Atterbury's amanuensis was the agent bought off by Horace Walpole. Such is not the case because the Sempill who acted as Walpole's spy mentions frequently in his letters to Horace the Sempill who became Atterbury's scribe (for example, Cholmondeley (Houghton) MSS, 1281, 13 February 1726, Sempill to Horace Walpole). H.C. Beeching in his biography of Francis Atterbury pointed out this error (321) and suggested that the Sempill in question was probably John Sempill who had served as Sir Robert Sutton's butler during his term of office in Paris.

In an attempt to identify this Sempill I was taken to certain letters printed in Henrietta Tayler's *Jacobite Epilogue* and her *Jacobite Court at Rome in 1719*. The letters printed on pages 224-5 and 137-8 she identifies as those of Robert Sempill, the father of Francis, Lord Sempill, the Pretender's agent in Paris. Certain expressions in these letters are identical with ones used in the spy's letters that appear in the Cholmondeley (Houghton) MSS – for instance, in one of his letters to Lord Dunbar at Rome (Tayler, *Jacobite Epilogue*, 225) he says he hopes Lord Dunbar will 'obtain me some small matter.' In a letter to Horace Walpole (Cholmondeley (Houghton) MSS, 1537) the writer says he hopes Horace will be able to let him have 'some small matter.' Was, then, one of Robert Walpole's major spies Robert Sempill who had been raised to the noblesse by the Pretender in 1712? A photostat of one of those letters, which Tayler identified as being Robert Sempill's (RA, Stuart, Box 2/496), when compared with the Sempill letters that appear in the Cholmondeley (Houghton) MSS proved that the handwriting was identical. But the identification was by no means complete. Robert Sempill died in 1731. Therefore, the Sempill who acted as Robert Walpole's spy could not possibly have been Robert Sempill since the one who acted as a spy continued to send letters as late as 1738. Several of these are to be found in the Waldegrave MSS (Chewton House).

A closer search of the Cholmondeley (Houghton) MSS revealed a letter of this agent for 20 March 1732. It is endorsed 'John' Sempill. He was probably a distant relative of Francis, Lord Sempill, for in another letter he says: 'As to my being his [Francis, Lord Sempill's] relation or not is of no moment my father was a gentleman, and if not what then' (Cholmondeley (Houghton) MSS, 1882, 24 April 1732, Sempill to William Morice). There is also evidence to show that he was the John Sempill who had served as Sir Robert Sutton's butler and who had been arrested by Walpole's government in 1722. In a letter from Horace Walpole to Robert Walpole, Horace says that Sempill often mentioned Sir Robert Sutton but said he knew 'nothing against him' (Cholmondeley (Houghton) MSS, 1180).

APPENDIX 2

The Norfolk List of 1721[1]

A List of Some Few of the Loyal Gentlemen in the County of Norfolk and their Estates (viz):

Sir Ralph Hare of Stow Bardolph £3000
Sir John Wodehouse of Kimberly £5000
Sir Thomas Robinson of Dearham Grange besides an annuity of £1200 p.ann. for life £500
Sir Edmund Baron of Gardboldesham first Barr. in England £1500
Sir Edmond Baron of Gillingham £1600
Sir Horatio Pettus of Rackheath £1000
Sir Basingborough Gandy of Harling £600
Sir Nicholas L'Estrange of Basham (nonjuror) £2500
Christopher Layer of Booton (nonjuror) £800
Thomas Coke of Holkham £1200
Roger North of Rougham £3000
Thornaugh Gordon of Letton £1000
John Berny of Westwick £800
Richard Dashwood of Coskly Cley £1200
Roger Pratt of Ryston £1000
Beaupre Bell of Outwell £1100
Samuel Taylor of Watlington £1000
Henry Heron of Ketteringham £2000
Samuel Burkin of Watlington £500

1 RA, Stuart 65/10 (The original spelling has been retained throughout.)

Hewer Oxburgh of Outwell £400
Erasmus Earle of Heydon £1400
Erasmus his son £500
William Kemp of Antingham £600
Benjamin Dethwick of Wereham £600
Thomas Swift of Mewell £600
Thomas Lake of Wisbitch (merchant) £400
Henry Safrey of Downham (merchant) £300
John Davis of Watlington £700
Dr Massey of Wisbitch £200
Thomas Wright of East Harling £1200
Thomas Hoogan of Dunham £800
John Ropps of Matlask £600
Peter Elwin of Tuttington £1200
Thomas Chute of Pickenham £900
Thurlow Stafford of Below £400
James Lodge of Swafham £200
Joseph Eldon of Aylsham £300
Robert Curties of Aylsham £200
Doctor Boys of Aylsham (nonjuror)
Robert Burrows of Diss £500
Roger Doune of Naxham £300
Thomas Stone of Beddingham £500
Robert Knights of Winterton £600
Charles Bladwell of Swannington £300
Robert Donne of Creak £200
John Welch of Ludham £200
Andrew Chambers of Homing £400
Henry Smith of Colishall (attorney-at-law) £200
John Green of North Walsham (attorney-at-law) £200
Robert Davy of Ditshingham (counsell-at-law) £800
Robert Suckling of Wooten £900
Stroud Bendingfeld of Ditshingham £1300
Henry Warner of Walsingham £3000
Mr. Tasburgh of Flixton £1000
William Gilbert of Moulton £400
– Neave of Loddon £200
– Wogan of Redding Hall £1000
John Layer of Eye £300
Christopher Beddingfeld of Wighton £700

Walgrave Britisse of Wighton £300
Thomas Palgrave of Pulham £400
William Palgrave of Pulham £300
Robert Disipline of Stanhon £400
Augustine Holl of Twyford £300
John Curties of Wells £1500
Thomas Harris of Burnham £800
Roger Manser of Walsingham £400
Richard Godfrey of Hindringham, now one of the masters in Chancery £500
Cleer Garnish of Heddenham £1000
Richard Ferrier of Yarmouth £600
Captain Clarke of Clippesby £300
John Clarke of Bale £200
Thomas Seaman of Heigham £1000
William Gibbon of Thursford £700
Edward Lomb of Melton £2000
Leonard Mapes of Rollsby £400
Sir Richard Palgrave of Barningham £700
Thomas Halcott of Castleacre £200
Henry Negus of Hoveton £600
Thomas Blofeld of Hoveton £500
Edmund Blackburne of Wymondham £400
Thomas Rant of Yelverton £800
Thomas Damant of Lamas £400
Phillip Vincent of Marlingford £300
Edward Osborne of Sedon £900
William Newman of Baconsthorpe £700
Mr Freeston of Mendham £1200

In the City of Norwich
Richard Berny (councellor-at-law) £500
Alderman Vere £600
Doctor Amyas £400
Alderman Beny £1000
Alderman Newton £400
Alderman Nall £300
Alderman Harwood £500
Thomas Seaman (merchant) £800
Robert Seaman his brother £300
Mr Russell £1000

William Rolfe (attorney-at-law) £400
Thomas Risebrow (attorney-at-law) £500

Parsons of the Church of England that have Temporal Estates in the County of Norfolk and the City of Norwich (viz):
John Beddingfield of Ditchingham £800
Thomas Arrow Smith of Storston £300
John Tolly of Long Stratton £200
Robert Monsey of Booton (nonjuror) £500
James Verdon of East Dearham (nonjuror) £100
John Robinson of Keepham £150
James Norris of Marsham £150
Mr Thorneton of Saxlingham £100
Mr Lake late of Sparham (nonjuror) £250
James Hunt of Sparham £50
Lawrence Nomack of Buxton £200

Estimate of Jacobite strength in England and Wales for an uprising in 1721

[What follows is the list that was prepared by a number of prominent Jacobites in 1721 and submitted to the Pretender. It is entitled, 'A State of England' and is found among the Stuart papers at Windsor Castle (RA, Stuart 65/16). In reproducing this I have retained the form of the original, including the spelling of surnames, except in cases where the individuals were either members of the House of Lords or the House of Commons. The form of spelling adopted for this latter group is based on Romney Sedgwick, *The House of Commons, 1715-1754*, 2 vols. London 1970. The following code is used to identify those who were members of parliament at certain times.]

*member of the House of Commons 1715-22
**member of the House of Commons before 1715
†member of the House of Commons after 1722
§member of the House of Lords

A STATE OF ENGLAND

1 *Cornwall* Strong in Tinners and Fishermen – a bold, hardy well affected people.

§ Lord Lansdowne (chief)
† Sir John St Aubyn
** Sir Richard Vyvian
* Alexander Pendarves
Mr Williams
Mr Basset
** Mr Tonkin

Mr Soleskinham
Mr Hawes
Mr Collins
Mr Paint
** Sir William Pendarves
Mr Macworth
Mr Killigrew

Mr Kemp
Major Saller
* Mr Rashleigh
† Mr Goodall
Mr Grills
Mr Glyn
* Mr Anstis

Major Nance
* Sir William Carew
* Sir John Coryton
Captain Piper
Mr Phillips
Colonel Whaddon
Captain Gilbert

Dubious

Mr Travanian
Mr Nicholas Vincent
Mr Trelawny
Francis Scobel

Henry Scobel
Mr Buller
Mr Mannaton

Whiggs

Mr Boscawen
Mr Moile

Mr Williams
Mr Gregore

2 *Devonshire* Numerous in Clothiers and Manufacturers – most idle at present and discontented.

* Sir William Courtenay
* Sir Coplestone Bampfylde
* Sir Nicholas Morice
† Sir John Chichester
Sir Thomas Bury
Mr George Courtenay
* Mr Basset
* Mr Northmore
Mr Carew
Captain Stafford

Mr Day
Mr Goold
* Mr Elford
Mr Prescott
Mr Wolcombe
Mr Tothill
** Mr Quicke
Mr Fownes
* Mr Northleigh
§ Lord Clifford

Dubious

E. Radnor
Sir William Pole

Mr Role
Mr Bueteel

Whiggs

Sir Francis Drake
Mr Edgecombe
Mr Treby

Sir George Chudleigh
Sir Walter Yonge

3 *Somersetshire* A trading populous county wherein the number of honest people is by much superior as in Bristol, Bath and Wells. Lord Lansdowne's credit is here as in the two former shires.

§ Lord Poulett
* Sir William Wyndham
E. Castlehaven
§ Lord Stourton
Colonel Saller
Captain Lansdowne
* Mr Horner
Mr John Horner
* Sir John Trevelyan
** Sir Philip Sydenham

* Mr Bampfylde
* Mr Fownes
† Mr Phelipps
* Mr Palmer
Mr Poo
Mr Farwell
Captain Farwell
Mr Newman
Captain Fox
Mr Page

Dubious

Mr Brewer

Whiggs

Captain Pigot
Mr Spike

Mr Bubb alias Doddington

4 *Gloucestershire* Numerous in discontented Clothiers and Manufacturers. All the towns in this shire are in the right way.

§ Lord Bathurst (chief)
§ Lord Conway
Lord Tracy
† Mr John Howe
Mr Chamberline
* Mr Master
Mr Coleman

Captain Burghe
** Mr John Berkeley
Colonel Pool
† Mr Chester
* Mr Snell
Mr Hyall

Whigg

Lord Berkeley

5 *Wiltshire* Inhabited by Clothiers and Manufacturers at Bradford, Tunbridge, Warminister, Westbury and Hindon.

§ Lord Bruce (first chief)
3 Pophams (** Francis Popham)
Mr Ernel

Mr Wainwright
Mr Jones
Mr Whitlock

* Mr Talbot
Mr Seef
* Mr Nicholas
Mr Halls
* Sir James Long
* Mr Rolt

* General Webb (second chief)
* Sir Richard Howe
* Mr Hyde
* Colonel Lambert
* Mr Swanton

Whiggs

The Trenchards

The Pitts

6 *Dorsetshire*
§ Lord Digby
* Mr Strangways
* Mr Harvey

* Sir Nathaniel Napier
* Mr Chaffin

7 *Hampshire and Sussex*
* Sir Henry Goring (chief)
Sir William Oglander
* Colonel Holmes
* Colonel Stephens

* Sir Peter Mews
* Mr Lewis
* Mr Fleming
Sir Symon Stuart

Whiggs

Bolton

Somerset

8 *Surrey and Kent*
§ Lord Winchilsea (chief)
† Sir William Hardres
* Major Hardres
Colonel Broadnax

Sir Richard Head
Sir Philip Boteler
Mr Scot
Mr Stuart

Whiggs

The Onslows

9 *Middlesex* No other particular of this shire but that the Tory party was commonly strongest for the election in the country when even that of the Whiggs was present in London. The genius of this people is at present pretty obvious.

10 *Essex* Observation is made of this shire that five years ago during the suspension of the Habeas Corpus Act about 20 of the gentleman here were confined on suspicion of dissatisfaction.

11 *Suffolk*

** Earl of Dysart
* Sir Robert Davers
** Sir John Rous
† Sir Robert Kemp
* Sir Edward Turnor
Mr Croft

Mr Firebrace
* Mr Corrance
Mr Bridgeman
Major Alston
Mr Waring

12 *Norfolk* Walpole and Townshend have great interest in this shire, however stake may be made on the fishermen about Yarmouth and manufacturers of Norwich.

13 *Cambridgeshire, Huntingdonshire and Bedfordshire*

§ Lord North and Grey (chief)
The Cottons in their several branches
** Sir Pynsent Chernock

* Sir John Hynde Cotton
Sir John Chester
* Mr Harvey

Whiggs

Lord Manchester

Lord Orford

14 *Hertfordshire* A shire filled with honest men and able horses.

§ Lord Salisbury
* Sir Thomas Sebright

* Mr Caesar
Mr Robbinson

15 *Buckinghamshire* Influenced by two great families of Duke of Wharton and Bridgewater.

* Lord Fermanagh
* Mr Drake
* Mr Fleetwood
Mr Warren

† Captain Chapman
Mr Lownds
Mr Woodner

16 *Berkshire*

§ Lord Craven (chief)
§ Lord Stawell
* Sir John Stonehouse

* Mr Packer
† Mr Blagrave
Mr Bennett

17 *Oxfordshire*

§ Lord Abingdon (chief)
* Sir Robert Jenkinson
* Sir Jonathan Cope
** Sir William Glynne

Mr Chephard
* Mr Rowney
the University

18 *Northamptonshire* The shire most inhabited by noblemen yet the people have more confidence in the following gentlemen.

§ Lord Strafford (chief)
* Sir Justinian Isham
† Mr Isham
Mr Washborne

Mr Robinson
Mr Gore
Mr Alicock
Sir Robert Clarke

19 *Leicestershire* Very well stored with good horses and honest gentlemen who carried the elections against the Duke of Rutland.

* Sir George Beaumont
Sir Woolston Dixey
Mr Morice
** Sir Richard Halford

† Sir Clobery Noel
Mr Boothby
Mr Philips
* Mr Bracebridge

20 *Warwickshire* This shire has hardly a whigg in it. Lord Denbigh and Lord Brooke have lost much of their credit. Lord Leigh leads a private life and Lord Digby is old though well affected. Mr Jennings and Doctor Davis, both nonjurors, have the chief interest at Birmingham, a city capable of furnishing 12,000 men and arms.

Lord Craven (first chief)
† Mr Mordaunt
† Sir William Keyt
* Mr Peyto
Mr Harvey
Sir Edward Boreghten
** Sir Fulwar Skipwith
Mr Gregory
Mr John Craven
Mr Green

Mr Bracebridge
Mr Reppinton
* Mr Inge
Mr Olderby
Mr Jessen
Mr Holden
* Sir John Pakington (second chief)
William Lane
Mr Hoo
** Sir John Wrottesley

These [last] four are men of spirit, principles and great interest amongst the Ironworkers.

21 *Worcestershire* This shire is adjacent to Warwickshire in the same principle and influenced especially by –

§ Lord Plymouth (chief)
Sir John Packington
Sir Henry Parker
Mr Green

Mr Savage
Mr Hickford
Mr Ellison

22 *Staffordshire* Noted for perpetuated loyalty and influenced by –

§ Lord Gower (chief)
Mr Crampton
Mr Manwaring
Mr Whiler

** Mr Sneyd
The Bagots
* Charles Bagot
† Sir Walter Bagot

23 *Shropshire*
§ Lord Gower
* Mr Corbet Kynaston
** Mr Cotes
Mr Owens
† Sir John Astley

† Mr Baldwyn
** Mr Cresset
Mr Clayton
Mr Waring
Mr Cotton

24 *Herefordshire* Is governed by Duke of Chandos and Lord Oxford. Since the death of Lord Scudamore and Sir Thomas Morgan the gentlemen are well affected but have no chief.

25 *Monmouthshire*
§ Lord Windsor
* Sir Charles Kemys
Captain Bourgh
Mr Coghran
Mr Jones

Mr Ray
Mr Gregory
Mr Hughes
Mr Price

26 *Glamorganshire*
* Lord Mansel's son
  (chief of one party)
* Sir Charles Keyms
  (chief of another party)

* Sir Edward Stradling
Mr Lewis
Mr Jones
Mr Powell

27 *Breconshire*
* Mr Vaughan
(These two govern all the shire.)

Mr Percy Williams

28 *Carmarthenshire* Is mostly infected by the Marquis of Winchester's interest the Tory party having no chief of repute.

29 *Pembrokeshire* Most inhabited by honest people and gentlemen very well disposed. Mr Barlow of Galby is become cautious since he married Lord Harcourt's daughter. Mr Barlow his uncle is right.
* Sir George Barlow

† Mr Campbell

Mr Phillips

Mr Wogan

Dr Powell

Mr Langhorne

Mr Lloyd

Mr Skirm

Mr Knolles

Mr Parry

30 *Cardiganshire* Since the death of the most worthy patriot Lewis Price who ruled all this shire the principals are –

* Mr Parry

Mr Lloyd

Mr Hedman

Mr Williams

Mr Powell

31 *Radnorshire* Thinly inhabited – of no great use and most under the jurisdiction of Lord Oxford.

32 *Montgomeryshire* Under the jurisdiction of [§] Lord Hereford and [*] Mr Pugh both worthy men and fit to be relied on.

33 *Anglesey, Caernarvonshire, Merioneth*

§ Lord Bulkeley

Mr BrynKyr

Mr Coitmore

Mr Holland

Mr Thomas

Mr Davies

34 *Flintshire and Denbighshire* Very useful shires. By the neighbourhood of Chester abundant in coal and lead mines wherein members are employed.

* Sir Richard Grosvenor

* Sir George Warburton

Mr Mostyn

Mr Robinson

** Mr Shakerly

Mr Egerton

* Mr Eyton

Mr Lloyd

* Mr Roberts

* Mr Watkin Williams

35 *Cheshire*

Lord Gower (chief)

Mr Leigh

Mr Thomas Ashten

Sir William Meredith

Mr Willbraham

† Mr Cholmondeley

Mr Massey

Captain Hueston

Captain Warburton

Alderman Bourroughe

Edward Fowke

(Note that before the case of Preston Lord Chomley tendered the oaths to the Militia of Cheshire who all unanimously refused to take them.)

36 *Lancashire* A county well known for a spirit and principle. The city of Manchester can furnish 15,000 fighting men.

Mr Holland Egerton   Mr James Warren
Sir Ralph Middleton

37 *Derbyshire*
§ Lord Scarsdale (chief)   Mr Baylis
Colonel Beresford   (the generality of the gentlemen)

38 *Yorkshire* The generality of the gentlemen even the whiggs whom Aislaby drew into the S. S. Scheme and ruined.

§ Lord Downe   * Sir John Bland
Lord Strafford   Captain Beaumont
§ Lord Carmarthen   * Mr Stapylton

39 *Nottinghamshire*
§ Lord Middleton   † Mr Borlase Warren
§ Lord Lexinton   Mr Lewis
* William Levinz   * Mr Digby

Whiggs

Duke of Newcastle   Duke of Kingston

40 *Lincolnshire* Well situated by the sea for service and most of the gentlemen and people [are] well affected.

41 *Durham*
§ [Lord Crew],   Mr Stedworth
  Lord Bishop of Durham   * Mr Baker
* Sir John Eden

42 *Cumberland, Westmorland, and Northumberland*
Plentiful in colliers and workmen.

* Mr Shippen   * Mr Wrightson

APPENDIX 4

Known Jacobites or individuals suspected of Jacobitism who were members of the House of Commons in the years 1715-45[1]

Sir Robert Abdy of Albyns, Essex
John Anstis of West North, Duloe, Cornwall
Charles Areskine of Tinwald and Barjarg, Dumfries, and Alva, Stirling
Sir John Astley of Patshull, Staffordshire, and Everley, Wiltshire
Sir Walter Wagstaffe Bagot of Blithfield, Staffordshire
George Baker of Crook Hall, in Lanchester near Durham
John Baker of East Langdon, near Deal, Kent
Acton Baldwyn of Stokesay Castle, Salop
Sir Coplestone Warwick Bampfylde of Poltimore, near Exeter, Devon
John Bampfylde of Poltimore, near Exeter, Devon
Sir George Barlow of Slebech, near Haverfordwest, Pembrokeshire
John Basset of Heanton Court, near Barnstaple, Devon
Sir George Beaumont of Stoughton Grange, near Leicester
Anthony Blagrave of Southcot, near Reading, Berkshire
John Bland of Hulme Hall, Lancashire, and Kippax Park, Yorkshire
Samuel Bracebridge of Lindley Hall, Leicestershire
Sir Henry Bunbury of Bunbury and Stanney, near Chester
Charles Caesar of Benington, Hertfordshire
Sir William Carew of Antony, Cornwall
John Carnegie of Boysack, Forfarshire
George Chaffin of Chettle, Dorset

1 This list is based largely on information contained in the biographical sketches of individual members of parliament found in Romney Sedgwick, *The House of Commons, 1715-1754*, 2 vols. (London 1970).

Thomas Chapman of Caldecote, near Newport Pagnell, Buckinghamshire
Thomas Chester of Almondsbury and Knole, near Bristol
Sir John Chichester of Youlston, near Barnstaple, Devon
Charles Cholmondeley of Vale Royal, Cheshire
Sir Jonathan Cope of Bruern Abbey, Oxfordshire
Clement Corrance of Parham Hall, Suffolk
Sir John Coryton of West Newton Ferrers, near Callington, Cornwall
Sir John Hynde Cotton of Madingley Hall, Cambridgeshire
Sir William Courtenay of Powderham Castle, Devon
John Crowley of Barking, Suffolk
Sir Robert Davers of Rougham, Suffolk
Henry Dawnay of Cowick Hall, Yorkshire
Hon. John Dawnay of Cowick Hall, Yorkshire
John Digby of Mansfield Woodhouse, Nottinghamshire
Montague Garrard Drake of Shardeloes, near Amersham, Buckinghamshire
John Eden of West Auckland, county Durham
Jonathan Elford of Bickham, Devon
Thomas Eyton of Lower Leeswood, Flintshire
Hon. John Fane of Mereworth, Kent
John Fleetwood of Missenden, Buckinghamshire
Richard Fleming of North Stoneham, near Southampton
Thomas Foley of Soke Edith Court, Herefordshire
Thomas Forster of Adderstone, Northumberland
John Fownes of Nethway and Kittery Court, near Dartmouth, Devon
John Friend of Hitcham, Buckinghamshire
William Godolphin, Viscount Rialton
John Goodall of Bull Hill, Fowey, Cornwall
Sir Henry Goring of Highden, Wappingthorne, near Steyning, Sussex
Sir Richard Grosvenor of Eaton Hall, Cheshire
Sir William Hardres of Hardres Court, near Canterbury, Kent
Edward Harley of Eywood, Herefordshire
Edward Harvey of Coombe, Surrey
John Harvey of Ickwell Bury, Bedfordshire
Michael Harvey of Coombe, Surrey, and Clifton Maybank, near Milborne Port, Dorset
George Heathcote of Walcot, Somerset
Henry Heron of Cressy Hall, Lincolnshire
Thomas Hesketh of Rufford, Lancashire
Henry Holmes of Thorley, Yarmouth, Isle of Wight
Thomas Horner of Mells, Somerset, and Melbury, Dorset

Sir Richard Grubham Howe of Great Wishford, Wiltshire

Archibald Hutcheson of the Middle Temple and Golden Square, Westminster

Robert Hyde of Hatch, near Hindon and Heale, Wiltshire

William Inge of Thorpe Constantine, near Tamworth, Staffordshire

Sir Justinian Isham of Lamport Hall, Northamptonshire

Sir Robert Bankes Jenkinson of Walcot, Oxfordshire

Sir Charles Kemys of Cefn Mably, Glamorganshire

Sir William Keyt of Ebrington, Gloucestershire, and Stratford-on-Avon, Warwickshire

Corbet Kynaston of Hordley, Salop

Edward Kynaston of Garth and Bryngwyn, Montgomeryshire and Hardwick, Salop

John Kynaston of Hardwick, Salop

Edmund Lambert of Boyton, Wiltshire

William Levinz of Grove, Nottinghamshire

Thomas Lewis of Soberton, Hampshire

Isaac le Heup of Gunthorpe, Norfolk

Richard Lockwood of College Hill, London, and Dews Hall, near Maldon, Essex

Sir James Long of Draycot Cerne, near Chippenham, Wiltshire

Hon. Robert Mansel of Margam, Glamorganshire, and Crayford, Kent

Thomas Master of the Abbey, Cirencester, Gloucestershire

Sir Peter Mews of Hinton Admiral, near Christchurch, Hampshire

Sir Humphrey Monoux of Wooton, Bedfordshire

Sir Nicholas Morice of Werrington, Devon

Edmund Morris of Loddington, Leicestershire

Sir Nathaniel Napier of Middlemarsh Hall and Critchell More, Dorset

Edward Nicholas of West Horsley, Surrey

Sir Clobery Noel of Kirkby Mallory, Leicestershire

Stephen Northleigh of Peamore, Devon

James Edward Oglethorpe of Westbrook, near Haslemere, Surrey

Robert Packer of Shellingford and Donnington, Berkshire

Sir John Pakington of Westwood, Worcestershire

Thomas Palmer of Fairfield Stoke Courcy, near Bridgwater, Somerset

Stephen Parry of Neuadd Trefawr, Cardinganshire

Humphry Parsons of the Red Lion Brewery, Aldgate, and the Priory, Reigate, Surrey

Sir John Parsons of the Priory, Reigate, Surrey

Alexander Pendarves of Roskrow, Cornwall

Henry Perrot of Northleigh, Oxfordshire
William Peyto of Chesterton, Warwickshire
Edward Phelips of Montacute, Somerset
Sir William Pole of Colcombe Castle, near Colyton, and Shute, near Honiton, Devon
Lewis Pryse of Gogerddan, Cardinganshire
John Pugh of Mathafarn, Montgomeryshire
Johnathan Rashleigh of Menabilly, Cornwall
John Rolle of Stevenstone, near Barnstaple, Devon
Edward Rolt of Sacombe Hertfordshire, Harrowby, Lincolnshire, and Spye Park, near Chippenham, Wiltshire
Thomas Rowney of Dean Farm, Oxfordshire
Sir Thomas Saunders of Beechwood, Hertfordshire
William Shippen of Norfolk St, London
Henry Slingsby of Scriven, near Knaresborough, Yorkshire
John Snell of Lower Guiting, Gloucestershire
William Stephens of Bowcombe, Isle of Wight
Sir John Stonehouse of Radley, Berkshire
Sir Edward Stradling of St Donat's Castle, Glamorganshire
Thomas Strangways of Melbury, Dorset
Francis Swanton of Salisbury, Wiltshire
John Ivory Talbot of Lacock Abbey, Wiltshire
Sir John Trevelyan of Nettlecombe, Somerset
Sir Edward Turnor of Hallingbury, Essex
Alexander Urquhart of Newhall, Rosshire
William Gwyn Vaughan of Trebarried, Brecknockshire
Ralph Verney of Middle Claydon, near Buckinghamshire
Sir George Warburton of Warburton and Arley, Cheshire
John Richmond Webb of Biddesden, in Ludgershall, Wiltshire
Daniel Weir of Stonebyres, Lanarkshire
Watkin Williams of Wynnstay, Denbighshire
William Peere Williams of Hoddesdon, Hertfordshire, and Northolt, Middlesex
Thomas Winnington of Stanford Court, Worcestershire
William Wrightson of Newcastle-upon-Tyne
Sir William Wyndham of Orchard Wyndham, Somerset

APPENDIX 5

Duke of Wharton's list of Jacobite support among the peerage in 1725[1]

Duke of Norfolk
Duke of Beaufort
Duke of Hamilton
Duke of Gordon
Duke of Athol
Earl of Shrewsbury
Earl of Salisbury
Earl of Exeter
Earl of Northampton
Earl of Denbigh
Earl of Berkshire
Earl of Winchelsea
Earl of Thanet
Earl of Scarsdale
Earl of Cardigan
Earl of Anglesea
Earl of Lichfield
Earl of Abingdon
Earl of Plymouth
Earl of Strafford
Earl of Oxford
Earl of Dartmouth
Earl of Uxbridge

Earl of Aylesford
Earl of Crawford
Earl of Eglinton
Earl of Cassilis
Earl of Murray
Earl of Wigtown
Earl of Strathmore
Earl of Galloway
Earl of Northesk
Earl of Kincardin
Earl of Dundonald
Earl of Arran
Earl of Pontefract
Earl of Kintore
Earl of Orrery
Viscount Hereford
Viscount Falkland
Viscount Stormont
Viscount Strathallan
Lord Willoughby de Broke
Lord North and Grey
Lord St John de Bletsho
Lord Compton

1   RA, Stuart, 83/89

Lord Brooke
Lord Bruce
Lord Leigh
Lord Berkeley de Stratton
Lord Arundell de Trerice
Lord Craven
Lord Osborn
Lord Stawell
Lord Ashburnham
Lord Gower
Lord Conway

Lord Mountjoy
Lord Middleton
Lord Lansdowne
Lord Masham
Lord Foley
Lord Bathurst
Lord Bingley
Lord Salton
Lord Sinclair
Lord Semple

Bibliography

MANUSCRIPT SOURCES

Archives du Ministère des Affaires Etrangères, Quai d'Orsay Correspond-
ance Politique d'Angleterre: vols. 291-374
  Mémoires et Documents Angleterre: vols. 33-7, 40, 46, 49, 75-7, 82-4, 86, 88, 91-3
Archivio Segreto Vaticano, Vatican City
  Reports of the Papal Nuncios: Fiandra, vols. 109-15; Francia, vols. 231-2,
  241, 467, 469, 623; Germania, vols. 278, 231; Spagna, vols. 225, 232
British Museum
  Additional Manuscripts
  Carteret Papers: Add. MSS 22,511-22,522
  Coxe Papers: Add. MSS 9,128-9,130; 9,150
  Gualterio Papers: Add. MSS 20,292; 20,294-20,295; 20,297; 20,242; 20,245
  Hardwicke Papers: Add. MSS 35,406; 35,584-35,585; 35,875
  Newcastle Papers: Add. MSS 32,686-32,687; 32,992; 33,033; 33,064; 33,199-33,200
  Whitworth Papers: Add. MSS 37,363-37,397; 32,253-32,247; 32,258-32,305
  Miscellaneous Historical Papers, 1642-1817: Add. MSS 34,713
  Deciphers of Dispatches with Cipher Keys: Add. MSS 32,258-32,305
  Correspondence of William Wynne (d 1765): Add. MSS 41,843
  Portland Papers
  Portland Loan 29/1-3
  Stowe Papers: vols. 158, 186, 222-232, 242, 246-7, 250-1
In the possession of Lt.Col. J.H. Busby
  Caesar Journals

Chewton House, Chewton Mendip, Somerset
  Waldegrave Papers
Cambridge University Library, Sir Robert Walpole's Archive
  Cholmondeley (Houghton) Papers
  Correspondence
  Domestic Papers: Parliamentary and Political Papers; Papers Relating to
  Conspiracy and Public Order; Miscellaneous Papers Relating to Jacobi-
  tism, Riots, etc.; Miscellaneous Domestic Papers
  Foreign Papers
Haus-, Hof- Und Staatsarchiv, Vienna
  Reports of Patrick MacNenny
  Belgien DD.Abt.B.Fz 91-92b; DD.Abt.B. 136½, 136b/2a, 92a, 93a, 94b, 145a, 145b
House of Lords Record Office
  Records 1716-17
  Item 249: Intercepted letters of Görtz, Gyllenborg, and Sparre
Public Record Office
  State Papers (Domestic) George I (1714-27); George II (1727-45)
  State Papers (Foreign)   77: Flanders, vols. 70-1; 78: France, vols. 160-5; 84:
  Holland, vols. 256-60; 85: Italian States and Rome, vols. 13-16; 88: Poland,
  vols. 21-4
Royal Archives, Windsor Castle
  Stuart Papers
Scottish Record Office, Edinburgh
  Stair Muniments. GD 135/141, vols. 1-29

PRINTED PRIMARY SOURCES

[Unless otherwise stated the place of publication is London.]
Ailesbury, T. *Memoirs of Thomas, Earl of Ailesbury*, II. Ed. W.E. Buckley. Rox-
  burghe Club 1890
Alberoni, J.M. *Lettres Intimes de J.M. Alberoni Adressées au Comte I. Rocca.* Ed.
  Émile Bourgeois. Paris 1892
Atterbury, Francis. *Letters of Francis Atterbury, Bishop of Rochester, to the Chevalier
  St. George and Some of the Adherents of the House of Stuart.* Ed. J.H. Glover. 1847
Atterbury, Francis. *The Epistolary Correspondence, Visitation Charges, Speeches, and
  Miscellanies of the Right Reverend Francis Atterbury, D.D., Lord Bishop of
  Rochester.* Ed. J. Nichols. 1783-90
Bentley, Richard. *The Correspondence of Richard Bentley, D.D., Master of Trinity
  College, Cambridge.* Ed. C. Wordsworth. 2 vols. 1842

Berwick, Maréchal de. *Mémoires du Maréchal de Berwick*. Switzerland 1778

Blundell, Nicholas. *Blundell's Diary and Letter Book, 1702-1728*. Ed. M. Blundell. Liverpool 1952

Boyer, Abel. *The Political State of Great Britain*. 1711-40

Burney Collection. Burney Collection of Newspapers. British Museum

[John Campbell] *Memoirs of the Duke de Ripperda: First Ambassador from the States-General to His Most Catholic Majesty, etc. . . .* 1740

Chance, J.F., ed. *British Diplomatic Instructions, 1689-1789. I: Sweden, 1689-1727.* 1922

Chandler, Richard. *The History and Proceedings of the House of Commons from the Restoration to the Present Time*. V, VI, VII. 1742

Cobbett, William. *The Parliamentary History of England from the Earliest Period to the Year 1803*. VI, VII, VIII, IX, X. 1806-12

Coxe, William. *Memoirs of the Life and Administration of Sir Robert Walpole, Earl of Orford*. II, III. 1798

[Defoe, Daniel] *The History of the Wars of His Present Majesty Charles XII, King of Sweden; From His First Landing in Denmark, to His Return from Turkey to Pomerania* by a Scots Gentleman in the Swedish Service. 1715

– *Mercurius Politicus: Being Monthly Observations on the Affairs of Great Britain; with a Collection of all of the Most Material Occurrences in Europe for the Month of February, 1717* . 1717

– *An Impartial Enquiry Into the Conduct of the Right Honourable Charles Lord Viscount Townshend*. 1717

– *The Case of the War in Italy Stated: Being a Serious Enquiry How far Great Britain is Engaged to Concern Itself in the Quarrel Between the Emperor and the King of Spain*. 1718

Dickson, W.K., ed. *The Jacobite Attempt of 1719*. Edinburgh, Scottish History Society, 1895

The Gentleman's Magazine: Or, Monthly Intelligencer. Ed. E. Cave. 1731-45

Hearne, T. *Remarks and Collections of Thomas Hearne*. Ed. C.E. Doble. 11 vols. Oxford, Oxford Historical Society, 1885-1921

Hooke, N. *Correspondence of Colonel Nathaniel Hooke, Agent from the Court of France to the Scottish Jacobites, in the Years 1703-1707*. Ed. W.D. Macray. Roxburghe Club 1871

Historical Manuscripts Commission: Second Report. 1871. Baker MSS, Cathcart MSS, Bromley-Davenport MSS, Stair MSS, Spencer MSS

– *Third Report*. 1872. De la Warr MSS, Orlebar MSS

– *Fifth Report*. 1876. Sutherland MSS

– *Seventh Report*. 1789, Appendix I: Finch MSS

– *Ninth Report*. 1883, Appendix I: Elphinstone MSS; 1884, Appendix II: Chandos Pole Gell MSS

- *Tenth Report.* 1885. Drummond Moray MSS, Weston Underwood MSS
- *Eleventh Report.* 1887, Appendix IV: Townshend MSS; 1887, Appendix V: Dartmouth MSS
- *Twelfth Report.* 1891, Appendix V: Rutland MSS; 1891, Appendix IX: Ketton MSS
- *Thirteenth Report.* 1892, Appendix III: Fortescue MSS; 1893, Appendix VI: Lonsdale MSS
- *Fourteenth Report.* 1894, Appendix III: Roxburghe MSS; 1894, Appendix IV: Kenyon MSS; 1895, Appendix IX: Onslow MSS, Hare MSS
- *Fifteenth Report.* 1897, Appendix II: Hodgkin MSS; 1897, Appendix V: Foljambe MSS; 1897, Appendix VI: Carlisle MSS; 1898, Appendix VII: Ailesbury MSS, Somerset MSS
- *Bath MSS.* 1907, III
- *Polwarth MSS.* 1911, I; 1916, II; 1931, III; 1940, IV; 1961, V
- *Portland MSS.* 1899, V; 1901, VI; 1901, VII; 1907, VIII; 1923, IX
- *Stuart MSS.* 1902, I; 1904, II; 1907, III; 1910, IV; 1912, V; 1916, VI; 1923, VII
- *Various MSS.* 1909, V: Graham MSS; 1909, VI: Matcham MSS; 1913, VIII: Wood MSS, Clements MSS

An Historical Narrative of the Tryals of Mr. George Kelly and of Dr. Francis Atterbury, (Late) Lord Bishop of Rochester, etc. 1727

The Historical Register Containing an Impartial Relation of All Transactions Foreign and Domestick. 1716-31

Hobson, M.G., ed. *Oxford Council Acts, 1701-1752.* Oxford, Oxford Historical Society, New Series, 1954

Howell, T.B. *A Complete Collection of State Trials and Proceedings for High Treason and Other Crimes and Misdemeanors from the Earliest Period to the Year 1783.* XVI. 1816

Kelly, Reverend George. *Memoirs of the Life, Travels and Transactions of the Reverend George Kelly, From his Birth to Escape from his Imprisonment out of the Tower of London, October 26, 1736.* 1736

Ker of Kersland, John. *The Memoirs of John Ker, of Kersland, in North Britain, Esq. Relating to Politicks, Trade, and History.* 3rd ed. 1727

Knatchbull, Sir Edward. *The Parliamentary Diary of Sir Edward Knatchbull, 1722-1730.* Ed. A.N. Newman. Camden Society, 3rd series, XCIV, 1963

Lamberty, M. de. *Mémoires pour Servir à l'Histoire du XVIII siècle, contenant les negociations, traitez, resolutions, et autres documents authentiques concernant les affaires d'état.* IX, X. Amsterdam 1735

Layer, Christopher. *A Faithful Account of the Life of Christopher Layer from his Birth to his Execution for High Treason* by a Gentleman of Norwich, his Schoolfellow. 1723

Legg, J. Wickham, ed. *British Diplomatic Instructions.* II:*France, 1689-1721*, 1925; IV: *France, 1721-1727*, 1927; VI: *France, 1727-1744*, 1930

Letters Which Passed Between Count Gyllenborg, the Barons Görtz, Sparre, and Others, Relating to the Design of Raising a Rebellion in His Majesty's Dominions, to be Supported by a Force from Sweden. Dublin 1717

Lockhart, George. *The Lockhart Papers: Containing Memoirs and Commentaries upon the Affairs of Scotland from 1702 to 1715 . . .* Ed. A. Aufrere. 1817

Macky, John. *Memoirs of the Secret Service of John Macky, Esq., During the Reigns of King William, Queen Anne, and King George I.* Published from his Original Manuscript; as attested by his Son, Spring Macky, Esq. 1733

Paul, Rev. Robert, ed. *Letters and Documents Relating to Robert Erskine, Physician to Peter the Great, 1677-1720.* Edinburgh, Miscellany of the Scottish History Society, 1904

Register of the Estates of Roman Catholics in Northumberland. Surtees Society, CXXXI, 1918

A Report from the Committee Appointed by Order of the House of Commons to Examine Christopher Layer, and Others; and to Whom Several Papers and Examinations Laid before the House, Relating to the Conspiracy Mention'd in His Majesty's Speech, at the Opening of this Parliament to be Carrying on Against His Person and Government, Were Referred. Reported on the First of March, 1722, by the Right Honourable William Pulteney, Esq., 1722

A Report from the Committee of Secrecy Appointed to Enquire into the Conduct of Robert, Earl of Orford; During the Last Ten Years of His Being First Commissioner of the Treasury and Chancellor and Under-Treasurer of His Majesty's Exchequer. 1742

Report from the Secret Committee on the Post Office; Together with the Appendix. (Ordered, by the House of Commons, to be printed, 5 August 1844). Parliamentary Papers, Session 1844, XIV

Rogers, James E. Thorold, ed. *A Complete Collection of Protests of the Lords. I: 1624-1741.* Oxford 1875

Saussure, César de. *A Foreign View of England in the Reigns of George I and George II.* Translated and edited by Madame van Muyden. 1902

The Speech of Mr. George Kelly Spoke at the Bar of the House of Lords, on Thursday, the 2nd of May, 1723, in His Defence Against the Bill then Depending for Inflicting Pains and Penalties Upon Him. 1723

Stackhouse, T. *Memoirs of the Life, Character, Conduct and Writings of Dr. Francis Atterbury, Late Bishop of Rochester, from His Birth to His Banishment.* 1723

Stair, Earl of. *Annals and Correspondence of the Viscount and the First and Second Earls of Stair.* Ed. J.M. Graham. 1847

Stanhope, Philip Dormer. *The Letters of Philip Dormer Stanhope, 4th Earl of Chesterfield.* Ed. Bonamy Dobrée. King's Printer Edition 1932

Swift, Jonathan. *Gulliver's Travels 1726.* Ed. Herbert Davis. Oxford 1959

Tayler, Henrietta, ed. *The Jacobite Court at Rome in 1719 . . .* Edinburgh 1938

– *Jacobite Epilogue: A Further Selection of Letters from Jacobites among the Stuart Papers at Windsor.* 1941

Ten Reports of the Commissioners Appointed by Act 25 Geo.3.c.19. to Inquire into the Fees, Perquisites and Emoluments Which are, or Have Been Lately, Received in the Several Public Offices Therein Mentioned. Tenth Report, Post Office, 30 June 1788

Thomlinson, Reverend J. *The Diary of the Reverend John Thomlinson.* Ed. J.C. Hodgson. Six North Country Diaries, Surtees Society, CXVIII, 1910

Timberland, Ebenezer. *The History and Proceedings of the House of Lords, from the Restoration in 1660, to the Present Time.* 1742

Tindal, N. *The History of England, by Mr. Rapin de Thoyras Continued from the Revolution to the Accession of King George II.* 1746

Toland, J. *The State Anatomy of Great Britain Containing a Particular Account of its Several Interests and Parties, Their Bent and Genius; and What Each of Them, with All the Rest of Europe, May Hope or Fear from the Reign and Family of King George.* 1717

Voltaire, M. de. *Histoire de Charles XII, Roi de Suede.* 1798

Walpole, Horace. *Letters of Horace Walpole, Fourth Earl of Orford.* Ed. Paget Toynbee. I II. Oxford 1903

Walpole, Horatio. *An Honest Diplomat at the Hague: The Private Letters of Horatio Walpole, 1715-1716.* Ed. J.J. Murray. Bloomington 1955

Williams, E.N., ed. *The Eighteenth-Century Constitution: Documents and Commentary.* Cambridge 1960

Williams, Robert Folkestone. *Memoirs and Correspondence of Francis Atterbury, D.D., Bishop of Rochester.* 1869

Williamson, Adam. *The Official Diary of Lieutenant General Adam Williamson: Deputy-Lieutenant of the Tower of London, 1722-1747.* Ed. J.C. Fox. Camden Society, 3rd series, XXII, 1912

Wodrow, Rev. R. *Analecta, or Materials for a History of Remarkable Providences Mostly Relating to Scotch Ministers and Christians.* III. Edinburgh 1842

Yorke, Philip. *The Life and Correspondence of Philip Yorke, Earl of Hardwicke, Lord High Chancellor of Great Britain.* Ed. P.C. Yorke. Cambridge 1913

SELECTED SECONDARY SOURCES

Baraudon, Alfred. *La Maison de Savoie et la Triple Alliance, 1713-1722.* Paris 1896

Baudrillart, A. *Philippe V et la cour de France.* Paris 1890

Beeching, H.C. *Francis Atterbury.* 1909

Carswell, J. *The South Sea Bubble.* 1961

Cassan, Stephen Hyde. *Lives of the Bishops of Bath and Wells: From the Earliest to the Present Period.* 1829

– *Lives and Memoirs of the Bishops of Sherborne and Salisbury.* 1824

Castagnoli, Pietro. *Il Cardinale Giulio Alberoni.* 3 vols. Rome 1929-32

Chance, J.F. *George I and the Northern War: A Study of British-Hanoverian Policy in the North of Europe in the Years 1709 to 1721.* 1909

– *The Alliance of Hanover.* 1923

Conn, Stetson. *Gibraltar in British Diplomacy in the Eighteenth Century.* New Haven 1942

Coxe, W. *Memoirs of the Life and Administration of Sir Robert Walpole, Earl of Orford.* I. 1798

Doran, J. *London in Jacobite Times.* 2 vols. 1877

Ellis, K. *The Post Office in the Eighteenth Century: A Study in Administrative History.* 1958

Foord, A.S. *His Majesty's Opposition, 1714-1830.* Oxford 1964

Forrester, E.G. *Northamptonshire County Elections and Electioneering, 1695-1832.* Oxford 1941

Fraser, Peter. *The Intelligence of the Secretaries of State and their Monopoly of Licensed News, 1660-1688.* Cambridge 1956

Hatton, R.M. *Charles XII of Sweden.* 1968

– *Diplomatic Relations Between Great Britain and the Dutch Republic, 1714-1721.* 1950

Hatton, R.M. and Bromley, J.S., eds. *William III and Louis XIV: Essays 1680-1720 by and for Mark A. Thomson.* Toronto 1968

Henderson, A.J. *London and the National Government 1721-1742.* Durham, NC 1945

Horn, D.B. *The British Diplomatic Service, 1689-1789.* Oxford 1961

– *Great Britain and Europe in the Eighteenth Century.* Oxford 1967

Hughes, E. *North Country Life in the Eighteenth Century. I: The North East, 1700-1750.* Oxford 1952; II: *Cumberland and Westmorland, 1700-1830.* Oxford 1965

Insh, G.P. *The Scottish Jacobite Movement.* Edinburgh 1952

Jones, G.H. *The Main Stream of Jacobitism.* Cambridge, Mass. 1954

Ketton-Cremer, R.W. *A Norfolk Gallery.* 1948

Lecky, W.E.H. *A History of England in the Eighteenth Century.* 1878

Lewis, L. *Connoisseurs and Secret Agents in Eighteenth Century Rome.* 1961

Mahon, Lord. *History of England from the Peace of Utrecht to the Peace of Versailles, 1713-1783.* 1853

McLachlan, Jean O. *Trade and Peace with Old Spain, 1667-1750.* Cambridge 1940

Michael, Wolfgang. *England under George I: The Beginnings of the Hanoverian Dynasty.* 1936

– *England Under George I: The Quadruple Alliance.* 1939

Murray, J.J. *George I, the Baltic and the Whig Split of 1717.* 1969
Nordmann, C.J. *La Crise du nord au début du XVIIIe siècle.* Paris 1962
Overton, J.H. *The Nonjurors.* 1902
Petrie, Sir Charles. *Bolingbroke.* 1937
– *The Jacobite Movement.* 1959
Plumb, J.H. *Sir Robert Walpole: The Making of a Statesman.* 1957
– *Sir Robert Walpole: The King's Minister.* 1960
– *The Growth of Political Stability, 1675-1725.* 1967
Realey, C.B. *The Early Opposition to Sir Robert Walpole 1720-1727.* Kansas 1931
Robertson, C.G. *England Under the Hanoverians.* 1948
Robinson, H. *The British Post Office: A History.* Princeton, NJ 1948
Sedgwick, R. *The House of Commons, 1715-1754.* 2 vols. 1970
Sykes, N. *William Wake: Archbishop of Canterbury, 1657-1737.* Cambridge 1957
– *Church and State in England in the Eighteenth Century.* 1934
Syveton, G. *Une Cour et un aventurier au XVIIIe siècle: le Baron de Ripperda.* Paris
    1896
Thomson, M.A. *The Secretaries of State, 1681-1782.* Oxford 1932
Ward, W.R. *Georgian Oxford: University Politics in the Eighteenth Century.* Oxford
    1958
– *The English Land Tax in the Eighteenth Century.* Oxford 1953
Williams, Basil. *The Whig Supremacy 1714-1760.* Oxford 1962
– *Stanhope: A Study in Eighteenth Century War and Diplomacy.* Oxford 1932
Wilson, Arthur MacCandless. *French Foreign Policy during the Administration of
    Cardinal Fleury 1726-1743.* Cambridge, Mass. 1936
Wilson, C.H. *Anglo-Dutch Commerce and Finance in the Eighteenth Century.* Cam-
    bridge 1951

Index

DATE DUE

ILL			
152793			
2/14/05			